T0330103

Organisational Transformation in the Russian Oil Industry

NEW HORIZONS IN INTERNATIONAL BUSINESS

Series Editor: Peter J. Buckley
Centre for International Business.
University of Leeds (CIBUL), UK

The New Horizons in International Business series has established itself as the world's leading forum for the presentation of new ideas in international business research. It offers pre-eminent contributions in the areas of multinational enterprise – including foreign direct investment, business strategy and corporate alliances, global competitive strategies, and entrepreneurship. In short, this series constitutes essential reading for academics, business strategists and policy makers alike.

Organisational Transformation in the Russian Oil Industry

Sarah Dixon

Director of Postgraduate Programmes, Faculty of Business and Law, Kingston University, UK

NEW HORIZONS IN INTERNATIONAL BUSINESS

Edward Elgar
Cheltenham, UK • Northampton, MA, USA

Published by
Edward Elgar Publishing Limited
The Lypiatts
15 Lansdown Road
Cheltenham
Glos GL50 2JA
UK

Edward Elgar Publishing, Inc.
William Pratt House
9 Dewey Court
Northampton
Massachusetts 01060
USA

A catalogue record for this book
is available from the British Library

Library of Congress Control Number 2008931912

ISBN 978 1 84720 592 6

Printed and bound in Great Britain by MPG Books Ltd, Bodmin, Cornwall

Contents

Figures

Tables

Abbreviations and key terms

AAR	Alfa/Access Renova	Alfa Group and Access Renova – two private investment banks
bbl/d or b/d	barrels per day	
	Baltic States	Lithuania, Latvia and Estonia
CAQDAS	computer-aided qualitative data analysis	
CEE	Central and Eastern Europe	Central Europe – countries East of the former Iron Curtain and West of former Soviet Union Eastern Europe – countries of former Soviet Union
CEO	Chief executive officer	
CIS	Commonwealth of Independent States	Economic association of countries of former Soviet Union except Baltic States and Georgia
COO	chief operating officer	
	Downstream	Oil company operations covering processing of crude oil (refining, petrochemicals, etc.)
EBITDA	Earnings before interest, tax, depreciation and amortisement	
E&P	exploration and production	The upstream activities of oil companies
ESP	Electric submersible pump	
FDP	Field development planning	Technical planning for oil production
FIG	Financial-industrial group	Large-scale business group integrating financial (banking resource), industrial and commercial elements
FSU	Former Soviet Union	Russia, Ukraine, Belarus, Moldova, Armenia, Georgia, Azerbaijan, Kazakhstan, Turkmenistan, Kirgizia, Tajikistan, Uzbekistan, Latvia, Lithuania, Estonia
	Frac	A treatment to stimulate oil production
GAAP	Generally accepted accounting principles	A set of widely accepted accounting practices and standards set in the USA

HR	Human resources	
HSE	Health, safety and environment	
	Insider privatisation	The process whereby most privatised state property ended up in the hands of 'company insiders', i.e. the existing enterprise management
IB	International business	
	Insider managers	Managers who had always been in the company, both pre- and post-privatisation
IRR	Internal rate of return	
	New Russians	A group of entrepreneurial Russians who have gained rapid wealth, not always legally: also conspicuous consumers
JV	Joint venture	
KPI	Key performance indicator	
MBO	Management by objectives	
NEP	New Economic Policy	
NIS	Newly independent states	A term used increasingly to describe the countries of the former Soviet Union (FSU)
	Oligarchs	A small group of men in Russia wielding both wealth and power. Russian oligarchs are businessmen who came to prominence during Yeltsin's presidency
OPEC	Organization of Petroleum Exporting Countries	
	Outsider managers	Managers who were new to the company, often acquiring the assets after privatisation
PR	Public relations	
RBV	Resource-based view	
SOE	State-owned enterprise	
TMT	Top management team	
	Transition economies	Economies of Central and Eastern Europe, Russia, other countries of former Soviet Union, China, Mongolia and Vietnam. Countries moving from a planned to a market economy
	Upstream	Oil company operations covering exploration and production of crude oil
WETS	Well evaluation tracking tool	

Key personae

Alekperov, Vagit	President, Lukoil Major shareholder, Lukoil
Bogdanov, Vladimir	General Director, Surgutneftegaz Major shareholder, Surgutneftegaz
Dudley, Bob	President and CEO, TNK-BP
Friedman, Mikhail	Chairman, Alfa-Bank Major shareholder, TNK
Khan, German	Executive Director, TNK-BP Shareholder, TNK
Khodorkovsky, Mikhail	CEO, Yukos Major shareholder, Yukos
Kukes, Simon	CEO, TNK
Mach, Joe	First Vice-President, Yukos E&P
Vekselberg, Viktor	Executive Director TNK-BP Major shareholder, TNK
Wolcott, Don	Senior Vice-President, Yukos E&P, in charge of Reservoir Technologies and Waterflood

Foreword

The political and social changes of the 1990s in Central and Eastern Europe have forced companies to reinvent themselves, and to create new identities as market-facing business organisations. This organisational transformation put exceptional demands on business leaders who had to create or acquire new types of capabilities and to develop new organisational structures that would allow the effective utilisation of their resources, especially their human capital. Yet at the same time, they had to face an ever-changing external environment, where not only market trends but also legal and regulatory institutions were often highly uncertain. This interdependence of external change and organisational change is a key feature of the transition process in this region, yet also provides a showcase that may yield lessons for companies elsewhere facing radical external change.

The dramatic organisational changes induced by economic transition have been particularly evident in the Russian oil and gas industry. The key players adopted very different strategies of coping with the new situation, some aiming to develop new resources and capabilities to prosper in a market economy, while others relied on a political strategy that left key elements of the organisational structures intact. In many ways, the organisational change in the companies of the Russian oil and gas industry is a microcosm of economic change in Russian society at large.

Yet, the Russian oil and gas industry itself is a key player in the economic transformation and the political sphere of Russian society. The growth of export revenues generated by this industry on the back of rising prices in world markets for raw materials – and oil in particular – have underpinned the economic recovery after the crisis of 1998. This economic success has helped to stabilise the political system during Putin's presidency. At the same time, the central role of the oil industry led to continued political interference, and forced businesses to operate in both a market sphere and a political sphere. These dual pressures require different types of leadership skills than those normally expected in a mature market economy.

This study by Dr Sarah Dixon provides unique insights into the evolution of the key players over a period of over a decade of transition. She is an industry expert having worked for the Royal Dutch Shell Group for over twenty years, including four years based in Moscow as Chemicals Manager Russia. Her expertise has been the foundation of this scholarly study and provided her with exceptional access to the leading players in the industry in Russia. This study presents unique in-depth case studies, interpreted by an industry expert, and analyses them on the basis of concepts and theories developed from contemporary research on organisational change and strategic management, notably the resource-based view of the firm.

The insights of this study are hoped to transcend the specific context. Many companies face radical change in their environment and dual pressures of markets and politics, though rarely as radical as Russia since the 1990s. Dr Dixon's study generates new ideas about the role of business leaders in managing dynamic change processes. Her cases illustrate how companies can break dysfunctional inherited structures and develop operational and dynamic capabilities that open new, profitable growth paths.

Professor Klaus Meyer, University of Bath
October 2007

Preface

The oil industry in general, and the Russian oil industry in particular, is the focus of much media attention, with an emphasis on political machinations, geopolitics, economic power and corruption. The turn of the century was a period of rapid change in the Russian oil industry, with the privatisation of the industry in the early nineties being followed by a return to a significant amount of state control from 2003 onwards. The chaotic days of Yeltsin's presidency in the nineties, when rampant capitalism was allowed to have sway, gave way to stricter rule under Putin from 2000. The early promise that Putin would bring much needed stability, but nevertheless continue to promote the market economy, failed to materialise. By 2003 Putin had already put Khodorkovsky, CEO of Yukos – the most successful Russian oil company, into gaol and started to nationalise the assets. The recent presidential elections in March 2008 have reinforced the status quo with the likelihood of a continuing strong involvement of the state in industries critical to the economy. This book provides a new perspective on the happenings from the early 1990s until 2005, looking at the Russian industry from the inside, examining the internal workings of four Russian oil companies in order to derive an understanding of how to achieve organisational transformation in conditions of radical institutional upheaval during the transition from a planned to a market economy. Sadly the most successful company no longer exists.

My interest in this research derives from my background as a Russian linguist, an oil industry practitioner and an academic. My association with Russia started when I chose to study Russian at Bradford University in the early 1970s. The rare (at that time) opportunity to spend some time studying in Moscow at the Maurice Thorez Institute of Foreign Languages laid the foundations for an enduring fascination for the country, its people and their language. My subsequent international career, working for the Royal Dutch Shell Group, provided opportunities to gain an in-depth knowledge of business practice in Russia both in the Soviet period and during the transition to a market economy. From 1992–96 I lived in Moscow, participating in the creation and management of two new Shell operating companies in Russia and experiencing first-hand many of the dramatic changes taking place at that time at the macro-environmental level, within industry sectors and within organisations. A career change in 2002, with a move to an academic position at Kingston University, enabled me to deepen my theoretical understanding of organisational strategy and to pursue my research interests which focused around strategy, Russia and the oil industry.

This book represents the outcome of that research, conducted in the course of obtaining my doctorate from Henley Management College. It draws on four longitudinal case studies of Russian oil companies to explain the process of organisational transformation in the context of transition from a planned to a market economy. For the academic audience, the research builds on the resource-based view by explaining the linkages between organisational learning, dynamic capabilities and the implementation of organisational transformation. For the practitioner, the rich comparative case studies provide insight into the constraints and enablers of organisational transformation.

In bringing this work to fruition I owe a debt of gratitude to many organisations and people. The 'Shell connection' helped to secure an entrée for the empirical research. The Russian language skills gained at Bradford University enabled me to conduct my interviews in Russian. Kingston University provided sponsorship and support for my research. I would also like to thank the two supervisors of my doctorate for their invaluable help and support – Klaus Meyer, Professor of Strategy and International Business at the School of Management, University of Bath and Marc Day, Associate Professor in the School of Projects, Processes and Systems at Henley Management College.

Above all I would like to thank the 84 managers who gave up their time to talk to me about their perspective on organisational change. Particular thanks are due to Bob Dudley, CEO of TNK-BP, and his team, for facilitating so many contacts, and to all the Yukos managers, who were struggling in 2003–04 for the survival of the company in the face of renationalisation of its assets.

Sarah Dixon

Acknowledgements

The publishers wish to thank the following who have kindly given permission for the use of copyright material.

EIA (2005), *Russia Country Analysis Brief*.
   Available from:http://www.eia.doe.gov/emeu/cabs/russia.html, accessed 24 September 2005.

International Energy Agency (2004), *IEA Oil Market Report*, May 2004.

Every effort has been made to trace all the copyright holders but if any have been inadvertently overlooked the publishers will be pleased to make the necessary arrangements at the first opportunity.

1. Introduction

Many economies in the world are undergoing some form of transition. However in some countries the degree of change has been unprecedented as they are changing from a centrally planned economy to a market-based system. These 'transition economies' include countries of the Former Soviet Union (FSU), Central and Eastern Europe (CEE), China, Mongolia and Vietnam. Most of these countries adapted some form of 'shock therapy' that included rapid price liberalisation, opening up to international trade, and mass privatisation. Organisations, faced with such radical institutional upheaval, frequently struggled to adapt, leading to sharp drops in countries' industrial output and dramatic economic decline. Nowhere was this more apparent than in Russia where, in the first decade of transition, industrial production dropped more than 50 per cent and the economy contracted by around 60 per cent.

In Russia privatisation proceeded rapidly – it took only three years to transfer most state enterprises into private hands. However, two key factors inhibited change inside the organisations at the time: first most companies ended up in the hands of 'insiders', mainly existing managers, who had no experience in a market economy. Second a relative absence of legal, regulatory and financial institutions allowed many managers to pursue their own interests with impunity. In the planned economy, firms were largely state-owned and had excess employment and inventories, dated physical resources, extensive social services and a non-competitive product portfolio.

Managers faced cognitive barriers to understanding the radically changed environment and existing resources lost their value, while firms lacked resources normally considered standard in mature market economies, such as marketing and finance functions, and a portfolio of products in demand on the market. The new market conditions and the collapse of the old supply relationships required organisations to radically reappraise their operations, change their approach to business, and thus transform their organisations in order to survive.

RUSSIAN OIL INDUSTRY RESEARCH SETTING

The process of organisational transformation was particularly rapid in certain of the Russian oil companies (Khartukov, 2001; Dixon, 2004; Grace, 2005), to the extent that some of the integrated oil companies were beginning to compare themselves with the Western oil majors (Khartukov, 2001). The Russian oil industry thus provided an opportunity to analyse, at a company level, a rapid process of organisational transformation over a short period of time. Organisational transformation has been defined by Newman as: 'intra-organizational change that leaves the organization better able to compete effectively in its competitive milieu' (2000: 603). The purpose of this book is to explain this process of organisational transformation in the Russian oil industry in the critical ten-year transition period from 1995, when the Russian oil companies were privatised, up to 2005.

The main theoretical perspective adopted for the company-level analysis was the resource-based view, which highlights how the deployment of unique and idiosyncratic organisational resources and capabilities generates competitive advantage (Wernerfelt, 1984; Barney, 1991). The Russian oil companies provided a particularly interesting quasi-experimental setting, in that four firms started from similar positions in the mid-1990s, but followed different paths over the next decade. Two of these companies – Yukos and TNK/BP – demonstrated, prima facie, a high degree and rapid pace of organisational transformation towards Western business models (I call them 'Western-style' companies). This permitted literal replication between the two cases (where similar results are predicted) (Yin, 2003). The other two companies – Lukoil and Surgutneftegaz – were changing more slowly (I call them 'Soviet-style' companies). This permitted theoretical replication where different results are obtained but for predictable reasons. Table 1.1 provides basic data on the four oil companies and illustrates that Yukos was the leading company in 2002 in terms of growth in oil production, production costs and market capitalisation. The production and financial indicators for the other Western-style company – TNK – lagged the other companies, partly due to the later privatisation of this company and its inheriting the rump assets. As I shall argue below, however, organisational learning within this company and its organisational transformation clearly distinguished it from its Soviet-style counterparts. Indeed, by the end of 2004, it had gained the leading position in the industry in terms of oil production growth.

Table 1.1 *Basic data on four Russian integrated oil majors*

	Yukos	TNK	Lukoil	Surgutneftegaz
CEO[1]	Mikhail Khodorkovsky	• Simon Kukes (German Khan Viktor Vekselberg)[7]	Vagit Alekperov	Vladimir Bogdanov
CEO background[1]	• 1963 – born Moscow • Mendeleev Institute of Chemical Technology • Deputy Head Komsomol • 1986 – first business/ private café • 1988 – import/export business $10 mn. • 1989 – Bank Menatep • 1996 – First VP Yukos	• 1946 – born Moscow • Moscow Chemical Institute • 1977 – Emigrated to USA • US citizenship • To 1995 – Work for US oil firms Phillips and Amoco • 1995 – Return to Russia 1995 as head Yukos refining • 1998 – President TNK	• 1950 – born Azerbaijan • Azerbaijan Institute of Oil and Chemistry • To 1979 – Caspian oil fields • To 1984 – Siberian oil fields • 1984 – General Director, Kogalymneftegaz • 1990 – Deputy/Acting Minister of Fuel and Energy • 1991 – President Lukoil	• 1951 – born Siberia • Tyumen Industrial Institute • 1973 – started as technician in Siberian oil fields • Rose to deputy general director and general director Surgutneftegaz
	• 'Western-style'	• 'Western-style'	• 'Soviet-style'	• 'Soviet-style'
Ownership/control[2]	Mikhail Khodorkovsky	Viktor Vekselberg Peter Aven Mikhail Friedman German Khan	Vagit Alekperov	Vladimir Bogdanov

3

Table 1.1   (continued)

	Yukos	TNK	Lukoil	Surgutneftegaz
	• Oligarch • Entrepreneur • Major shareholder	• Oligarchs • Entrepreneurs • Major shareholders	• Oligarch • Industry bureaucrat • Major shareholder	• Oligarch • Industry bureaucrat • Significant control of shares
Head office[1]	Moscow	Moscow	Moscow	Surgut
Oil production kb/day 2002[3]	1,392	753	1,515	987
Oil production growth 2002[4]	20.3%	9.1%	1.5%	11.7%[9]
Refinery throughput, kb/day 2002[3]	623	284	681	298
Production cost 2001[5]	$1.76/bbl	$3.63/bbl [8]	$2.50/bbl	$2.50/bbl
Market value 31 December 2002 (World ranking – PFC 500)[6]	$ 21 billion (no. 15)	n/a	$13.1 billion (no. 33)	$13.2 billion (no. 31)

Notes and sources: [1] Company data. [2] Grace 2005. [3] (Petromarket Research, 2003) [4] (IEA, 2004). [5] (Landes et al., 2004) Compare ExxonMobil $3.38/bbl (2001). [6] (PFC Energy, 2004) Compare ExxonMobil, $235.1 billion (No. 1). [7] Although Kukes was CEO, Khan and Vekselberg were the key decision makers. [8] TNK came late to the privatisation process and inherited the rump assets. [9]Surgutneftegaz increased production by excessive and inefficient drilling.

4

OVERVIEW OF RESEARCH

Research interest in the transition economies of Central and Eastern Europe is expanding rapidly and is not only influenced by existing organisation theory, but also attempts to influence it. Thus Meyer and Peng (2005) postulate that research into the resource-based view in transition economies makes a contribution to general theory development in strategic management and international business beyond the context of the CEE. Furthermore, the context of organisational transformation in transition economies provides an interesting setting for the empirical testing of the resource-based view, providing a societal quasi-experiment for testing and developing theories by engaging them in an unusual and changing context.

The objectives of this research were thus twofold: to investigate the process of organisational transformation in the Russian oil industry and to contribute to resource-based theory in the context of the Russian oil industry. In pursuing these objectives I sought to understand how and why the process of organisational transformation differed between Russian oil companies and to what extent the resource-based view helped to explain this.

The study is based on longitudinal and cross-sectional case studies of four Russian oil companies covering a ten-year period from full privatisation of the oil industry in 1995 to 2005. Interviews were conducted from 2001 to 2005 and respondents were asked to talk about organisational change since privatisation. A longitudinal and qualitative approach is one most often used for research into organisational change (Pettigrew et al., 2001; Dawson, 2003). Choosing a period of rapid change allowed me to conduct a processual analysis of change over a relatively short period of time. The novelty and complexity of processes in a transition economy suggested the use of an interpretive approach, which is appropriate where the phenomena to be investigated are complex and not well understood.

Semi-structured interviews were conducted as it was essential to gain an in-depth knowledge and understanding of the organisations and their processes (Rouse and Daellenbach, 1999). Respondents included managers at different levels (top, senior and middle managers), representing different functions (e.g. strategy, PR, HR, finance, manufacturing and production) at two types of location (head office and regional subsidiaries). External experts with knowledge and experience of the case companies were also interviewed to gain a triangulated view of the general context of the industry. This triangulation of source data avoided over-reliance on perspectives of senior managers who might present events in a favourable light. Seventy-one interviews were conducted in which seventy-four respondents were involved. Eight of the respondents had worked in two of the companies. In 2003, while the research was still being conducted, two important events happened: TNK merged with BP to form a fifty/fifty international joint venture (JV); and the CEO of Yukos, Mikhail Khodorkovsky, was jailed for alleged tax crimes. The subsequent partial dismantling of Yukos meant that several employees transferred from Yukos to the new TNK-BP JV providing a good source of comparative data.

The interviews were conducted in Russian or English, according to respondent wishes, and lasted around one hour. They took place mainly in Moscow but also in the regions (for example Siberia for oil production and European Russia for oil refining). Respondents were encouraged to talk freely about organisational change and were assured of anonymity in writing up the results. The interviews were taped and transcribed. Representative quotations are given in the text, with anonymised references to the respondents provided in brackets, as well an an indication as to whether the text was translated or not (trans) and whether the interview took place in the regions or not. More information on the research methodology and data analysis is provided in the Appendix.

A THEORY OF ORGANISATIONAL TRANSFORMATION

On the basis of the above research I developed an integrative theoretical framework of organisational transformation, that captures the complexity of organisational transformation processes in transition economies. The framework demonstrates the influence of the institutional context and the administrative heritage, illustrates the varying roles of management practices, and explains how their impact changes over time, in a three stage process. I contribute to organisational learning and dynamic capabilities theory by explaining the linkages first between exploitation learning and the deployment function of dynamic capabilities, generating the operational capabilities required for short-term survival in a market economy, and second between exploration learning and the search and selection function of dynamic capabilities, generating the strategic flexibility required for sustainable competitive advantage in an unstable institutional environment. A top-down management style may provide the initial impetus for short term survival, but at later stages of transformation an empowering approach appears more likely to secure sustainable competitive advantage.

The main theoretical perspective is the resource-based view, however it is supplemented with key insights from organisational learning, dynamic capability, organisational change, top management team (TMT), leadership and institutional theory to form an integrative framework for organisational transformation. Key concepts in the theoretical framework thus are the TMT, administrative heritage, institutional embeddedness, absorptive capacity, organisational learning, operational and dynamic capabilities and strategic flexibility. Their role and relationships evolve over the stages of organisational transformation.

This integrative framework addresses one of the current challenges of strategic management research: how to develop a theory of strategic management that reduces fragmentation and synthesises different views (Elfring and Volberda, 2001; Schoemaker, 2001; Hambrick, 2004). It integrates a range of theories to gain a fuller appreciation of the complexity of the processes. Furthermore three stages of transformation are identified, each with distinct change dynamics, thereby contributing to the organisational change literature by adopting a processual theory of change (Pettigrew, 1997) and explaining the temporal and organisational processes by which change unfolds (Greenwood and Hinings, 2006).

STRUCTURE OF THE BOOK

Chapter 2 describes the external (macro-environmental and industry) and internal (administrative and cultural heritage) context for the Russian oil companies. Primary and secondary data are interwoven with the literature to provide a rich description.

Chapter 3 presents an integrative theoretical framework to explain a three-stage process of organisational transformation in firms in transition economies. This framework was developed as a result of iteration between the literature and the empirical research.

Chapters 4–6 present stories of organisational transformation as individual case studies for the Western-style companies Yukos and TNK-BP and as a combined case study for the Soviet-style companies Lukoil and Surgutneftegaz.

Chapters 7–9 split the integrative framework for organisational transformation into three sections and demonstrate the empirical underpinning for the model. Chapter 7 explains the relationship between leadership, administrative heritage and absorptive capacity. Chapter 8 focuses on the links between different types of organisational learning and the development of operational capabilities and strategic flexibility. Chapter 9 explains the interrelationship of organisational learning and dynamic capabilities. Each chapter includes detailed time-ordered and conceptually ordered cross-case data displays to explain the process of organisational transformation and to draw out the key similarities and differences between the four companies.

Chapter 10 provides the overall conclusions and explains the implications for theory and practice. A postscript is added to put the study into the context of developments in the Russian oil industry since the research was completed in 2005.

2.   Transition context

The external context is important for organisational processes (Johns, 2001; Meyer, 2007) and strategic management research and the resource-based view have been criticised for not sufficiently taking into account industry and environmental effects (Dess et al., 1990; Miller and Shamsie, 1996; Johns, 2001; Tsui, 2004). This chapter therefore describes the external (macro-environmental and industry) and internal (administrative and cultural heritage) context for the Russian oil companies. There are six sections which describe the general characteristics of the macro-environment in a transition economy; the stages of development in the macro-environment from 1990 to 2005; the key characteristics of the international oil industry; the key characteristics of the Russian oil industry; the administrative and cultural heritage of the Soviet planned economy; and a conclusion.

Primary and secondary data are interwoven with the literature to provide a rich description, thus setting the scene for the subsequent analysis.

MACRO-ENVIRONMENTAL CONTEXT OF TRANSITION ECONOMY

Transition economies are faced with an unprecedented degree of change as they move from a centrally planned economy to market-based system. In the FSU and CEE, a major motivation for rapid liberalisation and privatisation was the political imperative to dismantle the socialist state as quickly and irreversibly as possible (Sachs, 1993; Brada, 1995; Hoffman, 2002). In these transition countries the main approach was 'big bang' or 'shock therapy', whereas China took the 'gradualist' approach (Peng, 2000). The shock therapy required to unleash market forces was manifested in price liberalisation and mass privatisation (Sachs, 1993). In the initial stages, the shock therapy resulted in dramatic economic decline, with steep drops in industrial output.

Privatisation Process

The political drivers for radical economic change were very strong in Russia. The reformers under President Boris Yeltsin, believing they had little time, set out to 'wreck the old system at any cost' (Hoffman, 2002: 3) They freed prices and property first, expecting that the rules and institutions of a market economy would be installed later: 'Russian capitalism was born into an airless apace, a vacuum without effective laws . . . In these early years, Russia was a state without the rule of law. Lying, stealing, and cheating were part of daily business, and violence, brutality, and coercion were often tools of the trade' (Hoffman, 2002: 6).

The lack of an institutional framework promoted opportunistic behaviour such as managers and employees taking state enterprises into their own hands through spontaneous privatisation (Peng, 2000). Private ownership came without rights and without responsibilities (ibid.). Transition countries lacked an institutional framework – the set of fundamental political, social and legal ground rules that establishes the basis for production, exchange and distribution (North, 1990). 'Russia never had any significant tradition of stable property rights, or institutions of capitalist development. Politically, institutionally there isn't the historical precedent on which to build' (newspaper correspondent, Western, 2004).

The privatisation of state-owned enterprises (SOEs) took place in the relative absence of legal, regulatory and financial institutions (Earle et al., 1993; DeCastro and Uhlenbruck, 1997). These institutions still had to be created and new 'rules of the game' introduced, including bankruptcy laws, property rights and financial reporting requirements. The lack of institutions meant there was little protection for private business: 'This is what's been hampering us extraordinarily big time . . . I feel like that we are working, and what's around us is not interested in us being successful . . . they can come to you and basically cause big damage to your company. Look what's happening with Yukos right now' (middle manager, TNK-BP, Russian, 2004).

The lack of a banking system was a major challenge for companies needing capital to expand or restructure; and such banking systems as existed were often in crisis, as witnessed by the Russian economic crash in 1998. In Russia, the newly privatised companies were desperately short of capital, since the privatisation process often handed ownership over to insider owners, and firms in consequence did not receive any fresh capital (Estrin, 2002). Their ownership status was ambiguous and unstable, with the managers mostly sharing legal ownership with their workers. The absence of a legal framework for corporate governance and bankruptcy meant that the new owners could get away with not paying bills, wages and taxes, and with not restructuring their companies or listening to their shareholders (Gustafson, 1999). In Russia, many companies had complex tax avoidance schemes which 'under Russian law seemed to be perfectly legal' (investment bank executive, Western, 2004). No company could have survived if they had paid all the taxes levied on them: 'When we first got into Russia if we'd have paid every tax, it exceeded revenue, 100% of revenue. So tax management – big issue . . . it was a quagmire' (top manager, TNK-BP, Western, 2005).

The institutional environment was lagging behind developments in some companies and constrained organisational development: 'These companies exist within a country and they cannot become Western companies within Russia that we have today. It will take huge political change, economic change' (newspaper correspondent, Russian/Western, 2001).

Privatisation in transition economies frequently took place in two steps (Peng, 2000). The first step, privatisation through management and employee buyouts, generally failed to provide the necessary governance mechanisms via investor control and the firms remained inefficient and un-restructured. In the second step, outside investors and managers came in and provided the impetus for reorganisation and rationalisation. However, given the hostile and uncertain environment, outside investors were rare. Thus the majority of companies remained under insider control (Earle and Estrin, 1996; Wright et al., 1998).

In Russia, the first phase of privatisation proceeded rapidly – within less than three years (1992–95) the state economy had passed largely into private hands – most often to insiders. The second phase of privatisation in Russia (1995–98) involved the state selling off its remaining stake in the commodity export industries. Under the infamous 'loans for shares' scheme, the Russian government, desperate to fend off regime challenges from the Communists, raised money from the heads of the powerful financial-industrial groups that arose in the first phase of privatisation, in exchange for shares in important oil and telecommunications industries. The country's assets were effectively sold off for a fraction of their worth since the loans were not repaid and the shares remained in the hands of the banks. The transfer of ownership of these resources from the state to the financial-industrial groups (FIG) led to the rise of the oligarchs,[1] men who wield both wealth and power (Hoffman, 2002).

Restructuring

Before transition, firms had excess employment and inventories, dated phys-ical resources, extensive social services and a non-competitive product port-folio (Peng and Heath, 1996). In many transition economies the rapid transition to a market economy largely destroyed the value of their resources and many firms were unable to adapt to the fundamentally new conditions.

Given the confusion and the lack of institutional frameworks, choosing a muddling-through strategy was a rational choice for many organisations

(Peng, 2000). Uncertainty and ambiguity made it difficult for managers to operate in the short run, and nearly impossible to plan for the longer run, therefore short-term ad hoc adjustments to immediate pressure were often more rational than undertaking large-scale risky changes in pursuit of long-run strategic objectives (McCarthy and Puffer, 1995; Whitley and Czaban, 1998). This is consistent with the institutional perspective – when the rules of the game are highly uncertain, organisations are not able to invest in new capabilities and skills and will therefore, by default, continue in their old ways (North, 1990; Scott, 1995; Peng and Heath, 1996).

Strategic restructuring was very slow, and rarely happened without the involvement of a foreign partner (Estrin et al., 1996; Meyer and Møller, 1998). It required the development of marketing and finance as functions in the company and the introduction of new products in demand on the market. Often assets and businesses needed to be divested because of the high degree of vertical and horizontal integration that was common in the planned economy. Four major gaps were identified in transition firms: lack of access to financial resources due to an underdeveloped financial sector and the high risk of investing in an uncertain environment; weak systems of corporate governance leading to ineffective control of owners over management, or conflicting interests of insider-owners; fundamentally different success criteria for management and entrepreneurship in a market economy compared to a planned economy; and interruption in relationships with customers and suppliers before new international networks had been established (Meyer and Møller, 1998).

Crime and Corruption

Network contacts were extensively used to coordinate economic activity before transition (Peng, 1994; Child and Czegledy, 1996; Martin, 1999). Gift giving to superiors, bureaucrats and the party apparatus was prevalent not in the normal sense of a bribe for immediate favours, but rather as an investment in a long-term personal relationship (Luo and Peng, 1999; Peng, 2000). During transition, network ties become even more important (Johnson, 1997; Sedaitis, 1998). Where formal market-regulating institutions are missing or inadequate, managers use their connections (*blat*) to obtain information, interpret regulations and enforce contracts. These network-based personalised exchanges serve to reduce uncertainties in economic exchanges in volatile times (Sedaitis, 1998). Networks may also involve corruption, which is defined as the misuse of public power and/or public resources for personal gain. A wider definition includes networks between state officials and entrepreneurs and enterprise directors. These networks may not be based on direct transactions (bribes for favours) but on mutual trust, on the knowledge that granting a favour will offer the right to demand a favour in return (Pleines, 1999) (see below for corruption in the Russian oil industry).

Corruption was endemic in the Soviet system – the inflexibility of the planned economy had to be overcome in order for managers to fulfil their plan (ibid.). Corruption and theft had become the norm: 'We have to deal with theft – we have to fight this daily. This is something that is superfluous for a Western company. Because it would just not enter anyone's head there to steal, but here we are engaged morning till night in ensuring that we are not being robbed' (top manager, TNK-BP, Russian, 2004, translation).

One respondent maintained that Russians were not by nature dishonest, but that the Soviet system had encouraged this behaviour: 'Russians are not thieves . . . by nature. It is just that the whole of the preceding Soviet period made them do traditionally what was customary in this country' (energy consultant, Russian, 2001, translation). Russians tend to talk about the Russian *spetsifika*, the specific characteristics of Russian life and the way of doing business: 'Russia is different, although on the surface Russians may look completely European, dress properly in European style, talk properly as Europeans do, have a European education, but the country is organised in a completely different way . . . there is a completely different relationship between power and business' (energy consultant, Russian, 2001, translation).

STAGES OF DEVELOPMENT IN THE MACRO-ENVIRONMENT

This section identifies four stages of development in the macro-environment from 1990, the time of the collapse of the Soviet Union, to 2005, as they emerged from the data.

Time of Troubles (1991–95)

After the collapse of the Soviet Union, Russia descended into chaos. The state planning system was destroyed. Privatisation was rushed through in record time but market mechanisms did not exist. Industrial production tumbled. 'Unfortunately between Soviet times and today there were ten years which you can't even begin to describe. If you know the history of Russia, in the time of Boris Godunov there was the 'time of troubles'.[2] There is no other word for these ten years than 'time of troubles' (senior manager, TNK-BP, regional, Russian, translation).

Many jobs were lost – in the Nizhnevartovsk Production Association, employee numbers dropped from 72 000 to 30 000. For months neither employees nor the city administration got paid, whilst at the same time money was being misappropriated, to investments in sanatoria in the Crimea for instance. Criminal elements were siphoning off cash throughout industry and business was being developed in both legal and illegal ways.

There was no social support – the State had disintegrated. The inability to pay wages partly resulted from the mutual enterprise indebtedness which crippled industry in the early 1990s. Barter was the only means to survive and the catchword was 'deficit', since many of the basic necessities were unavailable. People in Siberia were particularly hard hit. Not only were wages not being paid, but also the traditional benefits, which were a necessity to attract people to work in such inhospitable regions, also disappeared, for example paid holidays in the South of Russia, recreation centres and special pensions.

In the industrial heartland of European Russia industry was at a standstill, not least because of the collapse in demand for military equipment: 'There was a period when the military industrial complex almost died out. That was a difficult time for the city then' (senior manager, TNK-BP, regional, Russian, translation). Into this chaos were to step the young entrepreneurs – the future oligarchs – who first took advantage of new opportunities for private enterprise in the form of cooperatives and trading and then set up fledgling banks to support their trading operations, thereby positioning themselves for acquiring assets languishing idle across Russia.

Asset Grabbing and the Rise of the Oligarchs (1995–98)

Industry had ground to a standstill. Anyone with drive and enthusiasm could acquire assets for next to nothing: 'It was essentially a grab and run kind of thing. And everything was . . . on offer for a dime' (senior manager, TNK-BP, Russian). The collapse of the Soviet economy left companies without markets or suppliers. Intercompany indebtedness created opportunities for entrepreneurs with cash: 'This was the period . . . when these non-payments made it possible to invoke bankruptcy proceedings . . . The law was clearly favourable to creditors. Creditors . . . were able to determine the fate of a company. And we began to actively make use of this . . . we were one of the first' (top manager, TNK-BP, Russian, translation)

Thus the oligarchs began to amass assets: 'They got the assets by theft and corruption, by knowing people in the government' (investment bank executive, Western). The oligarchs were unpopular with the man on the street:

There is the feeling that the majority of the population in Russia has been robbed, although, of course, Ivan Ivanovich Ivanov [the man on the street] is no different at all from Berezovsky [an oligarch]. Just that Berezovsky made himself a billionaire, and Ivan remained poverty-stricken, although he was the head of a laboratory, just the same as Berezovsky was, in an Institute. (energy consultant, Russian, translation)

A contrary view came from the regions. Respondents there seemed to respect the oligarchs: 'People who are superior and cleverer than us found a way, found means to organise themselves, to self-fulfilment. Not everyone is born to that. Each to his own place in life' (middle manager, TNK-BP, regional, Russian, translation). In fact life had always been the same in the regions. All the wealth was generated in the oilfields, but the benefits were enjoyed in the capital: 'You come back home from work, you can go to bed, the next morning get up and go to work again. So it is a tradition for us that the fruits of the labour are enjoyed by others [laughter]. In that respect there has been no improvement' (senior manager, TNK-BP, regional, Russian, translation). Nevertheless the view was that the oligarchs were in a precarious position: 'an oligarch lives well, but not for long! [laughter]' (ibid.).

Yeltsin's 'loans for shares scheme' in 1995 gave the oligarchs an added boost. Yeltsin's hold on power was precarious and he needed funding from the oligarchs for his election campaign – in return they received shares in the key assets of the country. Once acquired, the assets need protecting and major security systems manned by ex-KGB members were set up to establish control and stop theft. It was from this time that rumours sprang linking the name of the Yukos CEO, Khodorkovsky, to contract killings, carried out to stamp out activities of criminal gangs who were siphoning off cash from the companies. Part of the process of establishing control meant combining many legal entities, created in the first phase of privatisation, into one large enterprise. Khodorkovsky, for instance, combined 153 legal entities into one in Yuganskneftegaz.

The 1998 economic crisis in Russia and the collapse of the banking system was the impetus for the next stage of development: the move towards the market.

Move Towards the Market (1998–2003)

The 1998 economic crisis focused attention on cost reduction: 'The 1998 crisis probably played a beneficial role for Russian business. All the surplus fat – perhaps not all, but a lot of it – was cut away . . . so that business immediately became more sinewy and wiry, more muscular' (energy consultant, Russian, translation). By 2000, the result of cost cutting and efficiency measures meant increased competitive advantage for the Russian oil companies in the global market – their production costs were beginning to drop below those of the Western oil majors:

> The Russian oil industry now is very, very different from what it was a decade ago . . . There's no question that they are basically now quite commercially focused . . . There's also been a number of policy changes that have allowed that supplier response to occur, like the devaluation of the rouble, certain kinds of tax reform, . . . legal reforms and so forth . . . it's been sufficient to allow the industry to completely change and revolutionise itself already. (energy consultant, Western)

At this stage the changes in the Russian oil companies seemed to be moving in tandem with the changes in the politico-economic environment. A positive business climate was linked with Putin's takeover of power in 2000. It was at this time that companies began to think of long-term growth, rather than short-term survival. Furthermore, criminal activities began to decline, heralding an end to the violent asset-grabbing period of the 1990s: 'Whereas in '93–'94 all business problems were resolved with a gun, now this phase has passed, or almost passed, so there are just a few marginal businessmen who sometimes get killed or some bureaucrats, linked with some suspicious outfits, get killed – things are changing' (energy consultant, Russian, translation).

Soon after Putin took power he struck a deal with the oligarchs that if they stopped meddling in politics he would not reopen any issues associated with the privatisation and asset-grabbing process. Thenceforward the oligarchs were to focus on business only. Not all oligarchs, however, kept to the deal, as described below.

Reversion to State Control (2003–05)

Although most interviews in 2001 had been positive about further moves to a free market, there was already a hint of the government's nervousness about the private sector: 'Even now the mentality of the state, even at this stage, is wary, not just with respect to the West, but also with respect to the private sector as a whole' (senior manager, Lukoil, Russian, translation). In the interviews in 2004/05 there was a sharp decline in the optimism about the move of Russia towards a market economy in the wake of the Yukos affair. Khodorkovsky had ignored Putin's deal with the oligarchs and spoke openly of his political ambitions, even to stand for President against Putin. This was not tolerated and in 2003 Khodorkovsky was jailed and the assets of Yukos frozen, pending settlement of large tax claims. The progress that had been made towards a market economy was under threat. The oil companies which had transformed themselves over a short period of time were hostage to fortune: 'But the thing that can stymie a lot of that are the government policymakers. In terms of all the risks and problems and how it can go round and double up, it returns back to that' (investment bank executive, Western).

A reversion to state control was evidenced in the re-nationalisation of significant segments of the oil industry. The main Yukos oil-producing asset, Yuganskneftegaz, was auctioned off to a bogus company which turned out to be part of Rosneft, the state oil company; Sibneft, whose merger with Yukos had collapsed, was acquired by Gazprom, the state gas company. The move towards increased state power threatened the fragile market economy. One respondent drew a parallel with the way Stalin had stamped out the New Economic Policy (NEP), which had allowed the brief flowering of the private economy in the 1920s: 'History can repeat itself. And sometimes thinking of Russian history, . . . when thinking of the Putin administration . . . more and more it's starting to look like Moscow 1930. The New Economic Policy is just coming to an end' (headhunter, Western). Exaggeration or not, the atmosphere was one of heightened political risk.

The official reason for the break-up of Yukos was their non-payment of taxes. It was generally acknowledged, however, that Yukos had acted no differently from its competitors in managing its tax issues. One respondent had an inside view of two companies: 'To be honest, all the oil companies were interpreting the law to their own advantage – which is what Yukos is now being accused of' (middle manager, Yukos, ex-Sidanco, Russian, translation).

The political climate was uncomfortable for all the oil companies. The shifts and changes in the political landscape seemed likely to continue and the early promise of stability and a move to the market economy when Putin came to power seemed unlikely to be realised. By 2004 there seemed to be little cause for optimism about any further moves towards a market orientation.

INTERNATIONAL OIL INDUSTRY CONTEXT

This section describes the international oil industry and its key players, and the effect of environmental instability on strategic planning.

The international Oil Industry and its Key Players

Energy and its deployment are the most critical of all wealth-generating activities (Economides and Oligney, 2000). Of all energy sources, oil has been the most problematic because of its central role in the economy, its strategic

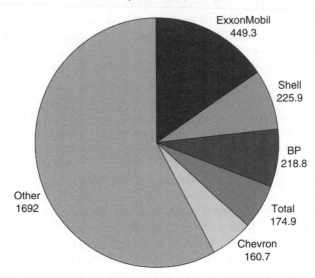

Source: PFC Energy, 2007

Figure 2.1   Five oil majors' share of top 50 energy companies,
January 2007

character, its geographic distribution, the recurrent pattern of crisis in its supply, and the irresistible temptation to grasp for its rewards (Yergin, 1991).

Two key groups influence the international oil industry – the independent oil majors and OPEC. The five independent super majors are: BP(Amoco/ Arco), ChevronTexaco, ExxonMobil, TotalFinaElf and Royal Dutch Shell (Figure 2.1). Between them, their market capitalisation represents 45 per cent of the top 50 energy companies (PFC Energy, 2007). (See Figure 2.1).

Penrose's (1968) classic study of the international petroleum industry indicated that large size is associated with economic power. The Organization of Petroleum Exporting Countries (OPEC), a cartel of 11 national oil producers, is one of the most powerful influences on the global economy, collectively supplying about 40 per cent of the world's oil output, and possessing more than three-quarters of the world's total proven crude oil reserves (OPEC, 2004). However, the independent oil majors have certain advantages over national oil companies – experience in new technology, domination of the refining industry and access to low-cost capital for investment (Turner, 1978; Economides and Oligney, 2000).

Much of the oil majors' domination of the industry derives from their history of vertical integration. Thus the multinational oil companies typically cover a range of activities in the oil value chain – crude oil production, crude oil transportation, refining, petrochemical production, oil products/petrochemicals distribution and wholesale, and gasoline retailing. The profit opportunities at the different levels of the oil industry have fluctuated continuously and for many years it was argued that vertical integration provided greater stability in earnings (McLean and Haigh, 1954).

Instability and Effect on Strategic Planning

The oil industry has been described as a precarious balance of programmed stability upset from time to time by conflict stemming from uncontrolled market forces (De Chazeau and Kahn, 1959). On this basis, these authors describe the desirable characteristics for oil companies as a combination of stability and flexibility, standardisation and uniformity on the one hand, and variation and diversity on the other. In 1986, the oil market was thrown into uncertainty and turbulence with a large fall in the oil price (Grant, 2003). This had far-reaching implications for the companies' strategies, structures and management processes (ibid.). The accuracy of macro-economic and market forecasts declined – as late as 1992, BP was brought to the brink of catastrophe as the result of a strategy that had assumed an oil price of $20/barrel. Increased environmental instability led to greater flexibility in strategic plans – they were less about projects and resource deployment, and more about strategic intent, setting aspirations and performance goals. Strategy making was transferred from the corporate centre to the business units – enabling faster decision making in response to fast-changing external circumstances (ibid.). Each business segment within an oil company had to justify itself on its own financial returns. The strategy had shifted from balancing operations in an integrated operation towards profit maximisation (Antill and Arnott, 2003), ensuring that each of the businesses in the portfolio is competitive and innovative while ensuring that the synergies deriving from common ownership are carefully managed (Rainbow, 2001).

RUSSIAN OIL INDUSTRY CONTEXT

This section describes the Russian oil industry in four parts: the Soviet heritage and the privatisation process, the global significance of the Russian oil industry, a comparison of Russian and Western oil companies, and the characteristics of the Russian oil industry.

Soviet Heritage and Privatisation Process

The structure of the Russian oil industry in Soviet times, prior to privatisation, was completely non-integrated – the industry was run by three separate ministries, one for exploration, one for production and pipelines, and
one for refineries. With the formation of the Russian Federation, the
opportunity was taken to create vertically integrated oil and gas companies
on the model of the leading Western oil companies in order to increase
operational efficiency and to be able to compete on world markets (Lane,
1999; Antill and Arnott, 2003). Yukos, for example, was created from five
production associations and five refining companies and Lukoil from four
production associations and seven refining companies. Since that time consolidation has continued, with the oil companies merging and investing in
upgrading or acquiring new refineries.

The privatisation of Russian oil industry started in 1991 when Lukoil set
up a joint stock company. Other companies followed but the state retained
a significant shareholding until the Yeltsin loans for shares scheme in 1995,
when ownership transferred to the financial industrial groups (Grace,
2005). Russian banks and financial institutions thus became the leading
institutional owners of some of the newly created integrated oil companies.
This was the case for Yukos, Sibneft and TNK, where the banks retained
control of the assets. These companies had financial managers, motivated
by profitability and shareholder value. In contrast, the existing managers of
Lukoil and Surgutneftegaz, who were professional oilmen, kept control
themselves as 'insiders' (Lane and Seifulmulukov, 1999). The resultant
industry was highly concentrated, 'divided between a few tenacious Soviet-
era managers and oligarchs' (Grace, 2005: 161).

The Global Significance of the Russian Oil Industry

The rise of the Russian oil industry from the mid-1990s was the most
influential new force in the world oil market since OPEC in the 1970s (Grace,
2005). Russia produces more than 10 per cent of the world's oil (*BP Statistical
Review of World Energy*, 2003) and is the second biggest oil exporter after
Saudi Arabia (Liuhto, 2003). Russia produced 11.4 million barrels per day
(bbl/d) in 1988, at which time it was the world's leading oil producer (Ebel,
2003). But the legacy of Soviet mismanagement, the economic collapse after
perestroika in the early 1990s and lack of investment capital constrained the
development of the industry (Ziener, 2001; Ebel, 2003). Crude oil production
fell from 11.3 million bbl/d in 1986 to 5.04 million in 1996 (Lane, 1999).

Led by the companies run by financial managers, a turnaround in
Russian oil output began in 1999, which many analysts have attributed to

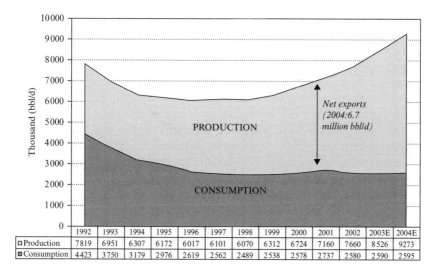

Note: E = estimate

Source: EIA, 2005, Fig. 1

Figure 2.2 Russian oil production and consumption, 1992–2004

rising world oil prices, which tripled between January 1999 and September 2000, as well as to the 1998 financial crisis with the subsequent devaluation of the rouble. The rebound in Russian oil production has continued since 1999, resulting in 2002's crude oil production of 7.7 million bbl/d (Figure 2.2). In 2004 production reached 9.3 million bbl/d (BP, 2005). Russian oil company managers speak of Russian oil production reaching 10 million bbl/d by the year 2010 (Ebel, 2003).

Russia has always been a major oil exporter, but the combination of a drop in domestic consumption (Figure 2.2) with the increased output means that Russia is becoming an even more important player on the global market. Exports of oil and oil products represent between 30–40 per cent of total Russian export revenues with oil-related taxes accounting for up to one quarter of the federal budget receipts (Khartukov and Starostina, 2003; Liuhto, 2003) The oil sector represents about 15 per cent of Russia's GDP (Khartukov and Starostina, 2003).

Despite these large export volumes, Russia does not provide a counterbalance to OPEC (Boue, 2004) because Russia cannot bring on surplus capacity in the short term, as Saudi Arabia can, to institute a price war. Russia thus remains susceptible to the volatility of oil prices (Mabro, 2001).

million tonnes

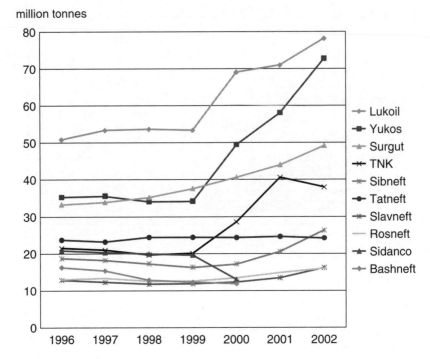

Notes:
a. Sidanco was acquired by TNK in 1997.
b. Slavneft is owned 50/50 by Yukos and Sibneft.
c. Rosneft is 100% state-owned.
d. Tatneft is the Tatarstan regional oil company.
e. Bashneft is the Bashkortostan regional oil company.

Source: Liuhto, 2003

Figure 2.3   Major Russian oil companies: production 1996–2002 (million tonnes)

In 2003, 80 per cent of oil production came from the five major private companies (Lukoil, Yukos, TNK-BP, Surgutneftegaz and Sibneft) (Figure 2.3) and two regional companies (Bashneft and Tatneft). The growth in oil production between 1996 and 2002 has been significant – an increase of 54 per cent for Lukoil and a doubling for Yukos (Figure 2.3). Figure 2.4 shows the increase in oil production in 2001 and 2002 for the Russian oil companies.

Russia lags the OPEC countries in oil reserves, with 5 per cent of global oil reserves compared to Saudi Arabia's 25 per cent (Liuhto, 2003). Most

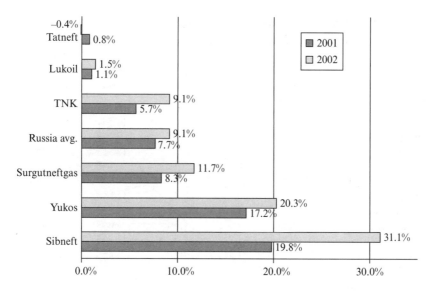

Source: IEA: (Murray, 2004).

Figure 2.4   Russian oil companies: oil production growth 2001–02

of Russia's oil reserves are located in Western Siberia, but there are also significant reserves in the North European part of Russia. The location and difficulty of exploiting the oil reserves means that oil production costs are higher than for the Middle East. However, the 1998 economic crash and the drop in oil prices led to lower costs and improvements in employee productivity (Gaddy, 2000). Average production costs dropped from $9.50 to $5.50 per barrel (Lane, 1999). This, combined with high oil prices from 2000 onwards, generated large cashflows (Brown, 2001).

Comparison of Russian and Western Oil Majors

The Russian oil majors are comparable with their Western counterparts in reserves and production, but lag on financial indicators, trading at large discounts (74 per cent) to the oil majors (Gladyshev, 2001; Nickolov and Kushnir, 2001) (Table 2.1). More recent market capitalisation figures as at end 2003 are shown in Figure 2.5.

The Yukos/Sibneft merger, announced in April 2003, had a combined capitalisation of $35 billion, putting it into seventh position behind the oil majors. By oil reserves it was no. 1 and by oil production no. 2. However, in November 2003 it was announced that Sibneft was withdrawing from the merger.

Table 2.1   Western and Russian oil majors compared (2000)

	Market capitalisation ($ million)	P/E (x)	EV/Ebitda (x)	Reserves (million bbl)	Production (million bbl)
Lukoil	7 347	2.7	2.1	14 202	502
Yukos	8 000	2.4	n/a	11 769	991
Surgut	10 104	3.6	1.9	9 078	278
TNK	n/a.	n/a	n/a	13 313	954
Tatneft	1 074	1.4	1.3	6 135	170
Sibneft	1 327	2.3	2.0	4 599	140
ExxonMobil	296 208	17.5	8.2	15 813	1 393
Royal Dutch	128 369	15.9	7.6	10 572	709
Shell T&T	81 902	15.6	7.5	7 048	473
BP Amoco	195 042	13.7	7.5	12 363	1 050
TotalFinaElf	103 147	14.3	n/a	8 438	643

Note: n/a = not available

Sources: Adapted from Nicklolov and Kushnir, 2001; Gladyshev, 2001; company data

Basic data on the four Russian majors under study were provided in Chapter 1, Table 1.1. Yukos led by market value at the end of 2002, and was the fifteenth independent oil company in the world by this measure. It also had the lowest production cost of the four majors (and lower than that of ExxonMobil the leading multinational oil major). Yukos' oil production had grown by 20.3 per cent in 2002, significantly ahead of its peers. The figures for TNK are rather less impressive. The likely reason is that TNK came later to the privatisation process, inheriting some of the poorest oil assets. In terms of oil production Lukoil is the largest company, but their oil production growth was the lowest of all, and production cost the second highest.

Characteristics of the Russian Oil Industry

The Russian oil companies are still heavily shaped by their Soviet history both in resources and capital base, but also in outlook on the technology, economic and politics of oil (Grace, 2005). The Soviet stewardship of the oilfields achieved high production levels in the 1980s, but at great costs. The industry was production-driven rather than profit-driven – oil was produced even if the production costs were higher than the world market price. Freedom from responsibility for costs at the field level led to wasteful operating decisions. Cost-based economics meant that 'the more you spend, the

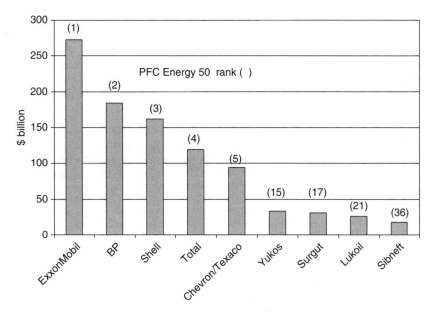

Source: Figures from PFC Energy, 2004

Figure 2.5 Comparison of market capitalisation of Western and Russian oil majors as at 31 December 2003

better for you' (middle manager, Yukos, Russian, translation). The attitude to planning differed from that in market economies. A plan involved a concrete forecast of what would be achieved. The requirement to achieve the forecast resulted in distortions of reality and conservative estimates. Failure was unacceptable and there were no incentives for extraordinary performance. The extensive use of water flooding to increase oil production has caused long-term damage to agriculture. The Siberian oilfields were developed by settling a large labour force in inhospitable locations. The reduction in workforce under market conditions has a huge social cost for the local people who have no prospects of work locally and no possibility to move. Lastly the Soviet oil industry was responsible for thousands of square miles of pollution (ibid.). This was the Soviet oil heritage facing the newly privatised oil industry.

The Soviet approach to oil production also differed from that in the West. A Western company might produce oil from a field for ten years, whereas a Soviet enterprise would take 30–40 years. This was due first, to lack of incentives to produce more and faster, since profit was not the objective. Second, it was feared that rapid well exploitation could lead to reduced recovery of oil over the field's lifetime. These concerns were magnified in towns in Siberia which existed only because of oil production. People wished to preserve their livelihoods and those of their children and grand-children. Lack of labour mobility (due partly to cultural factors and partly to housing shortages) further exacerbated the problem.

The privatised Russian oil industry can be compared with the early years of the petroleum industry in the USA, namely: 'Aggressive enterprise, ruth-less competitive tactics, often explicitly designed to eliminate competitors and obtain monopolistic control of markets, supplies or productive facili-ties, brilliant organising ability, technological progressiveness, and a stead-fast belief in the social and economic desirability of unregulated, uninhibited business enterprise' (Penrose, 1968: 26).

One respondent considered, however, that the lawlessness and excesses of the early days of privatisation were a transitory phenomenon and that busi-ness would gradually become more civilised.

> I think that processes are underway . . . The processes may come in surges, there may be excesses – they won't always be democratic processes unfortunately. But in principle there is an attempt to find the right balance between the interests of the state and the interests of business, and this balance should then . . . provide the basis for the further development of business in a conventional mechanism. (energy consultant, Russian, translation)

The aggressive privatisation and restructuring of the Russian oil indus-try was associated with theft, corruption, insider deals, networks between the oil elite and federal and regional officials, smuggling of oil exports, money laundering, capital flight and organised crime (contract killers) (Pleines, 1999). 'Corruption is a facilitating factor for most of these oil companies. I mean clearly there are large payments that get made to gov-ernment officials, regional officials, to the decision-maker effectively. And that's part of the nature of doing business in Russia' (newspaper corre-spondent, Western).

Increasingly, however, it has become clear to the oil companies that they can make more profits through legal means such as modernising the indus-try and stopping the decline in production (ibid.). To attract capital on the Western market for investments they need to institute systems of corpo-rate governance. One of the reasons Russian companies sought out Western partners was to increase their standing in the global capital markets: 'to help accelerate that process of respectability, having clearly been guilty of smash and grab raids and some pretty serious corporate misgovernance, abuse of minority rights, corruption and bankruptcy systems, corruption through the court system, asset stripping' (top manager, BP, Western).

Western companies with their business principles were unable to make the necessary facilitating payments to officials and legislative structures. However, they still had to deal with a system that was heavily reliant on relationships and networks:

> They cannot, to put it crudely, give bribes, not because they are such good people, but because it is disadvantageous for them, because this is not part of the rules of the game, this is forbidden. They are therefore obliged to find some Russian intermediaries . . . who will take on the dirty work, walking around the corridors of power. (energy consultant, Russian, translation)

Personal relationships were key to securing business deals, and often this might degenerate into facilitation payments: 'To do business in Russia . . . first of all you should find friends . . . People who for a long time had no economic stimuli to work . . . developed an unhealthy interest in personal material enrichment' (energy consultant, Russian, translation).

Good connections with the state are vital for the oil business (Pleines 1999): 'If you were making a risk matrix for a Russian company there'd only be one risk in the top right hand box, which would be government blessing' (top manager, Western Oil Company, Western). Good political relations played an important role in gaining access to pipelines, export quotas and production licenses. 'It's down to personal relations . . . there's a big bureaucracy here, a lot of people you have to know' (investment bank executive, Western). Russian oil companies had a source of competitive advantage compared to their Western counterparts operating in Russia, in that they had political connections 'although it's not worth as much now under Putin as it was with Yeltsin' (top manager, Western oil company, Western). But other respondents thought that political relationships were even more important under Putin, 'where you've seen a re-interest on the part of the government to maintain control over natural resources' (head-hunter, Western). Their importance was evidenced by Putin's crackdown on the leading oil producer Yukos, and its erstwhile CEO, Khodorkovsky. The jailing of Khodorkovsky for alleged tax crimes and the subsequent break-up and re-nationalisation of Yukos was a consequence of a more mono-cratic state under the government of Putin (Grace, 2005). The lesson of the Yukos story was clear – an oil company needed not just to maintain a normal level of cooperation with the government, but to actively cultivate 'a relationship which goes beyond normal cooperation . . . allowing it to deteriorate to something less than cooperation is potentially fatal' (top manager, TNK-BP, Western). In an interview in 2001, before the Yukos affair in 2003, the high risk of non-cooperation with the government was mentioned:

> In Russia the manager of a large company has to balance business and politics, because if he moves against some political current or other, or if he doesn't move in the same direction as all the others, then he runs the risk of dropping out, or his business will be destroyed, or he will be removed. This is no secret for anybody. (middle manager, Russian oil company, Russian, translation)

Whereas under Yeltsin the oligarchs had a strong influence on the government, under Putin, the government took control: 'The government is now stating the terms under which you act, if you act on those terms you'll be allowed to make your profits and if you don't, then you're out' (investment bank executive, Western). A critical success factor for operating in Russia was keeping in step with the government: 'There's a great phrase in Russia I use: "check with the Kremlin". That's exactly what the industry is about these days' (investment bank executive, Western).

A general trend was for the government to recapture oil and gas assets privatised in the 1990s. The short period of ten years of relative freedom to develop under a market system seemed to be coming to an end for at least some of the companies, with both Yukos and Sibneft being reabsorbed into the state. Yuganskneftegaz, the largest oil-producing subsidiary of Yukos, was acquired by the state oil company Rosneft in 2004 and Sibneft was sold to Gazprom, the state gas monopoly, in 2005. Surgutneftegaz, Lukoil and TNK-BP for the time being seem to have mastered the political skills vital to operations in post-Yeltsin Russia. Together these companies seemed to form the industry's long-term core (Grace, 2005).

ADMINISTRATIVE AND CULTURAL HERITAGE

The administrative and cultural heritage of the Russian oil companies shapes and constrains their actions. This section describes how the organisational routines and culture were at variance with those required in a market economy.

The market reforms undertaken by the Russian government failed to address three issues: the need for radical restructuring of the large state enterprises, the absence of any distribution, marketing and private financial institutions, and the lack of training and experience of Russian managers in the management skills and techniques needed in a market economy (Vlachoutsicos and Lawrence, 1996). The latter was a major problem, intensified by the lack of understanding of managers of market concepts. Russians retained a strong conservatism and it was difficult to change mindsets: 'Anything new is very difficult to introduce . . . There is a very pronounced conservatism, so that it is very difficult to drag people out of their normal way of thinking' (middle manager, TNK-BP, Russian, translation). Western practice was automatically rejected on the basis that 'this won't work here' (middle manager, TNK-BP, Russian, translation). The Soviet heritage of 70 years of the Communist system made people deeply suspicious of Western business and the concept of managers:

> The word 'manager', traditionally for a Russian person, it's a kind of incomprehensible word. Of course it's not a swear word, but all the same, people are disparaging about it, because 'manager' – no one understands what it is. No one understands that it is a bundle of knowledge such as HR for the management of human resources, or about corporate culture, and concepts of corporate governance. (top manager, TNK-BP, Russian, translation)

Cross-cultural studies highlighted a distrust of individualism in Russia – anyone showing signs of making themselves better than the group were viewed with suspicion and contempt (Elenkov, 1998; Naumov and Puffer, 2000). This reaction can be seen in the negative attitude towards the New Russians:[3] 'Many people . . . hold the deep-seated belief that the wealth and achievements of others are gained at the expense of those who have less' (Elenkov, 1998: 136). There was no concept of making money – the concept of profit was alien to the Russian culture.

> On the worker's level the Russians do not have a cult of money and enriching themselves, they don't care whether they can make more money or not, people would rather have an easier life. There is a joke in Russia that Russians would rather have their neighbour's house burned down than to build their own which would be just as good. (newspaper correspondent, Russian/Western)

In contrast, Western culture admires competitive individuals exploiting their own potential. The slogan 'don't live worse than your neighbour' is interpreted in opposite ways in Russia and the West (Naumov and Puffer, 2000).

Soviet organisations were characterised by a blame culture and consequently an aversion to risk taking:

> In Russia there's a tremendous opportunity for somebody to say no. A lone staff person can say no – and there's really no penalty for doing so. But if somebody was to say yes . . . you look around and you look over your shoulder and, have I done the right thing, and if I'm wrong will I be fired? (top manager, Western oil company)

It made sense to reflect the culture of conservatism in one's actions. Subordinates were discouraged from initiating dialogue with their superiors:

A subordinate would never allow himself to write a note to the President or even to a lower level manager, because the latter would say 'why are you writing to me? I don't know what this is all about. Why is he annoying me with his problems when I have enough of my own. And, by the way, make sure he doesn't do it again.' That is putting it mildly. More often than not, a much harsher approach is taken. (middle manager, TNK-BP, Russian, translation)

For Russians the boss was idealised as a father figure. No one challenged any of the boss's orders and there was no culture of delegation. Russian management style was rigidly top-down, aggressive and ideally suited to crisis situations: 'But when the crisis passes and the company is working normally again and needs to develop, then Russian managers are significantly less able to grasp the initiative' (middle manager, TNK-BP, Russian, translation).

In summary the Soviet administrative heritage was likely to be a considerable constraint on transition to a market economy.

CONCLUSIONS

The key macro-environmental factors affecting organisational change may be summarised as a lack of institutions, weak rule of law and inadequate financial systems. Companies operating in the Russian transition environment must deal with turbulence, opportunism, corruption, resource grabbing, disrupted relationships and differing concepts of organisational success. The four stages of development in the external context from privatisation till 2005 are illustrated in Figure 2.6.

A time-ordered data display links the key factors in the macro-environment to the different stages of development of the economy (Table 2.2).

The Russian oil industry makes a major contribution to the Russian economy. In all parts of the world oil is linked with power and politics, and especially so in Russia. The privatisation of the Russian oil industry resulted in significant improvements in performance, both in terms of production and efficiency. However, the new company owners, the oligarchs, were becoming too powerful and were perceived to be threatening the state. The actions of Putin to partially re-nationalise the industry can be seen in this light.

The Soviet administrative and cultural heritage was characterised by behaviours which were at variance with the requirements for success in a market economy and the prospects for organisational change towards a Western market-oriented model seemed poor. The key differences between the organisational routines and culture of Soviet and Western organisations are displayed below (Table 2.3).

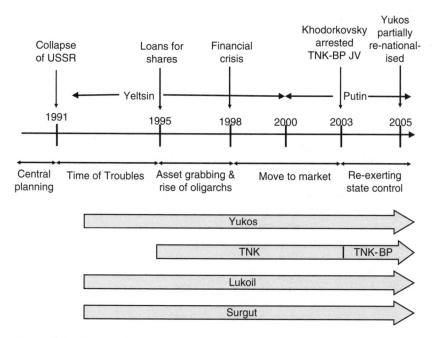

Figure 2.6   External context since the collapse of the USSR

The changes occurring in the transition economies are pervasive and cataclysmic. Organisations seeking to survive in the new order must undertake radical change. This requires more than just adopting the ways of a Western market economy, bringing in Western business practices and restructuring the organisation. It requires developing the strategic flexibility to adapt to political, legal, institutional and social instability on a scale unknown in the West. Although Western business models emphasise the need for strategic flexibility to cope with changes in the business environment, these changes are of a different order of magnitude from what is happening in the transition economies. In adopting the resource-based view, cognisance must be taken of the fact that the firm in a transition economy, and in particular in Russia, is beset by a continually changing set of environmental factors. The intertwining of the external context with the fate of the Russian oil companies implies that the resource-based view alone, focusing as it does on the internal capabilities of the organisation, is not sufficient for an understanding of the process of organisational change in the Russian oil industry. By including a consideration of the external context in the analysis this research addresses criticisms that strategic management research and the resource-based

Table 2.2   Time-ordered data display: summary of the external context

	Institutions	Politics	Crime and corruption
Time of troubles (1991–95)	• Privatisation and collapse of industrial production • Collapse of social services • Revert to barter	• Rival claims to power • Yeltsin vulnerable	• Insider privatisation • Widespread theft • Contract killings
Asset grabbing/ rise of oligarchs (1995–98)	• Combine legal entities • Divest social assets • Institutions undeveloped	• Yeltsin 'loans for shares' deal	• Contract killings • Bribery and corruption
Move towards market (1998–2003)	• Lack financial institutions • Banking crisis • Legal and fiscal framework under development • Move to market economy Institutions still lag	• 1998 economic crisis • 2000 Putin to power • Amnesty for oligarchs • Legal, tax and economic reforms	• Decline in criminal activity • Some introduction of corporate governance
Reversion to state control (2003–05)	• Partial re-nationalisation • Regression in market reforms • Opaque legal system	• Centralisation of power in state (Putin) • Oligarchs attacked • Heightened political risk	• 2003 Khodorkovsky jailed for tax crimes

view do not sufficiently take into account industry and environmental effects (Dess et al., 1990; Miller and Shamsie, 1996; Johns, 2001; Tsui, 2004).

This chapter has provided the external (macro-environmental and industry) and internal (administrative and cultural heritage) context for the Russian oil companies under study. This provides the background for the following chapters.

Table 2.3   Data display: Soviet vs Western organisational routines and management style

	Soviet organisation	Western organisation
Organisational routines	• Focus on production volume	• Focus on profit
	• Cost-based economics	• Profit-based economics
	• Social amenities provided	• Salaries only
	• Job security	• Job not guaranteed
	• No cult of money	• Cult of money making
	• 'Manager' dirty word	• Manager a bundle of skills
	• Understate plan to achieve target	• Incentives to stretch targets
	• Labour immobile	• Labour mobile
	• Knowledge is power – fiefdoms	• Teamwork
	• Knowledge sharing discouraged	• Knowledge sharing encouraged
	• Organisational silos	• Knowledge management
Management style	• Blame culture	• Mistakes tolerated if for innovation
	• Rigid hierarchy	• Flat and empowered organisations
	• Boss 'father figure'	• Boss can be challenged

NOTES

1. 'Business oligarch' – a business magnate, a wealthy person who significantly influences the life of a state. 'Russian oligarch' describes Russian businessmen who came to prominence during Yeltsin's presidency (http://en.wikipedia.org/wiki/Russian_oligarchs).
2. Boris Godunov was Tsar of Russia in the 1600s. During his reign there were many rival claims to the throne and discontent amongst the *boyars* (noblemen).
3. New Russian – a stereotypical caricature of the newly rich business class in post-Soviet Russia. (http://en.wikipedia.org/wiki/New_Russians).

3. Stages of organisational transformation in transition economies

This chapter introduces key theoretical perspectives on organisational transformation and presents an integrative theoretical framework to explain a three-stage process of organisational transformation in firms in transition economies. This framework was developed as a result of iteration between the existing literature and the empirical case study data. The case studies themselves can be found in Chapters 4–6 and the empirical grounding for the theoretical framework is presented in Chapters 7–9, which split the model into three sections.

The main theoretical basis is the resource-based perspective, which is combined with aspects of organisational change and learning theories as well as institutional theory. Key concepts in the theoretical framework thus are top management team, administrative heritage, institutional embeddedness, absorptive capacity, organisational learning, operational and dynamic capabilities and strategic flexibility. Their role and relationships evolve over the stages of the organisational transformation.

This integrative framework addresses one of the current challenges of strategic management research: how to develop a theory of strategic management that reduces fragmentation and synthesises different views. In contrast, most management researchers in transition economies have, to date, mainly conducted fragmented studies using either transaction cost theory, institutional theory or the resource-based view (Hoskisson et al., 2000; Meyer and Peng, 2005; Wright et al., 2005). However these fail to adequately reflect the complexity of the organisational change processes. Three notable exceptions adopt an integrated approach to organisational transformation. Filatotchev et al. (2003) examine the links between governance, firm capabilities and restructuring. Uhlenbruck et al. (2003) present a theoretical framework for organisational transformation combining resource-based and organisational learning theories. Newman (2000) develops a model combining institutional, organisational learning and organisational change theory to explain the effect of institutional upheaval on organisational transformation.

The framework of organisational transformation in transition economies presented in this book both builds on and extends these studies. It integrates a range of theories to gain a fuller appreciation of the complexity of the processes. Furthermore three stages of transformation are identified, each with distinct change dynamics, thereby contributing to the organisational change literature by adopting a processual theory of change (Pettigrew, 1997) and explaining the temporal and organisational processes by which change unfolds (Greenwood and Hinings, 2006).

The next section outlines key theoretical concepts that help to explain organisational transformation in transition economies, and that form the building blocks of the theoretical framework.

THEORETICAL PERSPECTIVES ON ORGANISATIONAL TRANSFORMATION

A number of lines of theorising have been applied to study organisational transformation, thus contributing complementary views on the phenomenon. This section introduces the key concepts which constitute building blocks for the model of organisational transformation in transition contexts.

Transformational change represents an organisational metamorphosis (Meyer, 1982; Meyer et al., 1993) or a change in organising templates (Greenwood and Hinings, 1996). It can be triggered by changes in the external environment (Meyer et al., 1993; Greenwood and Hinings, 1996) or by a change in leadership (Virany et al., 1992). Both triggers are manifest in transition economies and therefore both institutional theory and TMT/leadership theory are utilised in the elaboration of the model. Institutional theory is important because the behaviour of firms cannot be separated from their institutional environment – it is embedded in the broader socio-political environment in which competition takes place (Granovetter, 1985; North, 1990; Spicer et al., 2000). However strategic management and organisational behaviour research has largely failed to incorporate the institutional environment in its theoretical models and research designs (Miller and Shamsie, 1996; Johns, 2001; Tsui, 2004).

The top management team (TMT) – the dominant coalition of individuals responsible for setting firm direction – is an important organisational resource since the knowledge embedded in the team determines the organisation's ability to leverage and exploit other resources to adapt to changes in the environment (Penrose, 1959; Barney, 1986; Mahoney, 1995). This holds especially true in transition economies, where firms face transformation challenges of magnitudes rarely seen elsewhere. Thus, certain TMT characteristics have been associated with organisational transformation in transition economies (Filatotchev et al., 1996; Clark and Soulsby, 2007), yet precisely how they influence organisational transformation remains unclear.

Organisational transformation is constrained by organisational history, inherited routines and the bounded rationality of the managers. This represents the firm's administrative heritage, that is the configuration of assets and capabilities, the distribution of managerial responsibilities and influence, and the ongoing set of relationships, that continue even after structural change (Bartlett and Ghoshal, 1989). In transition economies, these constraints are magnified, as not only are the historical resources of firms inefficient, but also the inherited norms, values, and assumptions underlying economic activity are completely different to those required in a market economy (Newman, 2000). However no research has yet explained the process by which these constraints may be overcome.

An important element of this process is organisational learning. This is conditioned by the organisation's absorptive capacity – its ability to value, assimilate and apply new knowledge (Cohen and Levinthal, 1990). However, with the administrative heritage of a planned economy, these organisations lacked the prior knowledge that enabled them to interpret and apply new information (Filatotchev et al., 2003). Although the challenge of an administrative heritage with low absorptive capacity has been identified in transition economies, little empirical research has been conducted on this topic. Recent studies point to systems of corporate governance (Filatotchev et al., 2003) and partnering with foreign investors (Lane et al., 2001; Dixon, 2004) as possible avenues for overcoming administrative heritage to initiate and implement change. However, little is known about how managerial practices may increase absorptive capacity and help diffuse knowledge inside the firm (Minbaeva et al., 2003).

The organisational learning literature provides particularly relevant concepts for research into transition economies because it accounts for the history of a firm and how it adapts to a dynamic environment (Spicer et al., 2000; Makadok, 2001; Fey and Denison, 2003). Scholars have applied organisational learning concepts to transition economies, focusing on knowledge acquisition in alliances (Lyles and Salk, 1996; Hitt et al., 2000) and on knowledge sharing in firms acquired by foreign investors (Vlachoutsicos and Lawrence, 1996; Michailova and Husted, 2003). But only two theoretical models of organisational transformation of domestic firms in transition economies incorporate organisational learning. The Uhlenbruck et al. (2003) model of resource development of privatised firms in transition economies utilises concepts of the resource-based view and organisational learning to explain the process of organisational transformation, however it does not consider the institutional environment, the influence of the TMT or dynamic capabilities (see below). The Newman (2000) model combines institutional, organisational learning and organisational change theory to explain the effect of institutional upheaval on organisational transformation, but ignores the TMT and the need to develop dynamic capabilities.

Dynamic capabilities arise from organisational learning and constitute the firm's systematic methods for modifying operating routines (Zollo and Winter, 2002). They have been defined as 'the firm's ability to integrate, build, and reconfigure internal and external competencies to address rapidly changing environments' (Teece et al., 1997: 516). Helfat et al. (2006: 4) have redefined dynamic capabilities as 'the capacity of an organisation to purposefully create, extend or modify its resource base' and they distinguish between two functions of dynamic capabilities – the deployment function and the search and selection function, including resource creation. This distinction seems particularly relevant for the situation of companies in transition economies where companies both need to deploy the standard capabilities required for survival in a market economy as well as seek out and create new ones to secure competitive advantage in the specific context of institutional upheaval. My theoretical framework embraces these concepts and links them to exploitation and exploration learning respectively, thereby contributing to the growing dynamic capabilities discussion.

In transition economies, firms need to develop dynamic capabilities in order to create the operational capabilities which make the firm robust enough to survive in the short term in the new market conditions. Operational capabilities are defined as 'zero-level' capabilities, being the 'how I earn a living now' capabilities (Winter, 2003: 992). The concepts of operational and dynamic capabilities have become of pivotal interest to organisation scholars as well as management practice. However, the dynamics of their creation and their impact on organisational performance remain poorly understood.

Most studies of firms in transition economies focus on the development of operational capabilities (for instance, Hitt et al., 2000). An exception is provided by Newman (2000) who refers to the positive effect of strategic flexibility on organisational transformation in conditions of institutional upheaval. However little research has been undertaken to distinguish between the resource reconfiguration required for organisations in a transition economy to develop the basic operational capabilities for short-term survival in a market economy, and the resource reconfiguration required to develop strategic flexibility, defined as the capability to respond quickly to changing competitive conditions (Hitt et al., 1998).

The business environment facing firms in transition economies changed from a very stable plan-governed regime to a highly volatile environment where, in addition to market volatility, regulatory, political and social institutions frequently change. This gives premium opportunity for firms that are able to adapt flexibly (Newman, 2000; Uhlenbruck et al., 2003; Dixon et al., 2007). This book therefore aims to explain a process of organisational transformation that progresses from securing the basic operational capabilities required for short-term survival in market conditions to the creation of the strategic flexibility to provide for sustainable competitive advantage in a volatile environment.

THREE STAGES OF ORGANISATIONAL TRANSFORMATION IN TRANSITION ECONOMIES

The theoretical framework developed as a result of iteration between the literature and the empirical research on the Russian oil industry comprises three stages of organisational transformation with a focus on the changing role of the TMT over time (Figure 3.1).

In Stage I, 'Break with the past', the main challenge is to break with the administrative heritage, such as to increase the absorptive capacity of the

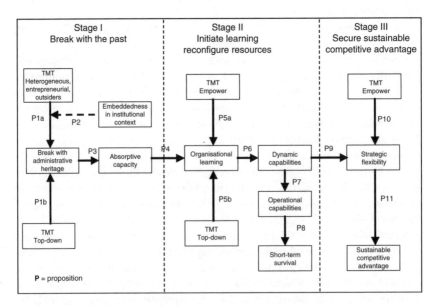

Figure 3.1   Stages of organisational transformation in transition economies

organisation, thereby allowing organisational learning to occur. At this stage, a top-down managerial approach may best move the organisational change forward.

In Stage II, 'Initiate learning and reconfigure resources', exploitation learning and the development of dynamic capabilities enable the organisation to reconfigure, leverage, and integrate resources thereby developing the threshold operational capabilities to ensure the short-term survival of the organisation in a market economy. At this stage, the change process may be advanced best if the TMT combines a top-down approach to initiate change, with the gradual introduction of delegation to empower the organisation as learning takes places and capabilities are acquired.

In Stage III, 'Secure sustainable competitive advantage', exploration learning and dynamic capabilities are important for the organisation to acquire the strategic flexibility to adapt continuously to changes in the environment. This enables the transformed organisation to secure sustained competitive advantage in a market economy with an unstable institutional context. At this stage of the process a TMT leadership style of empowerment brings into play the capabilities of the whole organisation, better equipping it to deal with environmental change.

Stage I   Break with the Past

Organisations adapt their organisational routines to their environment. When this environment undergoes radical change they may find themselves with a mismatch between the organisation and the new environment. Yet members of the organisation are well adapted to the old routines which therefore tend to endure. Thus the first requirement for organisational transformation is to break with this administrative heritage. At this stage, specific characteristics of the TMT determine whether it is possible for an organisation to break with its past and to create an absorptive capacity that facilitates organisational learning.

History, structure, culture, power and politics play a role in enabling and constraining change (Pettigrew, 1987). Historical endowments are 'sticky' in the sense that, in the short term, firms are stuck with their existing resources and structures, and the resultant processes that drive firm operations (Teece et al., 1997). This administrative heritage thus constrains organisational change processes. It is a particular concern in companies shifting from state to private ownership in transition economies, because they typically have a rigid organisational culture, and their resources and routines are not adapted to the needs of a market economy. These organisations have no related prior knowledge that enables them to interpret and apply new information in the context of their own organisation

(Filatotchev et al., 2003). Although managerial actions drive processes, these actions are embedded in contexts that limit information, insight and influence available to the decision-makers (Pettigrew, 1997). Contexts thus both constrain managerial action and are the result of managerial action (Giddens, 1979; Sztompka, 1991). As such they tend to be self-reinforcing.

In addition to the 'stickiness' of the historical and administrative heritage, managers may have difficulty adapting their mental models (Barr et al., 1992; Teece et al., 1997). Managerial cognition has an important influence on the ability of organisations to adapt (Tripsas and Gavetti, 2000). Managers have bounded rationality and rely on simplified representations of the world to process information (Simon, 1955). They often develop a system of beliefs or dominant logic for the organisation based on a shared history (Prahalad and Bettis, 1986).

In a transition economy, managerial cognition is bounded by the experience of working in a planned economy, therefore managerial action derives from the inherited way of doing things – firms behave according to the routines they have employed in the past (Nelson and Winter, 1982). Thus, managers who were brought up in the old system would be incapable of conceiving how to adapt to the new one. If top managers stay in power during the transition process, they are likely to be limited in their ability to change themselves or their organisations as they reinforce past routines.

Which TMTs are most likely to overcome the administrative heritage and extend the cognitive horizon of the TMT? Wiersema and Bantel (1992) suggest that strategic change is a function of receptivity to change, willingness to take risk, diversity of information sources and perspectives, and innovative decision-making. It is important for top managers to have an entrepreneurial orientation, which comprises innovativeness, risk-taking propensity and proactiveness (Miller, 1983). Heterogeneity and interactivity in the TMT enhances the firm's absorptive capacity – its ability to assimilate useful external innovations for knowledge, because of the broader set of experiences on which the TMT can draw to recognise, interpret and internalise new knowledge (Hambrick and Mason, 1984; Wiersema and Bantel, 1992; Uhlenbruck et al., 2003). The greater the heterogeneity of TMTs, the lower the level of psychological investment in the prevailing strategy and therefore the less likely is cognitive inertia (Hodgkinson and Sparrow, 2002). Research into TMT demographics suggests that post-socialist enterprises are more likely to change and restructure with a younger, marketing-oriented, short-tenured, well-educated and heterogeneous TMT (Clark and Soulsby, 2007).

Moreover, higher levels of TMT replacement are associated with greater changes in firm competitive strategy and firm structure and controls during turnaround attempts (Barker et al., 2001). TMT change results in the unlearning of old routines and thus may be associated with increased probability of strategic reorientation and discontinuous organisational change (Virany et al., 1992; Tushman and Rosenkopf, 1996). Indeed, studies in transition economies have shown that changing the TMT by bringing in outsider managers has a positive effect on organisational restructuring (Filatotchev et al., 2000; Filatotchev et al., 2003).

The characteristics of the TMT are therefore critical for breaking with administrative heritage and establishing a new dominant logic of the organisation. Heterogeneous TMTs are likely to have higher absorptive capacity and are more likely to entertain a wider range of ideas, to assimilate external innovations and to develop new capabilities, thus facilitating the emergence of a new dominant logic within the organisation. Entrepreneurial TMTs are likely to be more receptive to change, willing to take risk and innovative in decision-making. New TMTs, with a high share of outsiders, are more likely to be disconnected from the pre-existing dominant logic. Hence:

Proposition 1a   In the initial stage of organisational transformation a top management team that is heterogeneous, entrepreneurial and contains outsiders increases the likelihood of a break with administrative heritage.

Studies of TMT management style in the West have focused on transformational and transactional leadership (Bass, 1985, 1998). The transformational style is the most appropriate for radical organisational change (Vera and Crossan, 2004). Elenkov's (2002) analysis of leadership in 350 small single-business companies in Russia confirmed that transformational leadership (which involves changing the basic values, beliefs and attitudes of subordinates) predicted organisational performance over and beyond the impact of transactional leadership (which is founded on an exchange process in which the leader provides rewards in return for the subordinate's effort). The transformational style is described as charismatic, inspirational, intellectually stimulating and individually considerate (Avolio et al., 1999). Charisma and intellectual stimulation are linked with the entrepreneurial orientation described above, as one of the TMT characteristics appropriate for breaking with administrative heritage.

Traditional Russian organisations are characterised by a command-and-control approach which is manifested in authoritarianism, obedience to authority, the use of coercive power, and an emphasis on rank and status (Kets de Vries, 2001). Russian leaders have typically been highly directive, strong leaders with centralised decision-making and a rigid hierarchy (McCarthy et al., 2005). This corresponds to the 'authoritarian' style of leadership, as leaders take nearly all major decisions themselves, whereas democratic leaders make their decision jointly with their subordinates (Lewin et al., 1939). In the early stages of organisational transformation, such a top-down management style is more effective because it corresponds better to employee expectations by leveraging the command-and-control element of the administrative heritage. A top-down authoritarian leadership style may thus facilitate breaking with other elements of the administrative heritage.

Proposition 1b   In the initial stage of organisational transformation a top management team with a top-down management style increases the likelihood of a break with administrative heritage.

Pettigrew's (1987) starting point for studying strategic change is the notion that formulating the content of any new strategy inevitably entails managing its external and internal context and process – the 'what', 'why' and 'how' of change. The environment has also been found to be an important variable when examining the relationships between strategy and performance (Burns and Stalker, 1961; Emery and Trist, 1965; Dess et al., 1990). The rate and trajectory of change in an industrial sector facing significant boundary changes may be much faster than the sensing and adjustment pathways of individual firms to the regrouping of the sector (Pettigrew and Whipp, 1991). Such significant boundary changes are also found in the post-privatisation restructuring in transition economies. The relative slowness of the sensing and adjustment process of firms and their failure to recognise that the bases of competition have changed is a key factor explaining their loss of competitive performance and partially explains the dramatic drop in industrial production in transition economies.

The institutional infrastructure differs substantially between transition and developed economies. In transition economies, markets are continuously changing, emerging and disappearing while the rules of the game are not yet established. Strategic choice is embedded in the institutional framework, which has a strong influence on a company's 'genetic coding' (Peng, 2000). This 'genetic coding' explains why companies in transition economies differ radically from Western firms. For example, Whitley and Czaban (1998) maintain that in a setting where the state has no coherent set of policies and oscillates under different pressure groups, short-term ad hoc adjustments to immediate pressure may be more rational than undertaking relatively large-scale and highly risky changes in pursuit of long-run strategic objectives. This is consistent with the institutional perspective on business strategy – when the rules of the game are highly uncertain, organisations are not able to invest in new capabilities and skills and will therefore, by default, continue in their old ways (North, 1990; Scott, 1995; Peng and Heath, 1996). Entrenchment behaviour by incumbents may act as a barrier to the acquisition of the required resources and contribute to the maintenance of core rigidities (Filatotchev et al., 1999). Conversely organisation 'outsiders', particularly entrepreneurs, may bring a different genetic coding.

A basic tenet of institutional theory is that a set of values, norms and organisational templates exists outside particular firms and influences the way in which they are managed (Meyer and Bowman, 1977; Zucker, 1983). Organisations which adapt to institutional pressures are more successful than those that do not (Meyer and Bowman, 1977). However, Newman (2000) maintains that this cannot apply when the institutional context itself is changing radically. The institutional context no longer provides organising templates, models for action and sources of legitimacy (Greenwood and Hinings, 1993). The radical change in the institutional context also means that many existing resources and capabilities of firms become redundant and they lack the leadership required to compete. Therefore radical institutional change inhibits organisational transformation (Newman, 2000).

The rapid mass privatisation that took place in Central and Eastern Europe destroyed the old system, but did not create the institutional foundations which would enable it to achieve the required restructuring post-privatisation (Spicer et al., 2000). Privatisation from an institutional perspective highlights the inherent 'stickiness' of changing institutional templates (Johnson, 2000). Therefore those companies that manage to overcome the genetic coding of the organisation and interact with the emerging institutional frameworks of a market economy will be more successful than their peers that still cling to the old institutional frameworks of state ownership. Companies need to change and evolve, so that dynamic capabilities, the ability to learn continuously and the knowledge-based view of the firm will become more prominent in the study of emerging economies (Hoskisson et al., 2000). Once a company starts to embark on a particular type of change, it increases its competency in making that type of change, therefore further change follows (Ginsberg and Baum, 1994). However firms differ in the extent to which they adapt to the environment (Meyer, 1982; Meyer et al., 1990). In transition economies many of the big state-owned enterprises have become corporate dinosaurs, entrenched in old behaviours and unable to make the first steps of change to adapt to a changed environment. In their place a number of 'maverick' companies have emerged which have better foresight, set more ambitious strategic intent and stretch their resource bases (Peng, 2000).

It has been argued above that organisational transformation will not take place unless there is a break with the administrative heritage. However this ability to break with administrative heritage is inhibited by the degree of institutional embeddedness of the firm in the old system of the planned economy:

Proposition 2   The more an organisation has been embedded in the pre-transition institutions, the weaker the ability of the top management team to break with its administrative heritage.

Organisational learning is vital for companies in a transition environment that must adapt to new ways of doing business. However organisations interpret information based on prior knowledge or frames of reference. The absorptive capacity of companies in transition economies is limited by their experience and prior related knowledge from a different economic system. What an organisation knows how to do today is a function of what was learned yesterday (Pisano, 2000). Its ability to build new capabilities therefore depends on its administrative heritage. Organisational learning is limited by existing organisational structures and hierarchy, by organisational cultures that frequently encourage anti-learning values and routines, and by shared structures of organisational cognition (Salaman, 2001). In particular the administrative heritage of firms originating in the planned economy presents a major obstacle to learning and change since it includes routines developed for an economic system that is no longer in operation, therefore organisational transformation is inhibited both by the absence of absorptive capacity and the extent of the learning gap (Hitt et al., 2000; Newman, 2000).

Existing knowledge, that can no longer accommodate events in the environment, must be altered, and new understanding of the environment developed for effective organisational adaptation (Ellis and Shpielberg, 2003). This process is however constrained by the inertial nature of inherited resources and by cultural traits in Russian culture that inhibit change and knowledge sharing (Vlachoutsicos and Lawrence, 1996; Michailova and Husted, 2003). Socialist societies discouraged knowledge sharing, experimentation, innovation and change (Kornai, 1992; Kogut and Zander, 2000). An organisational culture that inhibits knowledge sharing can undermine organisational learning and cement existing routines. Thus the inherited resources, structures and cultures reinforce each other and further weaken the organisation's absorptive capacity. For an organisation to learn, it must be able to reconstruct and adapt its knowledge base, in so doing, creatively destroy outmoded practices and attitudes (Pettigrew and Whipp, 1991). Since firms in transition economies were organised fundamentally differently, they had to change even the inner logic from plan target fulfilment to profitability and efficiency (Meyer and Møller, 1998; Newman,

2000). New systems and procedures have to be adopted and the learner not only has to unlearn acquired routines and replace them with new ones, but also to reassess attitudes and value systems underlying behaviour under the old and new regimes (Lyles and Salk, 1996; Meyer and Møller, 1998; Lane et al., 2001). Thus the knowledge gap concerns skills that can only partially be transferred through active interaction between teacher and recipient, but rather require intensive learning by doing.

Levinthal and March (1993) argue that learning can improve performance, but may also limit future improvements – the self-reinforcing nature of learning helps sustain current core competence, but because of the reinforcing nature of success from learned behaviours a firm may become vulnerable to changes in the environment. Thus managers brought up in a planned economy will have learned the behaviours necessary for success in that environment. Changes in the environment require firms concurrently to both unlearn and learn – managers need a mindset that allows them to unlearn traditional practices, processes and strategies and to be receptive to new ones (Bettis and Hitt, 1995). In transition economies, organisations need to unlearn ways of the planned economy and learn the ways of the market economy. A number of studies of international joint ventures in Hungary have confirmed the 'unlearning' of existing routines and the absorption of new ones (Lyles and Baird, 1994; Lyles and Salk, 1996; Steensma and Lyles, 2000; Lane et al., 2001).

How does this unlearning occur and how can absorptive capacity be increased? Cohen and Levinthal (1990) maintain that a firm's absorptive capacity depends on the individual who stands at the interface of either the firm and the external environment or at the interface between subunits within the firm. Under conditions of rapid and uncertain change the interface function is centralised (ibid.), in this case in the TMT. As described above, a TMT that is heterogeneous, entrepreneurial and contains outsiders is more likely to be able to break with the administrative heritage of the organisation, encouraging the unlearning process. Breaking with the administrative heritage increases the absorptive capacity of the organisation by making prior knowledge obsolete and acknowledging the necessity to acquire new knowledge relevant to market conditions via the process of organisational learning.

Proposition 3 In the initial stage of organisational transformation, breaking with the administrative heritage increases the absorptive capacity of the organisation.

Proposition 4 In the initial stage of organisational transformation, an increase in absorptive capacity increases organisational learning.

Stage II   Initiate Learning and Reconfigure Resources

In the second stage of organisational transformation the role of the TMT is to initiate learning within the organisation to enable the reconfiguration of resources. At this stage the TMT takes a contingent approach to leadership, adopting a top-down approach for parts of the organisation where learning is slowest, but empowering parts of the organisation that are more advanced in their understanding of the requirements for survival under market conditions.

There are two types of organisational change: continuous, or first-order change, which is incremental and convergent, and discontinuous, or second-order change, which is transformational (Meyer et al., 1990). These two modes of change and learning can be linked to two leadership styles: transactional and transformational. Transactional leaders set goals and develop agreements about what is expected from the organisation, whereas transformational leadership is inspirational and helps the organisation to reframe the future (Bass, 1985, 1998). The transactional leadership style serves to increase the robustness of the existing organisation, whereas transformational leadership seeks to change it. Vera and Crossan (2004), in their investigation of the impact of TMT leadership styles on organisational learning, develop a contingent view of leadership. In times of change, when a firm's institutionalised learning has to be altered, transformational leadership is required. In times of stability, transactional leadership is appropriate for the process of refreshing, reinforcing and refining current learning.

I argue, however, that both leadership styles can *coexist* in addressing the contingent needs of organisations undergoing change. Thus at the intermediate stage of organisational transformation, transformational leadership is still evident in the parts of the organisation that have been slower to break with the administrative heritage and therefore slower to unlearn and change. However, transactional leadership becomes appropriate for parts of the organisation that have already acquired some of the basic operational capabilities required for short-term survival. At this stage empowerment of the organisation facilitates exploration learning enhancing organisational capability to react to and cope effectively with environmental change (see Stage III below).

Thus a combination of management styles is appropriate in the intermediate stage of organisational transformation, once parts of the organisation have started to learn what is required for survival in a market economy (for example, empowerment might be more appropriate in head office where a significant amount of organisational learning has already taken place, whereas the subsidiaries, where change happens more slowly, may still require a top-down approach). On the one hand, a top-down, transformational approach continues to encourage the break with administrative heritage and unlearning of old routines. On the other hand, a transactional approach, empowering those parts of the organisation, that learn and adapt faster than others, is also appropriate. The empowerment of these managers serves to further accelerate organisational learning in their part of the organisation.

Propositions 5a and b   In the intermediate stage of organisational transformation, a contingent leadership style (empowering some parts of the organisation and managing other parts top-down) increases organisational learning.

Organisational learning represents the process of improving actions through better knowledge and understanding (Fiol and Lyles, 1985) and occurs through organisational routines that are repeated and modified (Levitt and March, 1988). It is necessary for organisations to adapt their capabilities (Mahoney, 1995; Dosi et al., 2000; Eisenhardt and Martin, 2000; Pisano, 2000). Exploitation and exploration (March, 1991) have emerged as two organisational learning concepts underpinning organisational adaptation. They resemble Senge's (1992) description of adaptive (survival) and generative learning. Adaptive learning is about coping, i.e. exploiting. Generative learning, on the other hand, enhances creativity and corresponds to exploration learning. Both are necessary for organisational transformation in transition economies (Dixon et al., 2007). Exploitation learning is required to develop the operational capabilities required for survival in a market economy, but missing in a centrally planned economy, for instance marketing, finance and HR capabilities, corporate governance systems and information sharing. Exploitation involves selecting, implementing and adapting routines and structures that are already available in organisations operating in the Western market economies. Exploration, characterised by search, variation, risk taking, experimentation, creativity, flexibility, discovery and innovation (March, 1991), is discussed in Stage III below.

Most organisational learning is exploitation learning and often involves incremental change in routines within the existing schema. It is linked with first order learning (Lant and Mezias, 1992) or single loop learning (Argyris and Schön, 1978). But incremental change would not suffice to accomplish the radical changes required in a transition context. In fact there is a lack of consensus in the organisational learning literature as to whether exploitation refers to using past knowledge or whether it also refers to seeking and acquiring new knowledge 'albeit of a kind different from that associated with exploration' (Gupta et al., 2006: 693). Newman (2000) has suggested that firms undergoing change in transition economies need to primarily engage in exploration learning to accomplish radical changes to existing schema, however, she also suggests that extreme institutional upheaval inhibits second-order learning – the search for new routines and schema (Lant and Mezias, 1992) to achieve transformational change.

I argue, however, that the acquisition of operational capabilities already in existence in the West represents first order, or exploitation learning and is only the first stage of organisational transformation helping organisations to survive, but not to achieve sustainable competitive advantage. Knowledge acquired in this way is new to the organisation, but already exists in Western organisations. However it still may not totally fit the local context, and may not enable the organisation to continuously renew its capabilities in changing environments. For this, exploration learning would be required to develop new capabilities that fit the context, often by combining external and internal knowledge to develop new routines and practices (see Stage III).

Organisational learning, more specifically exploitation learning, enhances the development of dynamic capabilities that enable the organisation to adapt its routines and resources. At this stage the function of dynamic capabilities is the 'deployment' of resources to 'purposefully create, extend or modify its resource base' (Helfat et al., 2006: 4). I argue that the deployment function of dynamic capabilities involves the development of operational capabilities that are generally taken for granted in organisations in mature market environments. These operational capabilities are the threshold capabilities for short-term firm survival.

Organisational capabilities represent 'the ability of an organisation to perform a coordinated set of activities utilising organisational resources, for the purpose of achieving a particular end result' (Helfat and Peteraf, 2003: 999). Capabilities may be classified as either operational or dynamic (Helfat and Peteraf, 2003; Winter, 2003). Operational capabilities, called 'substantive' capabilities by Zahra et al. (2006), facilitate the efficiency and effectiveness of the use of existing resources and thus the 'robustness' of an organisation, that is its 'potential for success under varying future circumstances or scenarios' (Bettis and Hitt, 1995: 16). Winter describes operational capabilities as zero-level capabilities, being the 'how we earn a living now' capabilities (2003: 992). However, as explained above, many operational capabilities required in a market economy were absent in transition economies, thus organisational transformation had to create capabilities that are generally taken for granted in organisations in mature market environments. Organisations in transition economies need to develop two types of organisational capabilities. First, they need to develop the basic operational capabilities required for survival in a market economy. Second, since the institutional environment in transition economies is unstable, they need to develop the capability to respond quickly to changing competitive conditions, described as strategic flexibility by Hitt et al. (1998).

The development of operational capabilities is a function both of exploitation learning and of dynamic capabilities. Dynamic capabilities are those capabilities that constitute the firm's systematic methods for modifying operating routines (Zollo and Winter, 2002). Organisational routines and resources deriving from a planned economy are not suited to organisations operating in a market economy and thus require adaptation. Dynamic capabilities represent the process of new resource creation via 'reconfiguration, leverage, learning and integration' (Bowman and Ambrosini, 2003: 293) or the firm's ability to alter the resource base by creating, integrating, recombining and releasing resources (Eisenhardt and Martin, 2000). In transition economies, firms need to develop these dynamic capabilities to divest, acquire, upgrade and integrate resources (Uhlenbruck et al., 2003) in order to create the threshold operational capabilities which make the firm robust enough to survive in the new market conditions.

I argue, therefore, that in the intermediate stage of organisational transformation, exploitation learning contributes to the development of dynamic capabilities, which involve the reconfiguration, building and integration of resources to create the threshold operational capabilities for short-term survival in the new conditions of the market economy.

Proposition 6   In the intermediate stage of organisational transformation, organisational learning enhances the development of dynamic capabilities.

Proposition 7   In the intermediate stage of organisational transformation, dynamic capabilities of resource reconfiguration, building and integration enhance the creation of operational capabilities.

Proposition 8   In the intermediate stage of organisational transformation, operational capabilities enhance the chances of short-term survival.

Stage III   Secure Sustainable Competitive Advantage

While in the second stage of organisational transformation, the TMT is concerned with helping the organisation to acquire the operational capabilities required to survive in the market in the short term, in the advanced stage, the objective is to secure sustainable competitive advantage. At this stage the top-down leadership style may be less effective, and may thus be replaced by empowerment of the organisation in order to develop the strategic flexibility to adapt to changes in the environment.

In the intermediate stage, the main emphasis has been on exploitation learning, since firms had to acquire the operational capabilities that already exist in the West. However, at the advanced stage, companies start to engage in exploration learning, typified by new and original thinking, because the challenges of emerging economies require new business models that add value in the specific context (London and Hart, 2004; Prahalad, 2004). This form of learning would require the development of new capabilities that fit the context, often by combining external and internal knowledge to develop new routines and practices. It requires a systemic view of reality, and creative thinking, and it generates entirely new approaches rather than marginal change. Exploration learning is linked with second-order (Lant and Mezias, 1992) or double-loop learning (Argyris and Schön, 1978). This may best be achieved by learning through experimentation and internal development of new routines and capabilities, rather than by wholesale import of imported routines from others (Kogut and Zander, 1996).

March (1991) maintained that organisational change requires both exploitation and exploration to achieve continuing success. However there is a debate as to whether it is possible to simultaneously engage in both types of learning: the issue of ambidexterity versus punctuated equilibrium (Gupta et al., 2006). Authors suggesting a balance between the two – an ambidextrous organisation – include Benner and Tushman (2003) and He and Wong (2004). Burgelman (2002), on the other hand, concluded from his longitudinal study of Intel that exploitation and exploration learning were temporally differentiated in a process of punctuated equilibrium. In other words, a long period of exploitation learning is followed by a burst of exploration learning. I maintain that in circumstances of radical organisational transformation, exploitation learning precedes exploration learning.

Exploration learning enhances the dynamic capabilities that enable a firm to adapt rapidly in volatile environments. In the intermediate stage I described the deployment function of dynamic capabilities in terms of the reconfiguration, leverage and integration of resources to create operational capabilities. In the third stage, the crucial aspects are the search and selection function of dynamic capabilities (Helfat et al., 2006). Changes in the environment require a continuous rethinking of current strategic actions, organisation structure, communications systems, corporate culture, asset deployment and investment strategies. This requires flexibility and the ability to balance stable and fluid states of the organisation (Hitt et al., 1998). Dynamic capabilities enable organisations to develop the strategic flexibility which is necessary for long-term survival in an uncertain and changing institutional environment and thus provide a link between the capabilities of the firm, and what is going on in the environment (Kraatz and Zajac, 2001).

Proposition 9 In the advanced stage of organisational transformation, dynamic capabilities of search and selection lead to strategic flexibility.

Given the complexity and unpredictability of change in the institutional environment, I maintain that in the advanced stage of organisational transformation the TMT is no longer the sole arbiter of strategic flexibility. Heller and Yukl (1969) identified the use of different leadership styles on a continuum from no subordinate influence to complete subordinate influence in relation to specific situations. In the initial stage of organisational transformation I have explained that a top-down management style predominates, with little subordinate influence. In the final stage, subordinate influence is achieved by empowering the organisation. Empowerment has been described both as a relational dynamic and a motivational construct (Conger and Kanungo, 1988). As a relational dynamic it is the process by which a leader shares power with subordinates and as a motivational construct it implies an enabling, rather than just a delegating construct (ibid.). In order to secure sustained competitive advantage, the TMT empowers the organisation in terms of both delegation of authority to act and of increased motivation to act. The empowerment of the organisation thus increases its strategic flexibility, the TMT no longer being the sole arbiter of interaction with environment.

Proposition 10 In the advanced stage of organisational transformation, a top management team that empowers the organisation increases strategic flexibility.

Strategic flexibility is positively related to firm performance, helping companies to respond to crises in their competitive environment (Hitt et al., 1998; Grewal and Tansuhaj, 2001). As I stated above, strategic choice is embedded in the institutional framework. Being aware of, and adapting to the environment, is critical for newly privatised firms in transition economies. Strategic flexibility is particularly important for firms in transition economies because they face significant political and economic changes, an uncertain institutional environment and poorly developed markets. This places pressures on firms to adapt or proactively develop strategic responses to change, in order to secure sustainable competitive advantage, which is defined as the implementation of a value-creating strategy not simultaneously being implemented by competitors and which cannot easily be imitated (Barney, 1991).

Proposition 11   In the advanced stage of organisational transformation, strategic flexibility leads to sustainable competitive advantage.

CONCLUSION

I contribute to organisational change theory by developing an integrative framework of organisational transformation, that captures the complexity of organisational transformation processes in the transition context. The framework demonstrates the influence of the institutional context and the administrative heritage, highlights the interrelationships between management practices and explains the way in which these relationships change over time, in a three-stage process. By incorporating a range of management theories and concepts I address a criticism of strategic management theory that it is too fragmented.

I argue that a TMT, that is entrepreneurial, heterogeneous and contains outsider managers, is the key resource affecting the early stages of organisational transformation. Its role changes over time. The transformational top-down leadership style, necessary for breaking with the administrative heritage and increasing the absorptive capacity of organisation, gradually changes to a contingent approach in the intermediate stages of transformation, and ultimately develops into the transactional style, with the organisation empowered to adapt to changes in the uncertain institutional environment.

I contribute to organisational learning and dynamic capabilities theory by explaining the linkages first between exploitation learning and the deployment function of dynamic capabilities, generating the operational capabilities required for short-term survival in a market economy, and second between exploration learning and the search and selection function of dynamic capabilities, generating the strategic flexibility required for sustainable competitive advantage in an unstable institutional environment.

Despite the above contributions this framework suffers from a number of limitations. First, in attempting to clarify the key processes involved in organisational transformation over time it portrays organisational transformation as a simple linear process. In fact there are many areas where constructs overlap and interact with each other, for instance organisational learning and dynamic capabilities, dynamic capabilities and strategic flexibility. The three stages of organisational transformation are also likely to overlap. Second, although the importance of context is emphasised at the front end of the framework, for reasons of parsimony I did not attempt to show the constant interactions between organisation and context over time.

4.   Yukos case study

This case study describes the process of organisational transformation in Yukos. To facilitate understanding, the data display in Table 4.1 provides a time-ordered and conceptually ordered summary of the case uncovering the relationships between categories and contextualising the phenomenon of organisational transformation. The basic components of the paradigm (or organisational scheme) are the conditions (answering the questions: why, where, how come and when?), the actions/interactions (answering the questions: by whom and how?) and the consequences (answering the question: what happens as a result?). The process of organisational transformation is broadly linked to the stages of development in the external context. The table summarises the description of the case study. It should not be implied, for instance, that the TMT only played a role in the first period, or that organisational learning did not occur throughout the process of organisational transformation.

The starting point for the case study can be summed up as follows:

> The production of Yukos . . . was in long-term decline. . . .There was a big problem with cash flow; the company was close to bankruptcy. Salaries in many of the regions had not been paid for months and months. There was widespread discontent. There had been riots and even kidnappings . . . in the regions. There was really a big mess. Khodorkovsky was looking for a survival strategy and something which would help the company grow in the future. (top manager, TNK-BP, Western)

TOP MANAGEMENT TEAM

This section presents the findings on the Yukos TMT, describing CEO Khodorkovsky, the diversity and entrepreneurial orientation of the TMT and the management style. Khodorkovsky was the driving force in Yukos' turnaround: 'Khodorkovsky . . . actually strikes me as being one of the most dynamic managers that I've met in the oil industry, never mind in the Russian oil industry' (investment bank executive, Western). He was young, in his thirties, and a progressive thinker. He invited expatriates onto the board, onto the management team and into key positions, where transfer of know-how was important: 'Khodorkovsky was lucky with his management

Table 4.1   Time/conceptually ordered data display of stages of organisational transformation – Yukos

Sections	Conditions	Actions/Interactions	Consequences
TMT and break with administrative heritage	**1995–98 Asset grabbing and rise of oligarchs** • TMT heterogeneous, entrepreneurial, outsiders • TMT absorptive capacity high, unbounded by Soviet oil industry rationality • Organisation constrained by Soviet heritage	**TMT leverage administrative heritage** • Top-down leadership to implement change **TMT break with administrative heritage** • Promote move to market economy, acquire Western knowledge, remove blockers	• **Absorptive capacity** of organisation increases
Organisational learning	**1998–2003 Move to market** • 1998 economic crisis intensifies need to improve operational efficiency • TMT perceives need to raise foreign capital, i.e. corporate governance • Absorptive capacity of organisation increases	**Absorptive capacity** • Outsiders unconstrained by heritage, foster innovation, encourage decision-making **Knowledge acquisition** • Employ expatriates and Russians with Western experience • Strategic alliances • 100% training • 'Heriot-Watters' • Training for high-flyers **Knowledge internalisation** • Learn by doing	**Organisational learning** • Development of **dynamic capabilities:** reconfiguration, divestment, creation and integration of resources for survival in market economy

Organisational capabilities

1998–2003 Move to market
- Significant organisational learning
- Absorptive capacity increases

- Early successes
- Convince using Russian examples
- Project teams
- Learn from mistakes

Knowledge dissemination
- Break down silos
- Rotate managers
- Rotate meetings
- 'Heriot-Watters' into regions
- Working groups
- Technical means

Dynamic capabilities

Resource reconfiguration
- Asset acquisition
- Consolidation
- Restructuring
- New business systems
- Replace 'blockers'
- Job rotation to break down silos

Resource divestment
- Remove non-aligned employees
- Transfer social assets
- Hive off non-core activities

Resource creation
- Foster innovation introduce new systems

Organisational transformation
- **Operational capabilities** developed for survival in market economy – HR, marketing, production, finance, PR – leading to **efficiency and robustness**
- **Dynamic capabilities** further lead to **responsiveness and strategic flexibility**
- Altogether resulting in **competitive advantage** in the Russian industry

Table 4.1 (continued)

Sections	Conditions	Actions/Interactions	Consequences
		• Encourage ideas	
		• Create new training facilities	
		• Build future managers	
		Resource integration	
		• Integration of subcultures	
		• Alignment behind common goals, but integration not uniform across the company	
		• Improved telecoms	
		TMT	
		• Start to move away from top-down approach to **empowering the organisation**	
Epilogue	**2003–05 Reversion to state control**	2003 Yukos out of step with state Khodorkovsky jailed	Collapse of Yukos

team. They are a team of people with great professionalism, motivated not only by money, but with a huge desire for learning and self-development' (middle manager, Yukos, Russian, translation).

In the TMT there was a mixture of backgrounds (for example Western and Russian, financial and technical) and of age and experience. There was also an international board of directors with high-profile Westerners brought in to improve corporate governance. The TMT was characterised by an entrepreneurial approach, embracing new ideas and encouraging innovations: 'The company is simply innovative. And correspondingly this innovativeness is made up of the concept of flexibility, taking on board new things (top manager, Yukos, Russian, translation). This flexibility helped Yukos to monitor and grasp opportunities in the external environment and create competitive advantage: 'The competitive advantage in the case of Yukos was quite clearly (from 1999 through 2003) the innovativeness that was displayed, and the leadership in innovating in production methods and reservoir management' (energy consultant, Western).

Key decisions were under the supervision of one man – Khodorkovsky himself. This had the negative effect of encouraging people to bypass other managers and go directly to Khodorkovsky 'because that's both necessary and sufficient condition of your success' (senior manager, Yukos, Russian). Khodorkovsky both developed the strategy for the business and communicated it to the organisation. This resulted in great clarity: 'There was a very clear understanding of how each unit, each function would implement this strategy, and of what each unit had to do in order to carry out the tasks which . . . he, as the CEO . . . had set' (middle manager, TNK-BP, Russian, translation).

The crisis of declining oil production, the chaos of privatisation, the lack of alignment of regional managers and the constant theft required tight control: 'Khodorkovsky was a puppet master . . . he has strings attached to every part, every little manager there . . . keeping things very tight' (middle manager, Yukos, Russian). Khodorkovsky adopted the traditional Soviet command-and-control management style (see Chapter 2): 'It's like Stalin, big father and all . . . that. It's also intrinsic in the Russian oil industry because it's very macho, it's army style. You have to obey the commands . . . you must show you like the general' (middle manager, Yukos, Russian). He brought regional managers into alignment with his objectives through a combination of fear and personal relationships:

> We used to have those big board meetings . . . there was a jumbo jet taking all 400 managers out to a little town where we're going to be soon. So listen you guys we're coming, [threatening] Yukos is coming. And then it's really terrible, a dozen buses come through the town with sirens and every little policeman there are standing like that . . . And then they had big sessions there in the evening . . . when

everybody arrived from Eastern parts of Russia. Khodorkovsky would make a reception of a thousand people. And he is usually one or two hours late. Everybody is there by eight, and there they are waiting, people who have never met him. He's coming, okay . . . And then he would make his round, he would . . . say 'Hi, I'm so pleased to be with you'. It's only five minutes . . . and he literally would shake every hand. And that guy who shook his hand he will remember this for the rest of his life. . . . But it was a personal touch. 'I owe this to him. . . . It's very personal and it's my commitment to Khodorkovsky'. (ibid.).

A select group of managers had his special blessing and were given a certain amount of leeway in decision-making – the so-called clan:

Mikhail [Khodorkovsky] had this idea that . . . you can't trust Russians . . . I'm going to have a small cadre of people who I trust . . . and that's the people who will drive decision making. But they will be influenced greatly by a large cadre of expatriates, bright young expatriates or maybe even young Russians . . . thinking up all these wild thoughts, but they will have no power. The only power they will have is the power to influence me and my core of trusted individuals, who will make the key decisions. And the rest of the 110 000 people will be drones . . . worker bees. They will be given minimum amount of input with 'do this, and when you've finished with that come back and I will tell you the next thing to do'. (top manager, TNK-BP, Western)

This cadre of trusted people were friends, acquaintances and relatives and they formed the clan on whom Khodorkovsky could rely: 'It was trust, based on the clan principle' (middle manager, TNK-BP, Russian, translation). A clan member only had to go to Khodorkovsky: 'whisper into his ear and he would say, "yes, OK do this, do that"' (middle manager, Yukos, Russian). Employees who were not clan members were insignificant and easily replaceable and for that reason it was uncomfortable working in Yukos 'because you don't feel like a long-term employee, and you understand that you can be thrown out at any moment and that you will be of no use to anyone (middle manager, TNK-BP, Russian, translation).

Khodorkovsky's support and backing enabled other managers to achieve their goals: 'I had no problems introducing change because Khodorkovsky was behind me' (senior manager, Yukos, Western). This provided the Western expert, Joe Mach, with the authority to introduce changes in work processes to increase oil production: 'It was very directly the chain of command that ran from Khodorkovsky through Yuri Beilin,[1] through Joe Mach[2] and then down to the production directors at Yugansk[3] and elsewhere. And it was forced' (energy consultant, Western). Joe Mach's management style was as authoritarian as that of the Russian top managers. He believed that no other style was appropriate because of the extent of change required and the engrained behaviours: 'In a big company it is already difficult to bring about change. I am in charge of 15,000 Russians – and we are two expatriates. We cannot talk of consensus' (top manager, Yukos, Western).

The administrative heritage of the Soviet system was a powerful force counteracting change:

> You had this huge inertia from the senior and middle management who didn't necessarily share Khodorkovsky's vision and who didn't really appreciate people like Joe Mach and who had their own ideas about how things should be done. So there was a struggle and getting things done was sometimes very difficult. (top manager, TNK-BP, Western)

Aggression was needed to counteract aggression: 'It was a culture of force – it had to be to change things . . . because there is immediately opposition which has to be overcome' (middle manager, TNK-BP, Russian, translation). This was the only way to gain control: 'At that moment in time that was the medicine that Yukos needed, it was unpalatable medicine but it's what they needed' (top manager, TNK-BP, Western).

Over time, however, Khodorkovsky recognised that he needed to think about succession plans and delegating responsibility:

> He announced more than once that he understood that he was making mistakes, that perhaps he shouldn't be running the company, but that no one else would take on the responsibility. . . . Therefore this was a very big responsibility and he would have to develop a new generation of professionals in order to be sure of leaving the company in their hands. And then he could move on to something different. (middle manager, TNK-BP, Russian, translation)

It became increasingly clear that a centralised approach and reliance on the clan was not sustainable in the long term. It wasted intellectual capital. There were no incentives to build teams and share knowledge because only one man's approval was required. Khodorkovsky had recognised this problem and was beginning to address it:

> He was making efforts to go from a centralised one-man-show model of the early days of Yukos to a more effective management structure which would use most of the potential of other people. So he tried to consciously delegate certain aspects of decision making to other people. But . . . he is so important . . . as a manager, as a leader, as a founder of the company and a key shareholder, that of course for him it would take time and it was . . . difficult. (senior manager, Yukos, Russian)

The establishment of control systems and organisational processes was a prerequisite for Khodorkovsky to relinquish his control. New HR projects were being introduced, heralding the transition to a new style of management: 'The company had already . . . begun to move to a new culture – to a culture of initiative and responsibility . . . They had given us this to do, and the management was beginning to feel the changes . . . and the positive effects' (middle manager, TNK-BP, Russian, translation). But the jailing of Khodorkovsky came too early for the project of delegating decision-making to be fully implemented, leaving Yukos in crisis. The puppet master was no longer holding the strings and the puppets collapsed: 'Taking responsibility and decision making was difficult even at an operational level. Khodorkovsky's orders were needed for everything. . . . So when the crisis came with Khodorkovsky put into prison, there were practically no leaders – no one who could make any decisions' (middle manager, TNK-BP, Russian, translation).

This section has illustrated the entrepreneurial character of the TMT, and its clear understanding of the need for organisational change. At the same time it illustrated the command and control management style which was only in the later stages being moderated to empower the organisation.

ADMINISTRATIVE HERITAGE

The Soviet administrative heritage was described in Chapter 2. This section details how the TMT both broke with administrative heritage to bring about change and leveraged administrative heritage to increase the pace of change.

Break with Administrative Heritage

The administrative heritage was the main constraint on organisational transformation:

> In order to change the system . . . it required time to overcome the psychological resistance, because . . . [the oil industry] has its own traditions. There are people who have worked for years and years in the industry, who are used to certain ways of working, and here it is not so easy. It's not greenfield. (senior manager, Yukos, Russian, translation)

The main methods used to break with this administrative heritage were training, putting managers with a completely different approach into key positions and developing strategic alliances, for instance with Schlumberger, to gain access to Western expertise. As soon as positive results began to show, it became easier to persuade people to change. The main focus was on increasing oil production. Two expatriates were key in initiating change out in the oilfields. Soviet tradition was to extend the life of the oilfields and ensure that production targets could be met by concealing the real potential of the fields:

> And when the inspection comes from Moscow you should only expose to them the most obvious things. And you hide the best one even deeper, trick your reporting, don't show any of the maps, send this guy on vacation, he knows too much. You always have a lot of such ways to deal, and then you will live happily ever after. And you know for 20 years you are safe, you're going to deliver the plan, okay, that's life everybody dreams of. (middle manager, Yukos, Russian)

The status quo was shattered with the arrival of Joe Mach – an expatriate from Schlumberger, tasked with increasing oil production. 'It is not a case of success breeds success in changing people's mindsets. It is just a function of calculations. Russian managers didn't use the right physics – hydrodynamics. So I walked in the door and showed them with my calculations how to increase production. . . . The problems are in their heads' (top manager, Yukos, Western). Joe Mach would scrutinise all the well data and, ignoring all protestations, armed with a laptop, would do the calculations on the spot to establish the real well rate. 'And . . . nobody was able to resist' (middle manager, Yukos, Russian). Any managers who stubbornly refused to change were removed.

Because of the difficulty of changing the mindsets of managers who had experienced years under a different system, emphasis was placed on training young managers. They gained a master's degree in oil technology from a JV in Siberia, set up in partnership with Heriot-Watt University. Then they spent a further year training with the expatriates in Moscow. Some of these so-called 'Heriot-Watters' were fast-tracked into senior management positions in the regions: 'I came here, aged 26, and became deputy to the head geologist. This had never happened before. Probably in the whole history of Russia there hadn't been this kind of thing where the senior geologist was 26 years old' (senior manager, Yukos, regional, Russian, translation). Despite the resistance of the existing management cadre, this manager had the security of Khodorkovsky's backing. In contrast to their fellow managers, who had worked in the organisation in Soviet times, the young managers were prepared to challenge the experience of older managers, to ask questions and they were not afraid of making mistakes:

> I consider that it is rather rare for people [to admit mistakes] . . . who have worked in this sector for years and who think that they know everything. . . . These people always indulge in wishful thinking even if they know their decision is wrong . . . it is just forced through by their authority. . . . I am not afraid to

ask ordinary specialists what is the best thing to do in a given situation. Yes, I am a big boss, a big manager, but I simply do not know how to proceed in this situation, because I have never come across it before. . . . I think it is important to make it possible for people to come to me and say: 'we think that this is not right. Here are our calculations'. 'OK, lads, I understand, thanks a lot' and we come to a conclusion. (ibid.)

Another approach to breaking with the administrative heritage was getting local managers to work together on projects. Instead of issuing an order for something to be done, managers were encouraged to work together, were praised for their capabilities and challenged to make a new system work. The managers began to understand that the success of the project depended on all of them: 'These were innovative approaches which were easy to . . . initiate. It was just necessary to think it through clearly, present it in the right way, argue it correctly, and provide a budget for it' (middle manager, TNK-BP, Russian, translation). Not all initiatives were successful; for instance, the 'Corporate Leader' programme initiated in 2001 in the regions, which was designed to change managers' mindsets and attitudes, was admitted to have been before its time – managers were not ready for it, neither in the regions nor in Moscow. But in 2004 a new change management project was initiated: 'the development of a culture of initiative and responsibility at every level of management'. The project was run in two regions:

We analysed the culture existing in the regions – what was the culture? A culture of force. And what kind of culture do you want? A culture of order, a culture of initiative, etc. A lot of research was done and it was immediately possible to see what there was, what was wanted and what could realistically be achieved and by what means. (ibid.)

Another way of breaking with the administrative heritage was the introduction of incentive systems to motivate changes in behaviours. A bonus system was introduced, with the personal bonus representing 80 per cent and the group/company bonus 20 per cent.

Increasingly companies like Yukos . . . see that you have to incentivise people and provide them with a risk, but also obviously the commensurate return, to get them to produce the goods. And those are the companies that are now catching up and outperforming because they're providing share option schemes, bonus payments for out-performance, and are sacking people who aren't good enough. (investment bank executive, Western)

The carrot was offered, but the stick was still in evidence as part of the TMT's drive for control and results.

Leverage Administrative Heritage

The TMT's aggressive style had the benefit of leveraging the command-and-control aspect of the Soviet administrative heritage. This style fitted well with the expectations of employees brought up in the Soviet system: 'They are very implementation-oriented. The company says "do this", and they do it' (middle manager, TNK-BP, Russian, translation). The style also met the needs of the organisation for rapid implementation of change: 'I think that working groups are not very effective. A direct line of command . . . is always more effective . . . in management, direct commands are best – they go through without distortion and are implemented' (top manager, Yukos, Russian, translation). The Western approach of empowerment and involvement of employees in decision-making was not seen as appropriate, at least at the early stages of organisational transformation. The top-down approach helped to ensure rapid implementation: 'it is not acceptable if a decision is delayed by more than twenty-four hours by any part of the organisation' (top manager, Yukos, Regional, Russian, translation).

Administrative heritage was also leveraged with respect to hierarchy and respect for authority. The young Heriot-Watters were sent into the regions as senior managers but had the protection of Khodorkovsky and his team: 'All the managers who were above us, including the general director had quite clearly been given orders how to behave towards us' (ibid.).

Although there were not very many characteristics of the Soviet system which could be utilised in a market economy, nevertheless an attempt was made, where the administrative heritage was positive, to retain it: 'The good things are always kept. Keeping things is always easier than destroying them because . . . the good things are normally consolidated over years and years. We normally understood what was good, we didn't destroy things which had become traditions' (top manager, Yukos, Russian, translation). Thus Joe Mach would leverage the Russian administrative heritage by referring to the Russian origins of the calculations he was using to demonstrate how to increase oil production: 'He was saying, "That method . . . was invented by your Russian guy, that equation you are using is by that Russian guy, it's not American, it's you guys." And somebody from the audience says "Yes I remember . . . when I was at school, somebody mentioned the same"' (middle manager, Yukos, Russian). Leveraging the Russian scientific heritage in this way made it easier for the Russian specialists to accept change.

By leveraging the command-and-control elements of the administrative heritage the TMT were able to implement change more rapidly, involving a break with the administrative heritage.

ORGANISATIONAL LEARNING

This section describes the development of absorptive capacity, knowledge acquisition, internalisation and dissemination.

Absorptive Capacity

The absorptive capacity of an organisation, or its capacity to learn, is determined by its prior experience. But the company had no experience of a market economy:

> The biggest problem for Yukos . . . is the absence of a culture of normal management . . . This determines everything else. Because if a person does not understand this – [if] he does not understand why KPIs are necessary or why an MBO management system is necessary, how can you convince him that this is necessary if he doesn't know anything about it? And it is not just one or two people who do not know this, but 70 per cent of the managers in the company do not know it. (top manager, Yukos, Russian, translation)

To overcome the lack of knowledge of Western business practices, outsiders were needed to bring in the knowledge of how to do things and a climate had to be created which fostered innovation:

> All of this . . . is written about in books. But for this to happen you simply need to have the first person who understands it, who is an advocate of it. Khodorkovsky was this man . . . he advocated innovations . . . he promoted the 'Western' direction of development. And if he had not propounded and created this culture, Yukos would not have changed – I can say that unequivocally. (top manager, Yukos, Russian, translation)

What was much more important for organisational learning in Yukos than past experience was the capability of people to think, to analyse and make decisions: 'I make it clear to people that for me your experience is not the principal matter, nor your personal ambitions. For me the principal thing is your ability to analyse, to substantiate . . . to defend your point of view' (senior manager, Yukos, regional, Russian, translation).

Once the impetus was provided by the top management for the organisation to break with the administrative heritage, thereby creating absorptive capacity, organisational learning became possible. The next three subsections describe how knowledge was acquired, internalised and disseminated.

Knowledge Acquisition

Khodorkovsky and the TMT were not oil industry experts – their backgrounds were largely in banking. An anecdote was recounted about a group of 'bankers', i.e. the top managers, visiting an oilfield. A piece of equipment called a sputnik (a satellite) was used to measure the oil flow rate. It was just a large tank and the oil flow was measured by the speed at which the tank filled up. The 'bankers' asked how the flow rate was measured, 'and the operator says, "well as usual, through sputnik." "Oh, satellite communication – wow." Stupid, hey? So that's how they got treated, that's the degree of understanding of what the technology is' (middle manager, Yukos, Russian).

But the new managers recognised their own shortcomings and they themselves went on training courses and to conferences and seminars, as well as visiting Western oil companies to acquire knowledge. Khodorkovsky developed a strategic alliance with Schlumberger, an oilfield services company, to help re-engineer the business. Their expertise was in the area of oil production, but they also had strong HR and finance capabilities:

> Schlumberger . . . encouraged Yukos to do two things. The first was to apply basic petroleum engineering principles to the development of their fields . . . And so by simply applying the principles of petroleum engineering, which were widely accepted in just about every oil company worldwide, it was possible to catch a lot of low-hanging fruit . . . And the second thing was to persuade Mr Khodorkovsky that transparency in financial reporting was ultimately good for the success of the business. (senior manager, TNK, Western)

Knowledge was acquired from the Schlumberger employees, several of whom had been seconded into Yukos. Amongst them were two key figures: Joe Mach and Don Wolcott. The two were both offered permanent jobs in Yukos by Khodorkovsky: 'he offers them that much money they couldn't resist and they just ditched Schlumberger' (middle manager, Yukos, Russian). The two became legendary for the spectacular increase in oil production. The return on investment was huge:

> I mean the brilliant thing was Khodorkovsky, he hired maybe . . . I don't know, two dozen let's say, something on that order, expats. Let's say he pays them $1 million a year cash compensation, that's 25 million a year. And the technology that they brought, I mean there was so many multiples of that. I mean he just got it at a steal. (investment bank executive, Western)

Russians with experience of working abroad or for Western companies in Russia were recruited, as well as Westerners who had worked for other companies in Russia. Consultants were hired. Khodorkovsky did every-thing to encourage learning and adoption of Western management prac-tices: 'When we looked at all the Western methods we selected the best, and also the ones which could be implemented in the company. Plus the fact that management put absolutely no break, absolutely none, on any innovations' (middle manager, TNK-BP, Russian, translation). Yukos' performance was benchmarked against Western best practice. For instance Yukos' oil depot turnover rates[4] were less than once a year compared to European rates of 40 times a year for large depots. They set a target of achieving at least 15–17 in 5–6 years.

Yukos placed a heavy emphasis on training its employees: 'In Yukos, right from the beginning, Khodorkovsky set the target – 100% training' (middle manager, TNK-BP, Russian, translation). Everyone initially had a chance to have some training and to demonstrate their potential. Later, training was allocated as required, but was still at a high level. In 2004 65 000 of the total 100 000 employees in Yukos were undergoing training. Yukos had ten training centres and had relationships with leading Western business schools, such as IMD and Duke and universi-ties such as Newcastle and Edinburgh. A leadership programme was developed in alliance with IMD and Yukos became the first Russian company to join the IMD Learning Network as a full partner. In-house programmes were developed specifically for Yukos by IMD faculty. About 1000–1500 managers were identified as high-flyers and special development programmes were organised for them, accounting for about 80 per cent of the training budget. From 2003 the focus for training was on those employees demonstrating two competencies: 'openness to new ideas' and 'determination to achieve'.

Engineers were sent on training courses in Russian and Western univer-sities and technical training programmes for hundreds of regional special-ists were run by Joe Mach and his team. A one-year master's programme in petroleum engineering was set up in Tomsk, co-organised by Heriot-Watt University: 'and the graduates – I think we had 42 of them in the first year – are no differently qualified than those who graduate from Scotland' (top manager, TNK-BP, Western). The 'Heriot-Watters', as they became known, went on to further training in the Yukos FDP[5] centre in Moscow and then out to work in the field. With the later collapse of Yukos many of the 'Heriot-Watters' were recruited by TNK-BP: 'We've hired a lot of the graduates from Yukos now, because from that programme they're good' (top manager, TNK-BP, Western).

Knowledge acquisition thus proceeded on several fronts, including expa-triates, alliances, benchmarking and training and development.

Knowledge Internalisation

Reaping the benefits of training could only be achieved by internalising the knowledge and applying new skills. Much of the knowledge internalisation was a result of learning by doing: 'In Yukos we divided personal development into five areas: development on the job, development through business projects, development through learning from others, etc. So development was a broad process. And training courses, they are the least important ... The most developmental are business projects' (middle manager, TNK-BP, Russian, translation). A policy of job rotation enabled managers to gain experience in different environments. A key element of knowledge internalisation in the oilfields was learning by doing. Jo Mach would show the engineers the calculations and the engineers would calculate themselves and understand the logic of his argument.

> These people were experienced, highly educated Russians and the last thing they wanted to hear was this redneck from Oklahoma telling them how to do their business. And so they would argue with him using their own technical arguments and he would systematically shoot down their own technical arguments in a way which was undeniable. (senior manager, TNK, Western)

Learning from mistakes was another way to internalise knowledge. Khodorkovsky encouraged innovation and mistakes were allowable if learning derived from them: 'The good thing about Yukos ... is its efficiency, i.e. having recognised its mistakes Yukos tried to rectify these mistakes in as efficient a manner as possible and to take measures to ensure that these mistakes were not repeated' (senior manager, Yukos, regional, Russian, translation).

Knowledge internalisation was thus a function of learning by doing, project work, job rotation and learning from mistakes.

Knowledge Dissemination

Knowledge dissemination was challenging in a company with 100 000 employees, that had previously consisted of numerous small legal entities, and was spread over a huge geographical area from European Russia and the Baltics to West and East Siberia. The difficulties were magnified by organisational silos[6]: 'one of the features of Yukos is in every function, in every department, people have a rather narrow perspective' (top manager, Yukos, Western). One way of breaking down these barriers and transferring knowledge was to encourage a culture where communication and open discussion became part of life. 'I think people here understand the importance of communication, and if you have a set of common goals . . . then you have a chance, and the culture of discussing things, then I think it works towards just trying to work out mutual acceptable solutions' (middle manager, Yukos, Russian).

Job rotation helped to break down the silos as did the policy of rotating the directors' meetings around the different sites. 'Open up the eyes of some of the directors to what the real work was about, and that I liked, I thought that was a very powerful thing which many world class companies are doing' (top manager, Western oil company, Western).

Disseminating new management concepts into the field was aided by email, databases and web resources. There were several success stories about harnessing organisational knowledge. The Heriot-Watters, for instance, had set up a real-time online database on the technical status of every oil well: 'This data base is on line . . . you press a key and you get the latest technical programme . . . no one else has anything like this . . . we exchanged some information [with ExxonMobil and Shell] . . . and both companies were simply amazed' (senior manager, Yukos, regional, Russian). The Heriot-Watters also developed an unofficial website for the young engineers working in the company, for sharing knowledge in a community of practice.

In the finance department of Yukos RM[7] initiatives were undertaken to systematise and share financial data:

> When I arrived everyone had their own computer, each person was doing something or other for himself, so that his neighbour didn't know what he was doing. I made them create a common resource, we allocated disk space to them and sorted everything into folders. And I had to work at it for a very long time to get them to load general information which was useful for everyone onto this common disk. This seems like a minor thing, but people did begin to work differently. (middle manager, Yukos, Russian, translation)

To conclude, knowledge dissemination was a function of changing cultural attitudes to sharing information, breaking down organisational silos, communication systems and shared values, and technical facilitation.

Organisational learning provided the knowledge base for the development of organisational capabilities – the dynamic capabilities required to reconfigure, divest, create and integrate resources, and the resultant operational capabilities for survival in the market economy.

ORGANISATIONAL CAPABILITIES

Dynamic Capabilities – Resource Reconfiguration

After privatisation both the finances and the oil production of Yukos were in a very serious state. The company was hugely indebted, had falling production rates and had a very complex structure with difficult relationships between the centre and the regions. The Yukos takeover of Tomskneft[8] was an example of the harsh measures undertaken to turn around the company. In progressive steps contractors had to agree to a 30 per cent reduction in prices, a spread of debt repayments over three years and payments only covering their wage costs for the first year. 'It was . . . unpleasant, with a lot of cursing etc, but . . . it was done' (middle manager, TNK-BP, regional, Russian, translation). By 1998 all the legal entities, which had been privatised individually, were finally consolidated after an aggressive and complex process: 'Khodorkovsky put together small pieces, put together like a jigsaw that was there, this puzzle okay, this part went there. With the iron fist and forced financial and administrative controls. He was taking people out and depriving them of proxies [power of attorney], they couldn't run their entities' (middle manager, Yukos, Russian).

The successful consolidation of the company paved the way to organisational restructuring. 'It was only then that the serious work of transforming the company could begin' (senior manager, Yukos, Russian, translation). There was a lot to do: production needed to be increased, new technologies introduced and a thorough evaluation of the value chain undertaken. 'The restructuring was complex – on all fronts. This was both restructuring of human assets, for example training, development and classification, and it was restructuring of the material assets, and as well the improvement of business processes and reporting systems' (ibid.)

Rapid progress was made: 'If Khodorkovsky said he wanted something to happen – the criteria would be established and it would all happen in six months. The competency model and the succession plan, for example, were all set up in less than a year' (middle manager, TNK-BP, Russian, translation). There was always money available for new projects to improve business processes. However, sometimes the systems that were established were not properly applied, for instance the Hay grading system: 'the results were not always used correctly' (top manager, Yukos, Russian, translation). The system was not totally understood: 'it's not accepted by most people, it was just another administrative process in the minds of most' (top manager, Yukos, Western). The basic systems were all set up over a period of five years but were not fully embedded: 'They did not always become the norm and they are still changing. Therefore, unfortunately, Yukos has not progressed to full process management. There are a lot of rules and regulations, but process management, as a business process, has not been achieved' (top manager, Yukos, Russian, translation).

A more positive view came from one of the Heriot-Watters:

> Everyone now knows what is expected of him, where he should turn to, what he should say, how he should represent his company. . . . It is already in his consciousness, his corporate mentality, that this is the way things are and the way they should be. From this point of view I think that Yukos is closer to its Western analogues than any other Russian company. (senior manager, Yukos, regional, Russian, translation)

In head office, however, it appeared that many of the systems were more for show than for use. The performance management system was criticised by expatriates and locals alike. The elaborate computerised system was a mere formality: 'In no way is it linked to the real results of your work; everyone understands that their boss will allocate it in accordance with whether he likes you or not. No one discusses the results of your appraisal – this is not customary here' (middle manager, Yukos, Russian, translation).

Restructuring was most difficult in the regions. Radical action was undertaken if managers persisted in their old behaviours, as the following example demonstrates:

> In February . . . it became clear that Samaraneftegaz[9] may not be able to fulfil its plan. So a commission was sent there . . . which established . . . the general negative feature, that the team there was a dyed-in-the-wool, ossified team which had been working together for years and years. They had their own internal objectives, but not the objectives of the company. Therefore the management of the company took the decision to replace the local management completely . . . practically all of the key positions were replaced, with the exception of the General Director. So now essentially the whole Samaraneftegaz team has been totally replaced, because once the key positions were changed then the new key people replaced their team members. (senior manager, Yukos, regional, Russian)

Organisational silos represented a significant aspect of the Soviet administrative heritage – each part of the organisation hoarded knowledge. One method Yukos used to break down these barriers and transfer knowledge was job rotation:

> So the person at Nefteyugansk[10] was sent to Tomskneft[11] and so on and so forth. So they started rotating people into different operations so that they would start to network and understand the different people who were in different departments and . . . subsidiaries as a way of starting to knock down the walls that were . . . put up by the Soviet traditions. (consultant, Western)

A great deal of resource reconfiguration took place over a short period of time, and it is not surprising that all of the new systems and processes were still not fully implemented: 'To bring a Soviet company, a Soviet production unit, into a profitable, effective, really commercial business unit is a difficult transition. And it is a long slow process' (headhunter, Western).

In summary, resource reconfiguration involved asset consolidation, restructuring, the establishment of new business systems, the replacement of 'blockers' in the system and job rotation to break down organisational silos.

Dynamic Capabilities – Resource Divestment

Resources were divested in several ways. First it was necessary to remove employees who were not prepared to adapt to the new Western business practices: 'Many people had to change their approach totally – both their relationship to work and their relationships with other people – this is not always easy. Some couldn't take it, some could not make the transition. And that happened quite often' (senior manager, Yukos, Russian, translation). Most of the social support systems provided by Soviet companies were transferred to local town administrations (for instance kindergartens, leisure centres, hospitals). Many non-core activities were hived off, including repair and maintenance, transport and oilfield services: 'Yukos was the first to start this . . . hiving off their non-core enterprises into separate companies so that competition developed between them and new players' (senior manager, Yukos, Russian, translation). In Tomskneft, the process of outsourcing was particularly advanced: 'You go to Tomskneft and they're hugely efficient . . . they describe how they run their operations and you say "Well, outsourcing contractors, it's really complicated, how do your accountants manage?" "I don't know, we've outsourced those as well." So very lean and advanced the way they're operating businesses' (investment bank executive, Western).

The divestment of non-core activities was an important step in increasing the efficiency of Yukos operations.

Dynamic Capabilities – Resource Creation

Resource creation is considered in terms of innovation and the development of future management resources. Yukos actively encouraged employees to come up with new ideas and projects: 'After about a year I realised that Yukos was not like a company, but more like a business school where the challenge was to see what innovations and projects you could introduce to get access to the pot of money available for this' (middle manager, Yukos,

Russian, translation). The bonus system was oriented towards the introduction of new projects or innovations, rather than normal measures of operating efficiency. There were many opportunities to introduce new ideas: 'Yukos always had money available to try the things out that they wanted to' (top manager, Yukos, Russian, translation).

An example of successful innovation in the field was provided by a regional representative. Previously a work brigade had fixed broken-down wells either that were closest to where the brigade was currently operating or in the order in which the breakdowns occurred. A new database was set up which prioritised wells in accordance with their flow rate and thus served as a guide to the most important wells to be fixed. This innovation was a contributing factor to the dramatic growth in oil production: 'In 2002 we were increasing [production] in significant volumes – 41 thousand tons per day . . . that is, about 300 thousand barrels per day – the same as an average-sized oil company . . . And this was all in addition to what we were producing in one year!' (senior manager, Yukos, regional, Russian, translation).

Any employee could participate in the competition called 'A million for an idea' – the chance to win a million roubles for a good idea. Other competitions had prizes of two months at a Western business school. Several groups of 10–15 people went. 'For young people who had generally never travelled outside Russia and not seen anything of the world apart from their own region, to find themselves in a business school in Switzerland for a month!' (senior manager, Yukos, Russian, translation).

One expatriate in the organisation was, however, rather scathing about the innovation capacity of the organisations: 'There weren't many ideas coming up – creativity and innovation has been killed by the former system (top manager, Yukos, Western). Another criticism was that Yukos was trying too hard to develop a leadership position and spending too much on developing its own technology rather than taking a 'me too' approach. 'I do think . . . that we tried to take too large strides in this direction' (senior manager, Yukos, regional, Russian, translation).

Although Yukos fostered innovation there was some doubt about how much of it derived from the organisation as opposed to the TMT: 'They encourage . . . thinking along economic lines, and I think that's the big step change that has occurred. I would struggle to say that they were looking for people to suddenly come along with massive strategic ideas, that really does just happen at the top' (investment bank executive, Western). But encouraging people to think along economic lines was already different from the old system of production according to plan, regardless of cost. Innovation was being encouraged by challenging people to come up with ideas on reducing cost and increasing profits: 'And if you're telling me you're losing money on every barrel that comes out of that well, then don't tell me that, just turn it off. That's the kind of innovation they're encouraging. And that's a pretty significant first step' (investment bank executive, Western).

The development of future resources involved improving the quality of training centres. 'We studied Western centres, no one put any obstacles in our way, told us where to go, what to do' (middle manager, TNK-BP, Russian, translation). The training centres were redesigned and rebuilt at a cost of millions of dollars. A further innovation was to provide workers with practical training courses. Previously the only training had been on-the-job or theoretical training courses. 'As the production workers said, this was not just a step forward, but a great leap ahead. And what does this tell us? That management gave us complete carte-blanche for change' (ibid.).

Yukos were very concerned to develop the intellectual capital within the regions from which they might draw their future employees and introduced a system of subsidies for star students in the regions: 'We paid all A grade students, never mind which institute they were studying in. That was called a 'social grant' – the main thing [to qualify] was to live in the regions where the company was operating' (ibid.) In every higher education institution relevant to the oil sector, Yukos set up a student club. The clubs were involved in joint ventures with young specialists already working in Yukos: 'the students were learning about business, early on, they were preparing the future managers of the company' (ibid.: 292). The scheme later developed into a three-year structured development programme for young specialists.

In summary, Yukos had paid significant attention to innovation and the development of future resources for the organisation.

Dynamic Capabilities – Resource Integration

An important way of integrating resources was ensuring that employees were aligned with organisational goals: 'It's very clear that ultimately it's in the best interest of everyone involved to achieve certain key results in terms of profitability or market share, etc. So there are unquestioned common goals of the organisation' (senior manager, Yukos, Russian). However, given the different backgrounds of the employees, it was not an easy task to create a common corporate culture:

> There are two different formations of people in this industry. There are the old oil men with their good relationships and large production experience, and there is the young generation which does not have any significant production experience, but they do have current [business] knowledge . . . To survive . . . you need . . . to be knowledgeable in your professional sphere, but that is not

sufficient. You also have to be a good political player because . . . these companies within Yukos were very politicised. Now, if these people of the old formation . . . start to sabotage . . . (top manager, Yukos, Russian, translation)

The oil men and the young businessmen were examples of two subcultures in the organisation. In Moscow there was also the clan: 'Historically some of the managers . . . involved their friends. So the result . . . is you have sometimes groups of people . . . who share certain views, which are not necessarily in line with views of other groups' (senior manager, Yukos, Russian). The mixture of international managers and Russian locals provided a further challenge. Gaining understanding of the requirements to achieve a common goal helped to break down barriers. Making financial information available to a head office function was one instance where progress had been made: 'It's available, and not just available because it's available to everyone who wants to have it, but people understand what I am doing and they understand why I need this information, so they are open' (senior manager, Yukos, Russian).

Ironically it seemed to be the collapse of the company that put into high relief the fact that a strong corporate culture had in fact been developed at Yukos:

A corporate spirit . . . it is amazing that these legal disputes have been going on for more than a year now, but nevertheless, the whole company – like a unified whole – all of the employees . . . no-one is giving up . . . Everyone is ready to stand up and go and demonstrate in the streets if the company requires it – this is the sense of corporate belonging which we have developed – it is simply amazing. I myself am sometimes surprised at the extent to which the company was able to create the atmosphere of a very close family, that we were all aiming for the same thing, moving in the same direction. (senior manager, Yukos, regional, Russian, translation)

The biggest challenge to the creation of a corporate culture was in the regions where conservatism predominated. However even there the culture had changed, particularly at the managerial level, because managers were in constant communication with the Moscow office, travelling there frequently. Improved telecommunications were also important for developing closer relationships with the regions. The availability of company telephone and email directories facilitated communication. Although quite normal for Western companies, these were extremely rare in Russian companies. Job rotation had also been a key factor in promoting a common culture. However, certain locations were more difficult to bring into line, either because they had been acquired more recently or because they were not given the same priority for development, for instance some of the downstream locations. Relationships between the regional managers of the refineries and the expatriate in charge of refinery operations in Moscow were difficult: 'I get stuffed' (top manager, Yukos, Western).

In summary, resource integration involved aligning the organisation behind common goals although the process was not uniform across the company.

Operational Capabilities

Organisational learning and dynamic capabilities enabled Yukos to develop many of the basic operational capabilities required for success in a market economy. As early as 1997 Yukos had already begun to introduce modern Western HR systems and Yukos 'was leagues ahead of the other companies' (middle manager, TNK-BP, Russian, translation). Khodorkovsky had given priority to HR, so all the new processes were introduced within two years 'at a gallop' (middle manager, TNK-BP, Russian, translation). Financial systems were established and GAAP accounting was introduced. The early priority was to achieve centralised control of cashflows. The financial crisis in 1998 shifted the focus to cost efficiency: 'The big obvious changes in Yukos date from 1999. But from that point on the evolution was phenomenal, and genuine' (energy consultant, Western). Significant progress had been made in corporate governance: 'In terms of . . . transparency we are getting to the level of a normal Western company. The only thing, perhaps, is that we lag behind a little in getting our reports out' (senior manager, Yukos, Russian, translation).

New technology and systems significantly increased oil production. Yukos' integrated approach to increasing production was considered one of their sources of competitive advantage versus their domestic competitors. For example, increasing the oil flow rate required a simultaneous increase in capacity of the surface facilities.

> We are growing about two times faster than the industry as a whole . . . because early on we re-evaluated our approach to working in the oilfields. We succeeded in 2–3 years in building a new management system and a new technological system. This is a complex integrated system which allows us to achieve results. We began to change, earlier than others, the system which used to exist in Soviet times (ibid.).

The systemic and integrated nature of the changes was a recurring theme. 'What was particularly distinctive was the systematic approach. Everything was systematic. In Yukos it was impossible for one process to be ripped out of the circle' (middle manager, TNK-BP, Russian, translation).

Russian competitors acknowledged that Yukos were well ahead in developing Western capabilities: 'Everyone agrees that they [Yukos] made a significant breakthrough from the point of view of establishing a normal . . . corporation by Western standards' (top manager, TNK-BP, Russian, translation). Due diligence for the acquisition of Sibneft[12] had also demonstrated the superiority of Yukos:

> We saw that they were . . . 3–4 years behind us. We had already passed that stage, exhausted those ideas. On the one hand it was difficult talking to them, finding common ground with them, but on the other hand . . . we were . . . bursting with pride that we had already progressed past that stage. (senior manager, Yukos, Russian, translation)

Yukos promoted the image of a very successful company: 'Khodorkovsky did a very, very good job of promoting Yukos. Promoting it to the West in particular' (top manager, Yukos, Western). However, there were some doubts as to the extent to which change had been embedded in the organisation: 'I call it the western veneer on Yukos. Yukos looks Western, this is not a Western company' (top manager, Yukos, Western). This insider view was shared by most Western experts, although they recognised that in the key area of oil production, Yukos standards were very high: 'the way it looks at its wells and its reserves and its field planning seems very good . . . so that part of the company . . . they are very Western in the way they do their business' (investment bank executive, Western). One respondent claimed, however, that under circumstances of high oil prices anyone could make money: 'My 18-year-old daughter could have run this company successfully . . . up until about a year ago . . . because crude prices were so strong' (top manager, Yukos, Western).

One relatively neglected area in Yukos was HSE[13] for which no KPIs were set: 'There is no such evaluation, it is not used. All Russian companies, the whole world, are evaluated by concrete indicators, and what are we supposed to say to the world? Evaluate us differently? . . . They evaluate us . . . on 3–4 indicators: profitability, share price, reserves – that's all' (top manager, Yukos, Russian, translation). There was thus little understanding at top management level of the importance attached to HSE in the West.

Although operational capabilities had generally improved, overmanning remained a cause for concern. For instance, the downstream business had 38 million tonnes of refining capacity and employed 40 000 people – ten to twelve times the number of people that would have been needed in the West. Priority for the development of operational capabilities had been given to increasing oil production because that was where most money could be earned. The downstream was relatively neglected and consequently there had been much less change towards a Western model. For instance, an average Western company would run units in the refinery for three to five years between maintenance shutdowns, whereas Yukos units were closed for maintenance every year.

It was particularly difficult to deal with the behaviour of the management in the refineries. The expatriate in charge of operations had made little progress: 'I've had no major breakthrough to success' (top manager, Yukos, Western). The reluctance of the refinery managers to change their attitudes was due 'in part because of Khodorkovsky's view that refineries add no value, Yukos doesn't even calculate a gross margin on its refinery, they purely view it as an operating cost centre' (ibid.). Without Khodorkovsky's support it was difficult to convince the refinery managers to think in terms of profit and efficiency.

Bureaucracy was a major issue for the whole organisation: 'Look at the bureaucracy in Yukos – at how many signatures are necessary to get anything done – you probably need more than 12 signatures' (top manager, Yukos, Western). Some employees would only take action if requests were made formally, with a number and date, 'so some people play games just based on that' (senior manager, Yukos, Russian). On the other hand, by Russian standards the bureaucracy had been considerably reduced. 'I can tell you for certain, 100 per cent, that by comparison with other companies we have no bureaucracy at all. By comparison with TNK-BP, with Lukoil, I can tell you with 100 per cent certainty' (senior manager, Yukos, Regional, Russian, translation). Whilst acknowledging the bureaucracy, a manager who had come from Sidanco was nevertheless very impressed by Yukos' business processes:

> I was simply struck by how well developed the processes were in Yukos. On the one hand . . . very many bureaucratic procedures . . . But on the other hand, just the scale of it all, very many processes have been specified. There is a very good control system. The financial control is significantly greater than I saw in Sidanco. (middle manager, Yukos, Russian, translation)

In summary, in a short period of time Yukos had managed to implement the main business systems required to operate in a market economy, with the exception of HSE. Although not all of these were totally embedded across the organisation, Yukos was still considered to be ahead of its peers. The systematisation of business processes had as a consequence an element of bureaucracy, but this was less than that which prevailed in other Russian organisations.

ORGANISATIONAL TRANSFORMATION

This section examines the organisational transformation of Yukos in terms of efficiency and robustness; responsiveness and strategic flexibility; and performance and competitive advantage.

Efficiency and Robustness

These findings illustrate the organisational efficiency of Yukos in terms of the operational capabilities required for survival in a market economy. Yukos was universally regarded as the leading Russian oil company in organisational efficiency and operational capabilities. The company was thus the most robust in the context of a market economy. ['*So have they gone further than the other Russian oil companies?*']. . . 'Certainly in terms of all those kind of factors in terms of transparency and internal systems and starting to put in place some accounting, approach to shareholder management, investor relations, all of those factors were looking pretty good' (newspaper correspondent, Western). Organisational transformation was comprehensive – complex restructuring programmes were implemented despite the constraining factor of the administrative heritage: 'Not everything happened straight away, not everything went smoothly, not everything went quickly and well. Of course there were all kinds of problems and arguments and opposition from employees. But . . . it was a serious complex programme for restructuring the whole company' (senior manager, Yukos, Russian, translation).

Yukos emulated Western business practice, leveraging the expertise of the expatriates they had recruited.

> I think what strikes me is the fact that they were able to change so quickly and adapt so quickly. Everything from bringing in foreigners at very senior levels to their close relationship with Schlumberger, really trying to bring those management styles and that knowledge inside of the company, but doing that within a more or less Russian structure. And then I think after doing that, trying to change and adjust the structure to a more Western style of management. (headhunter, Western)

The general view was that Yukos had made a remarkable transformation in a very short period of time: 'Yukos these days is a very proud company. It went from being a basket case, frankly, in 1997 to being a $30 billion industrial powerhouse a year ago' (top manager, TNK-BP, Western). However, not all the business processes had had time to become fully embedded in the organisation. Some respondents felt that Yukos merely has a veneer of Westernisation, sufficient to convince investors of its high value and to increase its market capitalisation: 'This is an old Russian company with all the old Russian stuff, but we've got this veneer of Western management, this veneer of very deliberate and thoughtful external affairs communications . . . to depict the company in a certain way, but it's a veneer nonetheless' (top manager, Yukos, Western). The new business processes coexisted side by side with bureaucratic remnants from the Soviet past: 'The more enlightened organisational development issues are cohabiting with some of the old Soviet bureaucratic processes that deal with the command-and-control mentality and the need to have passes and permission for rather trivial administrative activities' (consultant, Western).

In summary, Yukos had made great progress in moving towards a Western business model and developed many of the operational capabilities required for survival in a market economy. However, not all new business systems were fully embedded in the organisation.

Responsiveness and Strategic Flexibility

This section describes the ability of Yukos to respond to changes in the external environment. The high political, economic and social profile of the industry[14] meant that a certain strategic agility was required to keep pace with changes in the environment.

> It is an extremely specific thing, oil. It is always politics. Conditions in the country were changing, they were changing depending on each period. The company had different strategic goals and tasks. The company grew and developed and the managers who led the company also improved themselves. They studied this and that, they made a few mistakes, they learnt by doing, so to speak. Therefore to say that there is one key criterion for survival . . . at each concrete period of time they might have been completely different things. (senior manager, Yukos, Russian, translation)

The TMT's top-down management style had negative implications for the strategic flexibility of the organisation as a whole: 'Only the top management team has the capability to react to changes in the environment. It will take a long time for the organisation to develop such that lower parts of the organisation will be able to react and take decisions in accordance with changes in the environment' (top manager, Yukos, Western). But one positive feature of the command-and-control style was that the organisation could be mobilised rapidly. An example was given where there was an urgent need to produce an extra 2 million tonnes of oil. At 4 o'clock in Moscow, money was allocated to the project, and by 7 o'clock in the evening the tractors and excavators were already getting to work in

Yugansk: 'probably there isn't this kind of efficiency anywhere else in the world' (senior manager, Yukos, regional, Russian, translation).

There was some evidence that Yukos was moving towards greater empowerment and employees were being entrusted with more responsibility. 'The main thing was that there should be no failures, i.e. my boss, he was answerable for me having no failures, and in this sense I was given total and absolute support' (middle manager, TNK-BP, Russian, translation).

As has been mentioned earlier, innovation was encouraged. This was linked with strategic flexibility: 'The company was simply characterised by innovation. And the concept of innovation includes flexibility, openness to new things and being prepared – all of this exists' (top manager, Yukos, Russian, translation).

In summary, the strategic flexibility of the organisation as a whole was still relatively limited due to the slow transition from a command-and-control style of management to empowerment of the organisation. However, the command-and-control style had advantages in quick implementation. The success of the organisation in a rapidly changing environment was largely a reflection of the strategic flexibility of the TMT rather than that of the organisation as a whole.

Performance and Competitive Advantage

This section reviews Yukos' performance and explains why it was the benchmark for success in organisational transformation in the Russian oil industry: 'If you look back to the time when TNK-BP was formed . . . just over a year ago, the norm for success in Russia was unquestionably Yukos – unquestionably' (top manager, TNK-BP, Western). It was Khodorkovsky's objective that Yukos should be the leading oil company in Russia: 'we were one step ahead of everyone else . . . Yukos chose the most difficult strategy – to be the leader' (senior manager, Yukos, regional, Russian, translation). In fact if the deal to acquire Sibneft had proceeded, Yukos would have achieved world recognition as the No. 4 company in the world by oil production and No. 1 or 2 by reserves. It undoubtedly impressed Western observers: 'Yukos was seen as one of the stars on the horizon when it came to what was more of a Western style company' (consultant, Western).

Yukos management enhanced the attractiveness of its stock by introducing more transparency, inviting Westerners onto its board and management team, and developing investor relations. It was Khodorkovsky's objective to get the stock listed on the New York or London stock exchange in order to enhance the value of the company and to gain access to the international capital markets. 'Their market capitalisation was number one among all the Russian companies. They were certainly attracting the attention of Western companies, so it seemed to be really making the right steps' (headhunter, Western). In 2003 Yukos was in talks with potential Western partners with a view to selling off part of the company.

A more critical view of Yukos' performance came from an expatriate inside the company: 'Yukos in its essence, it's an option on crude price . . . The rest of it is window dressing' (top manager, Yukos, Western). This may have accounted for the popularity of oil stocks in general; however, it did not explain how Yukos came to have the leading position in the industry, unless from the point of view of window dressing. For one of the core competences of Khodorkovsky was managing PR: 'Selling it. UK, Europe, America, talking about it, talking about it. And he made it the poster job' (top manager, Western oil company, Western).

In terms of attracting the interest of international investors the first priority was to increase production rates: 'The Russian oil industry was in a deep slumber. Yukos led its revival' (top manager, Yukos, Western). Yukos increased production at rates far in excess of those achieved by Western companies: 'Yukos production was growing at close to 20 per cent year-on-year, which was unprecedented in Russia, in fact unprecedented almost anywhere in the world . . . That's staggering. BP, Shell, Exxon are nowhere near that' (senior manager, TNK-BP, Western). Not only was production increasing, but costs were coming down and profitability increasing: '[Yukos are] a third the cost of Exxon for example, their operating costs are $1.50 compared to $5. About 60 per cent of the level of Lukoil and TNK-BP' (investment bank executive, Western). 'If you look at the raw profits of companies like Yukos in 2002, 2003, the profits were unmatched by any major oil company in the world, incredibly profitable. And so if that's a measure of success then they have been incredibly successful, much more so than their large Western competitors' (top manager, TNK-BP, Western).

Yukos set the benchmark for other, more qualitative measures of competitive advantage, for instance corporate governance:

[Yukos] was the first to introduce it [corporate governance] in this country. OK, TNK-BP are now moving in the same direction, only they are late. Yukos foresaw the need for Russia in '98 – they are six years ahead. That's a long time for Russia. Six years ago only a few companies understood that this was necessary for Russia. Now everyone understands. You just need one example for everyone else to follow. (top manager, Yukos, Russian, translation)

Yukos was also the leader in human resource management:

I think that today Yukos is the undoubted leader in the development, training and qualification of its employees. HR issues were put as priority number one

by the company . . . I think that nowhere else in Russia – that's for certain . . .
is there such a large-scale programme for increasing qualifications and education as there was in Yukos. (senior manager, Yukos, regional, Russian,
translation)

Overall. Yukos had a clear competitive advantage in the Russian oil
industry. It was difficult to imitate – one of the criteria for sustainability:

> What Yukos has achieved cannot be replicated because it's already been done
> and the bar has moved upwards. Also I think we will never again have the com-
> bination of people like Khodorkovsky with his vision and his dynamism com-
> bined with people like Joe Mach with their dynamism and refusal to take no for
> an answer. I don't think you will find that particular combination again . . . I
> mean to go from close to bankruptcy to $30 billion capitalisation in about four
> years was a significant achievement. (top manager, TNK-BP, Western)

Unfortunately their competitive advantage turned out not, after all, to
be sustainable. Externally imposed measures by the State meant that the
CEO was put into jail and the company was broken up.

EPILOGUE

In late October 2003 Khodorkovsky was arrested. At the end of 2004
Yuganskneftegaz, the main production subsidiary, was sold in a rigged
auction to a bogus company representing the state oil company Rosneft.
Yukos was effectively being re-nationalised. At the end of 2005
Khodorkovsky was sentenced to nine years in prison, of which he had
already served one and a half. This epilogue to the success story of Yukos'
organisational transformation towards a Western model describes some of
the causes of Khodorkovsky's and Yukos' downfall, describes the situation
in Yukos at the end of 2004 and discusses why Yukos' competitive advantage was, after all, unsustainable.

The exact causes of Yukos' downfall are not known, but many associate its demise with the fact that Khodorkovsky was beginning to present
a political threat to Putin. Respondents confirmed that Khodorkovsky
was preparing to run for the presidency in 2008. Some suggested that he
had become a victim of his own PR: 'I think that they allowed their
PR people and their Western partners, their western lackeys almost, to
persuade them that they could walk on water and the ice wasn't as
thick as they thought' (top manager, TNK-BP, Western). Ostensibly,
however, Khodorkovsky was arrested for fraud and tax crimes. Ironically
Yukos' high standards of corporate governance and transparency had

contributed to its downfall: 'Most of the information that the procurator general used against Yukos in the first instance came right from the website of Yukos and their disclosures from their US GAAP reporting' (consultant, Western).

At the time of conducting the majority of the interviews in the third and fourth quarters of 2004 Yukos was struggling to survive as most of its bank accounts and assets had been frozen pending payment of the massive tax claims.

> We are in a very critical situation. We find ourselves, however absurd it might seem given how high our sales revenues are, on the verge of bankruptcy . . . You simply cannot imagine how terrible the situation with Yukos is . . . Well if you can imagine it, then multiply it by ten times and then you will have an idea of how complex it is. (top manager, Yukos, Russian, translation).

Given the intractable nature of the crisis, it was surprising how the company seemed to be surviving against all odds, at least till the end of 2004:

> I told you about our innovation capability. Yes, well this capability has been helping us to work for two months without any money, and we are feeling more or less confident. Isn't this one of our competitive advantages? . . . Because on the one hand we are more flexible, and on the other hand we are more able to withstand pressure and attack than any Western managers. Because we grew up in a different environment. We grew up as managers in a very aggressive environment, in the period of the first formation of capital in the country. (top manager, Yukos, Russian, translation)

Within the organisation there was still an immense loyalty to Khodorkovsky and to the company. A top manager proudly claimed that not a single senior manager had left the company even a year after Khodorkovsky had been jailed and compared this with the situation when Enron collapsed. This situation was confirmed by a headhunter:

> I really expected that our office . . . would be a revolving door, but it hasn't been . . . I think also the unique thing is that no one is really at fault at Yukos. They are seen as victims of a game, a political argument, but it's not a situation where management has decided that it has destroyed the company or things like this. (headhunter, Western)

The corporate spirit was typified by what one of the Heriot-Watters had to say in defence of his company:

> I, at least, am never embarrassed to say where I work . . . I always pronounce the word loudly and with pride, even today, knowing what a difficult situation the

company is in, knowing that many people are criticising the company. I have never removed the badge from my jacket, never . . . I will always remember this company as the one which made me the person I am. Not anything else, but Yukos. I joined Yukos, I developed, I trained and I grew up in Yukos. I have no one other than Yukos to thank. (senior manager, Yukos, regional, Russian, translation)

In summary it appeared that Yukos' downfall was more politically motivated than anything else. Despite overwhelming difficulties the company managed to retain its key personnel for over a year, demonstrating the loyalty and pride in a company that had become the benchmark for success in Russia.

CONCLUSION

The organisational transformation of Yukos proceeded rapidly – in a period of 7–8 years the company developed many of the operational capabilities required for survival in a market economy. The top-down management style which had been necessary at the outset to force through a break with administrative heritage was beginning to change towards increased empowerment of the organisation which would have lead ultimately to increased strategic flexibility. The jailing of Khodorkovsky in 2003 and the re-nationalisation of major Yukos assets precluded further progress.

Table 4.1 above provided an overview of Yukos' organisational transformation showing the interrelationships between the TMT, administrative heritage, organisational learning and organisational capability. A further data display in Table 4.2 presents a conceptually ordered summary of the evidence of organisational transformation in terms of efficiency and robustness; responsiveness and strategic flexibility; and performance and competitive advantage. The implications of the case study are explained further in Chapters 7–9.

Table 4.2 Conceptually ordered data display of Yukos organisational transformation

Construct	Evidence
Efficiency and robustness	• Development of basic **operational capabilities**: transparency, corporate governance, HR, finance, production, marketing, PR • Industry consensus that Yukos was the leading oil company in terms of move to a **Western operating model** • **Robust** in the context of a market economy • Signs that TMT moving away from top-down leadership style to Western leadership style, **empowering** the organisation • Some concern that operational capabilities not completely **embedded** in the organisation
Responsiveness and strategic flexibility	• Constant **adaptation to changes in unstable environment** – learning by doing • **Strategic flexibility** vested mainly still in the TMT, although signs that organisation beginning to be **empowered** • **Top-down management style** permitted **rapid implementation**
Performance and competitive advantage	• Successful strategy to be the **leading Russian oil company** • Leader by growth, operating costs, capex efficiency, marketing approach, market capitalisation • Oil production growing by 18–20% pa • Operating costs below Western oil majors • Profits higher than Western oil majors • Leader on corporate governance, HR, training and development • Employee loyalty • **Competitive advantage** in the industry

NOTES

1. President of Yukos E&P, the upstream company.
2. Vice-President Yukos E&P Operations, Western expatriate.
3. Yuganskneftegaz, Yukos' largest oil-producing subsidiary, West Siberia.
4. Depot turnover rates are a measure of inventory management efficiency. The higher the rate, the better use the company is making of its fiscal assets.
5. Field Development Planning.
6. A company with organisational silos is characterised by poor information flow between units. Information is stored, as in a grain silo.
7. Yukos RM is Yukos Refining and Marketing – the downstream company.
8. An oil-production subsidiary in Siberia.
9. Oil-producing subsidiary in European Russia.
10. Oil-producing subsidiary in Siberia.
11. Oil-producing subsidiary in Siberia.
12. One of the Russian oil majors. This acquisition did not proceed when Yukos' CEO, Mikhail Khodorkovsky, was arrested in 2003.
13. Health, Safety and Environment.
14. Due to the dependence of whole towns in Siberia on the industry.

5.   TNK/TNK-BP case study

INTRODUCTION

This case study traces the process of organisational transformation of TNK/TNK-BP. TNK[1] was created from the privatisation of several oil enterprises in 1995. In 1998 the financial investors Alfa Group and Access/Renova (AAR) gained control of the company in an auction of its shares. Sidanco, later acquired by TNK, was created in the privatisation process in 1994. BP's first involvement was a 10 per cent shareholding in Sidanco in 1997, subsequently increased to a 25 per cent shareholding plus one share in 2002 to give it blocking rights. The 50/50 JV TNK-BP was set up in February 2003 involving three companies: BP, TNK and Sidanco.

The case study format follows that for Yukos. In each section the elements of the framework are applied firstly to TNK and then to TNK-BP. Sidanco, which had a chequered history under TNK with a partial BP shareholding, is included under the TNK-BP sections because of BP's involvement in turning around the company in the later stages of their relationship. An overview of the organisational transformation process is provided in the time-ordered and conceptually ordered data displays in Tables 5.1 (TNK) and 5.2 (TNK-BP). Organisational transformation in TNK lagged that of Yukos, but the arrival of BP in 2003 speeded up the process.

TNK was the last of the integrated oil majors to be privatised. It was an inauspicious amalgamation of assets that were left over in the privatisation process. This was the starting point for the case study:

> The bumpy birth of TNK . . . This is a company that sort of arose almost by accident. It was slapped together as a second best . . . and the idea was to take the remnants because all the good stuff had run away . . . So what they were left with was the remnants of a handful of properties in South Tyumen Province and so they formed what was called the Tyumen Oil company [TNK]. (energy consultant, Western)

TOP MANAGEMENT TEAM

This section reviews the TMTs of TNK and TNK-BP, describing key personalities, the diversity and entrepreneurial orientation of the teams and management style.

TNK was a company driven by 'the very strong personalities of the two top managers' (senior manager, TNK-BP, Russian/Western). One was German Khan and the other was Viktor Vekselberg. Khan was described as extremely aggressive by numerous respondents: 'He has too much of the wrong kind of charisma. He inherited his brutality not from the Soviet era of aggressive Red Directors, but from the asset-grabbing days of the '90s (middle manager, Yukos, Russian, translation). Vekselberg, on the other hand, was calmer: 'Viktor is very wise, very analytical, very structured. I guess the word wisdom would be the one to describe the guy' (senior manager, TNK-BP, Russian/Western).

Khan was a hands-on micromanager who had the company under tight centralised control:

> It was very centralised. If someone knew the right people, the right routes to get to Khan himself, he could solve a problem quickly. You had to quickly get access, quickly explain the problem to him, he said 'yes', and everything was sorted just like that. You only had to say 'German said . . .' and everyone's mouths opened. (middle manager, TNK-BP, Russian, translation)

Managers in the regions, used to a command-and-control approach, viewed Khan's management style positively. He was regarded as capable and hard-working: 'It is practically impossible to have such a working capability. He was a workaholic, who worked for 15–18 hours a day. A computer. We didn't regard him as an oligarch. He was a very clever manager' (senior manager, TNK-BP, regional, Russian, translation).

Both Khan and Vekselberg were highly entrepreneurial: 'He [Khan] certainly came from an entrepreneurial background – both of them did. No one in Russia was born rich . . . They came from very ordinary backgrounds and they became billionaires at a fairly young age, 40 . . . So they are entrepreneurial. They had to be entrepreneurial' (senior manager, TNK-BP, Russian/Western). Khan in particular was entrepreneurial and action-oriented: 'He could take anything which seemed like a bad business and ignite it all over again' (ibid.).

Neither had any experience in the oil industry. An anecdote was recounted in the refinery about their lack of knowledge. They had sent a plan to the refinery requiring higher volumes of gasoline, but the original quantities of kerosene and mazut.[2] 'They are told: "That's not possible."

Table 5.1 *Time/conceptually ordered data display of stages of organisational transformation – TNK*

	Conditions	Actions/Interactions	Consequences
TMT and break with administrative heritage	**1995–98 Asset grabbing and rise of oligarchs** • TMT – heterogeneous, entrepreneurial, outsiders • TMT absorptive capacity high, unbounded by Soviet oil industry rationality • Organisation constrained by Soviet heritage	**TMT leverage administrative heritage** • Top-down leadership to implement change **TMT break with administrative heritage** • Promote move to market economy, acquire Western knowledge, remove blockers, learn from mistakes	**Absorptive capacity** of organisation increases
Organisational learning	**1998–2003 Move to market** • 1998 economic crisis intensifies need to improve operational efficiency • TMT perceives need to raise foreign capital, i.e. corporate governance • Absorptive capacity of organisation increases	**Absorptive capacity** • Outsiders unconstrained by heritage, open minds, fresh approach **Knowledge acquisition** • Employ some expatriates and Russians with Western experience, share knowledge with Yukos, use Western consultants and oil service companies, some training **Knowledge internalisation** • No evidence • Command-and-Control	**Organisational learning** Some development of **dynamic capabilities:** started reconfiguration, divestment, creation and integration of resources for survival in market economy

Organisational capabilities

1998–2003 Move to market
- Significant organisational learning
- Absorptive capacity increases

Knowledge dissemination
- Command-and-control
- Rotate Managers

Dynamic capabilities
Resource reconfiguration
- Asset acquisition and consolidation, restructuring, paying off debts, replacement of 'blockers', set up controls, upgrading facilities

Resource divestment
- No evidence

Resource creation
- No evidence

Resource integration
- Integration of acquired entities

Organisational transformation
- Limited **operational capabilities** developed to make company attractive to Western investor – production, finance, PR and marketing

2003–05 Reversion to state control
- 2003 – TNK-BP JV formed with state backing

See Table 5.2 for data display of organisational transformation for TNK-BP

Table 5.2   Time/conceptually ordered data display of stages of organisational transformation – TNK-BP

	Conditions	Actions/interactions	Consequences
TMT and break with administrative heritage	**2003–05 Reversion to state control** • TNK-BP JV established 2003 • TMT – heterogeneous, entrepreneurial, outsiders • TMT absorptive capacity high, unbounded by Soviet oil industry rationality • Although organisation constrained by Soviet heritage, absorptive capacity had increased under TNK management	**TMT leverage administrative heritage** • Top-down leadership to implement change **TMT break with administrative heritage** • critical mass of Western experts, begin to empower the organisation, openness, leading by example, encouraging 'thinking out of the box', demonstrable value/success	• **Absorptive capacity** increases • **Organisational learning** accelerates • **Dynamic capabilities** develop • **Operational capabilities** improve
Organisational learning	**2003–05 Reversion to state control** • Absorptive capacity of organisation increases • Significant influx of Western expertise from BP • BP acquires control and exerts influence on the JV	**Absorptive capacity** • Critical mass of Western expertise, 'thinking out of the box', demonstrable value/success **Knowledge acquisition** • Many expatriates, secondees and Russians with BP experience, Yukos specialists (Heriot-Watters), technology block expertise, supplement tertiary education, work shadowing, fewer training programmes than Yukos, focus on upstream not downstream **Knowledge internalisation** • Learn by doing, involvement in	**Organisational learning** • Development of **dynamic capabilities**: reconfiguration, divestment, creation and integration of resources for survival in market economy

90

projects, finding cultural key, demonstrable success

Knowledge dissemination
- Masterclasses/networking, job rotation, publication of best practice, working groups, focus on communication, change agents

Organisational capabilities	2003–05 Reversion to state control

2003–05 Reversion to state control
- Absorptive capacity continues to increase
- Significant organisational learning
- Operational and cultural integration commences

Dynamic capabilities

Resource reconfiguration
- Resolve charter issues to give BP control
- Span-breakers
- Clamp-down on corruption, organisational restructuring/remove silos
- HSE regulations
- Open-plan offices

Resource divestment
- No evidence, considering divestment of oilfield services

Resource creation
- Technology block

Resource integration
- Resolve partner conflicts, operational and cultural integration
- Language training
- Deal with different management styles
- Expatriates vs locals
- Synergies

Organisational transformation
- **Operational capabilities** developed for survival in market economy – increasing empowerment, knowledge sharing, HR, HSE, project management – leading to **efficiency and robustness**
- Dynamic capabilities further lead to **responsiveness and strategic flexibility**

- Likely to lead to **competitive advantage** in the Russian oil industry

"Why is it not possible, can't you make any more gasoline?" "We can." "And can't you make the same amount of mazut?" "We can." "Well go on then." "But we can't do both at the same time" (senior manager, TNK-BP, regional, Russian, translation). It had to be explained to them that crude oil is divided into fractions – if there is more of one, there is less of another. They also had no Western experience, so they brought in managers from the West such as Simon Kukes, who was Russian by origin, but had a US education and had worked for US oil companies. His role was to provide Western gloss and PR to impress the capital markets: 'For external financing we need to have somebody we can put up there and say look we're Western' (top manager, TNK-BP, Western). The finance director was also Russian by background, but with a US education. The TMT were outsiders, new to the company, and many of them new to the oil business. They were focused on short-term profitability: 'These are all financial investors . . . They are looking at assets and then will sell them to somebody also' (investment bank executive, Western).

TNK had a top-down, centralised management style: 'The first trick, before . . . decentralised initiatives, is rigid centralisation, strict control of cashflows, transparency in operations, and . . . driving international management techniques top-down through the company' (senior manager, TNK, Western). This process was aided by the fact that TNK employees were used to taking orders. Effectively, ten to 15 people ran a company of 60 000 (top manager, TNK-BP, Western). 'All decisions were taken only at the top' (middle manager, TNK-BP, Russian, translation). This top-down approach facilitated rapid decision-making: 'TNK was a very dynamic company. Decisions were taken very quickly. People got used to decisions being taken in a matter of hours, not days' (middle manager, TNK-BP, Russian, translation).

The focus was on increasing production, reducing costs and improving financial performance and it was very task-oriented:

> with a focus on rapid achievement of short-term results – it was such a short-term sprint that now when we talk about strategic issues or five-year plans people are just not used to thinking in this way, they are used to seeing a concrete, practical task, and away with it. (middle manager, TNK-BP, Russian, translation)

An example of this task orientation was the focus on one goal for improving oil production – the improvement of the submersible pumps: 'He [TNK expatriate] found the biggest gap, focused right on that one gap only, and ordered, command-and-control. Thou shalt optimise the wells . . . And they were measured. If you didn't fix those wells, man, you got yelled at, screamed at' (top manager, TNK-BP, Western).

Every operational decision had to be endorsed by Khan himself, or by those managers whom he trusted closely. Middle managers were simply afraid to take decisions: 'He is quite a tough guy and many people suffered as a result of his difficult character – the price for making a mistake was very high' (middle manager, TNK-BP, Russian, translation). The culture was very rough. An example was provided by a respondent, a Russian with Western experience, who had an unpleasant confrontation with Khan on his first appearance at the management board:

> I was asked to come along for that presentation and the guys who prepared that presentation asked me to sign on the front page, which I did. And the message which they delivered wasn't exactly what German [Khan] expected . . . And right at that management board he was like, f***, you're a bunch of f***ing idiots, get the f*** out of here, you know, all of you, you know, including you who just came in, you'd be better off sitting in your f***ing London. And stuff like that . . . And that was all this company was about. (senior manager, TNK-BP, Russian/Western)

Nevertheless the TMT had had a positive effect on oil production and regional employees were grateful for the improvements, such as wages being paid. In a play on words (TNK – TANK), a number of respondents compared TNK managers with tank crews in the army:

> It wasn't for nothing that they called the employees [of TNK] *tankisti*, tank troops, because it was really a very aggressive company in the positive sense of the word. And probably we were very lucky . . . that our top management were all young guys, all smart, all goal-oriented and therefore they were successful in introducing . . . everything new. (middle manager, TNK-BP, regional, Russian, translation)

Although useful for establishing control in the early days, the top-down style was a limiting factor on the further development of the company. Strategic decisions could be taken quickly, but operational decisions had to find their way up the hierarchy. However, by about the time that the TNK-BP merger took place, it was noticeable in the regions that TNK's management style was changing slightly, as manifested by their intention to give the regional subsidiaries greater autonomy:

> There was an evolution from the point where Alfa-Group came and stuck their noses into a different environment where . . . no one would be trusted, to an understanding that all key positions were occupied by good people, who could be trusted, and that excessive centralised decision making was beginning to have a negative effect. (middle manager, TNK-BP, regional, Russian, translation)

When TNK-BP was formed some of the Russian owners took a top management role in the new company – Mikhail Friedman of Alfa Group as Chairman of the Board, and Vekselberg and Khan as Executive Directors. In 2004 there were 14 people on the management committee, seven BP, six AAR, and one independent ex-Chevron. The President and CEO was Bob Dudley of BP. There was a good mixture of Western business skills, professional oilmen and Russian local knowledge.

One problem was the clash of cultures. TNK's style was aggressive, entrepreneurial and top-down: 'Keeping the AAR partners on board . . . that's very tough to do because those guys are entrepreneurs. They are very high energy and like most entrepreneurs they are completely undisciplined' (energy consultant, Western). BP's style, on the other hand, reflected respect for employees, openness in communication, and empowerment: 'This is becoming a reality – extensive communication within the company, the possibility for people to express their opinions, the possibility not only to receive orders and carry them out, but express an opinion, i.e. more actively involve employees in decision-making' (middle manager, TNK-BP, Russian, translation)

It was difficult, though, to involve TNK managers in decision-making. In one meeting Khan had walked out because he had already seen a particular presentation: 'and all the people that were with him, therefore all the Russians in the room, got up and left the meeting . . . the expats were left in the room looking at each other' (consultant, Western). Junior managers had to do what their bosses did. The top-down style of TNK differed significantly from BP's democratic approach: '[BP has] a more democratic style, than it was in TNK. There is more serious support of initiatives from below' (middle manager, TNK-BP, Russian, translation). However this democratic and consensus-building style was considered by Russian managers to slow down decision-making to an unacceptable level: 'The majority of Russian managers are completely convinced that expats don't like making decisions . . . They are convinced that expats prevaricate, drag things out and delay taking a decision in all possible ways. I personally think that it is a reluctance to take on responsibility' (middle manager, TNK-BP, regional, Russian, translation). Staff who had come from Yukos were disappointed by their inability to get anything done quickly. Although initiatives were welcomed, they took too long to be agreed and implemented:

> Here in TNK-BP everything is slower and dampened down . . . To get something done here you have to have meetings with managers and try to come to an agreement. A very detailed and careful process. It takes a long time to persuade people of a course of action – and even then there is no clear decision taken. (middle manager, TNK-BP, Russian, translation)

In the refinery the employees had got used to a very clear style of instructions: 'yes, no, this way, that way' and not what they called the 'humane' way where you had to work it all out for yourself. The standard BP form was: 'They would thank you for your attention, for the importance of the question, but then you could not understand whether to do it or not. It's very nice that they are polite, but then what?' (senior manager, TNK-BP, regional, Russian, translation). The same frustration with BP's bureaucratic approach was articulated in the oil-producing region: 'for them [BP] it was the process that was important . . . endless discussions about how everything should be' (middle manager, TNK-BP, regional, Russian, translation).

ADMINISTRATIVE HERITAGE

This section describes how the TMTs of TNK and TNK-BP were able both to break with administrative heritage to bring about change and to leverage administrative heritage in order to increase the pace of change.

Break with Administrative Heritage

Breaking with the Soviet administrative heritage and introducing a Western approach was the first priority for TNK: 'Russia cannot be changed overnight, but it's extremely important that these people, who went through these horrendous times, created the company, they realised that they needed to be thinking. . . West' (middle manager, TNK-BP, Russian, translation). Enterprises had been used to calculating costs and adding on a 15 per cent margin. Suddenly they were confronted with market concepts: '[When TNK came] it was the first time I had come across people asking: "But what are the market prices?" "What market prices? There's no such thing." "And how much is he prepared to pay?" ' (middle manager, TNK-BP, regional, Russian, translation).

Market prices and profitability were alien concepts. The introduction of Western business techniques required a substantial change of mindset – this was easier to achieve with a top-down approach:

> The first thing to do is to stop the leakage, sloppiness, the bad business practice of the past. You need the old managers in place, you can't replace them all, and they're very good technically, but some of them just don't have the financial or the managerial understanding to work in the new system, and some of their interests . . . aren't completely aligned with our shareholders, and therefore we go for centralised management. (top manager, TNK, Western)

Uncooperative managers, resistant to change, were removed: 'All procedures were designed to replace non-loyal managers with loyal ones. And the
only method of stopping the theft was to create a harsh regime, very harsh'
(top manager, TNK-BP, Russian, translation). Changing people's mindsets
was difficult, but once improvements started to manifest themselves, the
new ways of doing things became easier to accept.

> It is a characteristic of conservative people that they are hostile to all new
> demands. But I am convinced that people will get used to it, and they will get to
> like it . . . Anything new is always met with a hostile reception. But then people
> get used to it and say: 'Things have turned out well' . . . But it's hard – I am also
> conservative. (middle manager, TNK-BP, regional, Russian, translation).

BP brought further changes. BP's openness was particularly shocking for
managers brought up in the Soviet system: 'We [TNK] achieved a lot . . .
we were rather successful, developing rapidly. And we only need you [BP]
for your technology and technical skills. And then suddenly – wham! –
everyone starts to live by new rules, even to the extent that all office doors
are open' (top manager, TNK-BP, Russian, translation). TNK-BP had
moved into new open-plan offices at the end of 2004. Even the top managers' offices, which had glass walls and doors, were indeed left open
(researcher observation).

Western-type incentive schemes were also important for breaking with
administrative heritage. They were introduced early on in Sidanco: 'The
incentivisation . . . was aligned with the programme of change . . . It's complicated in Russia . . . The Soviet history in that sector . . . generated behaviours that were absolutely 180 degrees out of phase with what I needed' (top
manager, Western). In Soviet times, employees were entitled to an annual
bonus, but it was often reduced by failure to deliver on target. When BP
took control of Sidanco there was a backlog of pay and bonuses. They
decided to pay both the wages arrears and 50 per cent of the bonus:

> The Soviet management went nuts. They said, 'You can't do that.' I said, 'Why
> not?' They said, 'Well . . . we have no leverage left, how are we going to punish
> them in the future?' 'I said we're not going to punish them in the future, the object
> in the future [is] to incent[ivise] them to do even more'. (top manager, Western)

This had a powerful motivational effect on the workforce. At the same
time the pay scale was adjusted, so that although many people were made
redundant, the ones that remained were given incentives: 'so fewer people
but better paid with incentivisation toward performance . . . their success,
company success were tied together' (top manager, Western). In TNK-BP
a bonus system was also set up to align employees' interests with those of

the company with 20 per cent personal bonus, 50 per cent departmental bonus and 30 per cent based on company performance.

Another big change introduced by the new Western managers was a gradual move to encourage decision-making lower down in the organisation: 'It is a centralised approach, but it is an approach which teaches people at every level to take some management decisions . . . Now decision making is stimulated not only at senior levels, but also lower down the organisation' (middle manager, TNK-BP, Russian, translation). However, empowering employees was not easy, because people were so used to carrying out orders, and being punished for stepping out of line.

> Many of these people have incredibly good educations, but . . . they were turning off their brains the day they walked in . . . So we're going to give them the opportunity to turn it back on. Now that's another problem because in the Soviet period every initiative was punished, so . . . Don't take the initiative . . . Stay invisible if possible. (top manager, Western)

Asking people to make suggestions about what to do 'terrified them' (ibid.). An example of the reluctance of employees to come up with any ideas was given in connection with the establishment of the first working groups in TNK-BP to develop solutions for technical problems. Initially the attempt to involve Russian managers in defining a project met with incredulity and silence:

> It just was very difficult to herd this group to a resolution. But they had a day and a half and they had to stand and present to myself, the COO, Bob Dudley [CEO] . . . So the pressure cooker was in place . . . And they did it, X [expatriate in charge] told me he had the worse headache he'd ever had that night when he went home. He laid in bed almost in tears because he just couldn't fathom . . . what was happening. This barrier between Westerner and Russian was trying to be closed at a lightning pace. (top manager, TNK-BP, Western)

In the end some of the working groups were very successful. Their success was helpful in persuading others to change: 'We had some early successes, we had things that worked and they saw behaviours change and they saw people perform, given the right set of circumstances and processes' (top manager, Western).

Planning was another area where there was a gulf between Soviet and Western practice. BP set aspirational targets, without defining exactly how they would be achieved. In the Soviet system the plan had to be delivered exactly on target and as defined:

> Something . . . that rings out in the Russian culture. If you don't deliver exactly what you've said you'll deliver, and I mean exactly, you've failed. . . . Last year

our target was 9 091 000 tonnes. We delivered just slightly over 9 000 000, so 99 per cent, but we failed. Now that target of 9 091 000 was stretched, I mean really stretched, but in the BP world, 'You guys did great'. Right – we increased production over 14 per cent. But last year in the Russian culture – we failed. I think that component probably makes change difficult, because often when you change, you have to take risks. (top manager, TNK-BP, regional, Western)

In Sidanco a Russian management consultant was helpful in persuading people to change. He had headed his own company in Russia in the 1990s and later moved into international consultancy and academia (at INSEAD):

He had a track record as an executive of being successful . . . And *he* was able to bring the connection to what I was trying to say to my Soviet history executives: 'Wait a minute, this isn't from the moon, this actually works in Russia, and I've done it.' He, as a Russian, had a credibility of, 'Yeah, it does work you guys, it will work'. (top manager, Western)

Given the strength of the Soviet administrative heritage it was not surprising that a state of confusion reigned because the old ways of doing things were being abolished, but the new ones were not yet fully assimilated:

Probably, because everything being introduced is new, there is a rejection of it, because – well they have taken away the old practices – there was an iron horse, they melted it down, and promised to cast a cockerel, but the cockerel is not yet in the kiln. So there you are, the cockerel is not there yet, and the horse has gone. There is this feeling that the old has been taken away, and in exchange they haven't been given something new, which works properly. (middle manager, TNK-BP, Russian, translation)

The metaphor of the iron horse represented the administrative heritage that was being broken down.

Leverage Administrative Heritage

By adopting a top-down approach the TNK TMT was able to leverage a key aspect of the Soviet administrative heritage – the command-and-control management style: 'The buy-in in TNK was an executive order . . . that's the Russian style, more a military style, and very much TNK style' (senior manager, TNK-BP, Russian/Western).

BP also soon realised the benefits of adopting a similar stance, at least in the short term, in order to ensure rapid implementation, given that employee mindsets were unlikely to change quickly. An example was given of the implementation of new HSE regulations:

We consider, and BP acknowledges, that we are at the evolutionary stage called 'supervision'. What is the character of this supervision? The management is committed to safety, is taking steps to resolve these issues, but the structure is such that we have to use force for the time being – to force people to meet all the safety requirements because they cannot change their attitudes in a day. (senior manager, TNK-BP, regional, Russian, translation)

Although BP managers were keen to introduce Western styles of management, including decision-making lower down the organisation, they also recognised that the traditional top-down management style was a powerful tool for implementing change:

That's very powerful because once the group decide to do something, they implement – it's one of the strengths of the Russian culture. When they decide, they go, it happens. And it comes from the order, because when an order came down . . . it would become law . . . And so once the working group had set the standard, it got implemented. (top manager, TNK-BP, Western)

This manager gave the example of a well evaluation tracking tool (WETS) that was implemented in three months in Russia whereas it had taken much longer in other parts of BP; 'and BP has had WETS for I don't know how many years, but they've never got it fully implemented across the company' (ibid.).

The command-and-control approach was therefore a useful lever for rapid implementation of change in the short term.

ORGANISATIONAL LEARNING

The break with administrative heritage increased the absorptive capacity of the organisation, facilitating organisational learning. This section covers the development of absorptive capacity, knowledge acquisition, internalisation and dissemination.

Absorptive Capacity

The TNK TMT had no history, no established way of doing things and was therefore not hampered by the administrative heritage of the Russian oil industry:

The main thing [about TNK] is . . . they have no history . . . and they are prepared to solve a problem in a new way, which in many cases is very positive . . . They know, of course, the local conditions, they know how you can resolve things here. They have no traditions . . . that is, they view problems with a fresh approach. (middle manager, TNK-BP, Russian, translation)

Because of this fresh approach and their top-down management style they were able to increase the absorptive capacity of the organisation. The openness to new ideas of the TMT had a positive effect on the rest of the organisation:

> TNK had some very high quality people. It's not so much the intellectual capacity or even industry expertise, it's the way you open up your mind to a different view. So by that I mean the ability to recognise that someone can do it better . . . And that happens . . . I've seen some critical cases initially that they were considered really diehards. And after a few months of talking it out they would convert on both sides. (senior manager, TNK-BP, Russian/Western)

By the time of the merger the organisation already understood the importance of Western management techniques to improve performance: 'What it isn't doing is running them as effectively as a Western company would, . . . because it's probably where a Western oil company was in the 1960s. But it knows the paths to go down so it won't take 40 years to get to where the industry is today' (investment bank executive, Western).

BP brought a different outlook, but by that time the organisation was more ready for change: 'TNK started to transform itself quite quickly, because the things that BP brought were desired and expected by many people' (middle manager, TNK-BP, Russian, translation). The CEO himself set an example: 'He builds compromises . . . he doesn't . . . unilaterally take decisions, he consults, he engages people, he gives an example . . . he gives a learning by doing it himself. That example is followed by Russian executives who are now more into the mode of consultations and consensus building' (senior manager, TNK-BP, Russian/Western). Even Khan was seen to be changing '*a lot*' (ibid.: 153), becoming more Westernised, yet still keeping his core strengths. Other top managers were also beginning to understand key concepts of Western management: 'No one understands what a "manager" is. No one understands that it is a complex of knowledge of HR in the management of human resources, and of concepts of corporate culture, and corporate governance. All of this we – I personally – began to understand only when they arrived (top manager, TNK-BP, Russian, translation).

The presence of expatriates and Russians with Western experience was key to helping managers to understand why and what change was needed:

> Without the kind of people who know in practice how a Western company works, changing a Russian company is very difficult, because it is not realistic to think that you can do everything just by reading the textbooks . . . There needs

to be a critical mass of people who are prepared to change the company, other-wise it won't work. (middle manager, TNK-BP, Russian, translation)

BP brought a detailed approach which was 'very very helpful to the Russian staff here to organise themselves, to discipline themselves, to actu-ally see what the standards that Western businesses are running at are' (senior manager, TNK-BP, Russian). However, it was not just the Russian staff who needed to think differently. The expatriates too were faced with a steep learning curve: 'This is a different mindset than any place else you will go in the oil business, in the way that things are done here, . . . just very different. And it doesn't fit a lot of people's frame so you have to be able to exit the frame of thinking in order to see both sides' (top manager, TNK-BP, Western).

Training Russians to 'think out of the box' was important because their frames of reference were restricted to the Soviet system: 'They were used to thinking in their little boxes. When they were confronted with case studies . . . they would say "That won't work here, that's not for us, that works for them, but not for us" ' (middle manager, TNK-BP, Russian, trans-lation). Two training programmes, that were set up jointly with INSEAD for senior managers and high-flyers, were designed to address this problem.

Demonstrating the creation of value was important for changing behav-iours: 'It's all about understanding how this is going to help me . . . So if you can get them convinced that this is going to bring some value, they're all for it and they will attack it. They will just soak it up like a sponge' (top manager, TNK-BP, regional, Western). Demonstrable success also increased the readiness of the regional enterprises to support change: 'With the use of new technology, new methods, new developments, the produc-tion of oil compared to the previous year grew by about 12 per cent this year. . . . It is obvious that this is only welcomed and is supported in all ways possible' (middle manager, TNK-BP, regional, Russian, translation).

The foundations for absorptive capacity were created by the TNK TMT who brought a fresh approach. The arrival of BP provided a critical mass of Western experience which helped to increase the understanding of the organisation for the need for change. Increased absorptive capacity opened up the organisation to learning.

Knowledge Acquisition

In the early days in TNK there was little formal training. The urgency of the need to establish control over the operations of the company meant there was no time for anything else. Debts had to be paid off and oil production increased. They relied on the resources of the new managers and people brought in from other Russian companies: 'We were learning by our mistakes, and by the example of others' (middle manager, TNK-BP, regional, Russian, translation). In the early days there were no foreign specialists out in the oilfields. Instead TNK learned from what Yukos was doing, and vice versa. 'We would always meet and say: "What's new with you? That? OK, we'll start that as well"' (ibid.). In time the financial managers who had acquired the company realised that they needed more than just trial and error to bring about performance improvements and began to call in Western expertise, for instance the oil services company Halliburton and the consultants McKinsey: 'The investors realised that they do not know anything about the industry. They just happened to have bought a goose that lays a lot of golden eggs. So they brought in some proper goose keepers if you want to call it that. And so they brought in professionals' (consultant, Western). Of particular value were former Soviet citizens who had lived and worked in the West, but who spoke Russian and understood the Russian environment: 'They [TNK] resolved the problem of production and management experience by hiring people who knew something both about the oil industry and Soviet mentality. TNK quite quickly got on track with Western management techniques' (energy consultant, Russian, translation).

When the finance department was set up in TNK, everyone in the department was able to speak English, and many of them had a Western education or experience in Western companies (top manager, TNK, Western). A drilling specialist of Russian extraction was brought in who introduced the supervising system:

> He was an American, but Russian-speaking, and of course, that gave him the possibility to converse with our specialists in one language . . . his knowledge, his experience and his experience of working in Russia. He came and was in the situation where he understood the Russian soul, Russian specialists, the so-called Russian mentality. He contributed a lot. (middle manager, TNK-BP, regional, Russian, translation)

Overall, however, there were relatively few expatriates or Western-trained Russians working in TNK. In 2001 the feeling was expressed that an even stronger infusion of management skills was required, which could come only from Western equity participation: 'In order for Russian oil companies to become . . . competitive we need a stronger infusion of international management skills, of international technology, and the only way that you can . . . get that in a strong enough dose is through equity participation by Western oil companies' (senior manager, TNK, Western). This was later to occur when in 2003 the TNK/BP JV was created.

To summarise, TNK knowledge was acquired from a few expatriates and Russians with Western experience, from peers (Yukos), and from Western consultants and oil service companies. A limited training programme was set up.

The availability of Western knowledge and expertise increased with BP's arrival: 'There has been a significant influx of management and leadership talent from BP – expatriates, typically from the UK and the US, . . . who have brought with them the BP way . . ., BP technologies, the access to the BP network of expertise, which will unquestionably over time deliver significant value and improvements' (top manager, TNK-BP, Western). Thus TNK-BP had a critical mass of Western expertise, far greater, for example, than Yukos. Forty-five BP managers and 80 BP secondees came into the JV (top manager, TNK-BP, Western). Further expertise was acquired from 2004 with the recruitment of trained professionals from the leading Russian oil company, Yukos: 'We [Yukos] had trained specialists, spent a lot of money on them, and then the specialist went off happily – he was simply bought out. Our friends TNK-BP are the leaders in this direction, i.e. they have whole departments which consist totally of Yukos specialists' (senior manager, Yukos, regional, Russian, translation). Despite the recruitment of these trained professionals, there was still perceived to be a lack of technical expertise: 'The problem is there's not enough of them, we need hundreds of them. And the problem isn't just in engineering, we need geoscientists – there's a real lack of geological skills and geophysical skills that take us to the next level' (top manager, TNK-BP, Western).

The technology block, located at head office, was an important source of knowledge and expertise. It coordinated technological issues across the company. In the regions the technical centres had been revamped but no decision had been made about whether to copy the Yukos/Heriot-Watt model.

The BP connection had great potential in terms of both developing intellectual capital and in offering prospects for career development.

> It's a very distinctive thing to have BP because BP could take somebody for a year in Sunbury[3] and really give them a different way of thinking, give them a different way of doing things and train them in a modern world-respected oil company. Maybe it's too ambitious, but my vision is that this little JV – not really little JV – but one day could . . . be as powerful or better than BP. (top manager, TNK-BP, Western)

The availability of secondees from BP in TNK-BP and the possibility to second Russian managers to BP was a competitive advantage that TNK-BP had over all other Russian oil companies. But the BP secondees were very costly resources and in some cases, where they had a particular speciality, a rare commodity. Therefore the intention was to extract the maximum benefit from their presence by instituting a work-shadowing programme for promising young specialists (ibid.).

According to an ex-Yukos manager, much less general management training and development was offered than in Yukos (middle manager, TNK-BP, Russian, translation). Nevertheless BP initiated a substantial number of training programmes. For example, detailed training programmes were developed for high-flyers in the regions and formalised in a dual-language booklet (TNK-BP, 2004b). An important emphasis was on project management training which was delivered by Western specialists using interpreters (top manager, TNK-BP, Western).

In the refinery, however, there appeared to be little training and transfer of best practice except for project management for new plant construction: 'Here in the production units . . . the influence of the BP culture on us, from the point of view of bringing something new . . . is non-existent' (middle manager, TNK-BP, regional, Russian, translation). This may have been due to prioritisation of the upstream business.

In summary, BP's arrival had provided a significant boost to the knowledge acquisition process, bringing access to BP's global network and expertise.

Knowledge Internalisation

No evidence was found of knowledge internalisation during the TNK period. This may be accounted for by the fact that the management style was command-and-control. Employees implemented orders without questioning them. In TNK-BP the main emphasis was on learning by doing. For example, when a new strategic planning system was being introduced the issue was discussed, the broad outline taken from the BP approach and then it was 'learn as you go . . . various people got involved and they try to understand what exactly they were supposed to be doing in their section of work' (senior manager, TNK-BP, Russian/Western).

In Sidanco one of the most difficult things for Russian employees to internalise was the concept of safety management. 'We were *killing* people, *injuring* people in a fairly large way, just *awful*' (top manager, TNK-BP, Western). They brought in DuPont, the world leaders in HSE, and extensive training was undertaken. But no breakthrough was achieved. 'They were . . . giving it lip-service . . . but it just wasn't getting there. And constantly . . . accidents happened' (ibid.). There were many debates about what could be the 'cultural key', what was the element that would cause people to engage in this activity in a real way, and not superficially?

> And it turned out to be pride. I said . . . 'Anywhere in the world this level of production, this number of people, this could be an incident rate that you see almost around the world and we're way above it so what's wrong with us?' 'There's nothing wrong with us, we can do anything those guys do'. (ibid.)

Once that was recognised it was possible to put the right incentives in place to start improving safety performance.

Demonstrable success from using new approaches in the field was also a key way for the technical specialists to internalise knowledge: 'If I'm doing it one way and you can't demonstrate to me how . . . you're proposing it's going to be better, why should I change?' (top manager, TNK-BP, Regional, Western).

In summary, the main methods of knowledge internalisation were learning by doing, which included involvement in development projects, finding the cultural key, and demonstrating success.

Knowledge Dissemination

Knowledge dissemination in TNK was mainly by order from the top. For example, new Western business techniques were pushed out into the region and managers were ordered to adopt different performance criteria:

> We really are . . . driving cash flow analysis down to the level of our subsidiaries when they make investment decisions. People all know in the field now, what our IRR is, and what the criteria are. . . . The criteria aren't 'how do I increase production 5 per cent this year?', the criteria are 'how do I put in place higher IRR projects?' And they're already starting to think with the correct tools. (top manager, TNK, Western)

Managers were also rotated from one location to another to gain experience and transfer best practice.

TNK-BP took a different approach to the job rotation system by organising 'masterclasses' in centres of excellence for groups of people. Training was planned: 'how it should be organised, what format it should take, how to transfer one's knowledge' so that people could learn from each other, 'but it is not direct training, but indirect learning, more like professional networking, linked with the implementation of innovations' (middle manager, TNK-BP, Russian, translation). However, job rotation of senior managers still took place and was the subject of ribald comments in the regions: 'I think that the company resolves the problem [of transferring best practice] by transferring top managers . . . from time to time from one main sector to another [laughter]. He goes from one division to another. He is just about being recognised there, when he has to start learning things here' (senior manager, TNK-BP, regional, Russian, translation).

Improvement projects presented at a technical conference were published in a booklet (TNK-BP, 2004a): 'This is what is called sharing, when we take the presentations from different regions and publish them together so that the knowledge does not stay just within the region' (middle manager, TNK-BP, Russian, translation).

The technology block in Moscow, staffed mainly by expatriates, was responsible for disseminating technology and best practice throughout the company. Working groups were also used as a forum for transfer of best practices. About six technical working groups were set up based on specific projects such as electric submersible pumps (ESPs), water flood excellence and corrosion failure prevention (Dupree, 2004). 'We have people that are from basically every business unit . . . and they get together on a routine basis and try to . . . establish . . . baseline information, . . . benchmark and identify areas of excellence and areas that have fallen below the norm, to try to drive performance' (top manager, TNK-BP, regional, Western). The working groups sponsored pilot projects and visited them as a group. Some were sent overseas to view best practice. Working groups were used not just in the area of technology, but also in other functional areas, such as HR. 'Now if we are developing anything new we try to include people from the regions. Indirectly, this works as training for them' (middle manager, TNK-BP, Russian, translation).

The size and geographic spread of the organisation represented particular barriers to change. Therefore communication played a major role:

> People shouted out 'No, our way was better, what we had was good, and what is it you are now offering us?' And that is everywhere. There's approximately the same reaction to every initiative, so we need to undertake serious communication work with people. This is where the problem of our large size and geographic spread comes in, because communicating is extraordinarily difficult. (middle manager, TNK-BP, Russian, translation)

Another key method of disseminating knowledge and bringing about change was the use of change agents:

> There are always . . . some leaders within the organisation who take on the responsibility to drive things. And they are not necessarily leaders by virtue of their position. . . . They are informal leaders. And we have such informal leaders who are unafraid to take the responsibility, who are unafraid to take the heat for it, who aren't afraid to stand up and defend their position in front of very important, very powerful opponents. (senior manager, TNK-BP, Russian/Western)

To conclude, knowledge dissemination in TNK-BP was a function of networking, job rotation, publication of best practice, masterclasses, working groups and the use of change agents.

ORGANISATIONAL CAPABILITIES

Dynamic Capabilities – Resource Reconfiguration

TNK first had to establish control over the disparate entities acquired in the privatisation process:

> All efforts were directed at stopping the theft within the company. All procedures were directed at replacing disloyal managers with loyal ones . . . and the only method of stopping the theft was to set up a very harsh regimen, very harsh. . . . All efforts, all internal corporate regulations were directed to (a) preventing stealing, (b) installing the toughest financial discipline possible, and (c) . . . reducing costs. (top manager, TNK-BP, Russian, translation)

When TNK took over the company in Nizhnevartovsk, a major oil-producing enterprise, it was bankrupt and there were long delays in paying wages. Large credits were obtained from Eximbank (US) and gradually debts were liquidated and wages began to be paid. 'It went through many stages. Each positive step and positive action by the company was interpreted correspondingly by the employees' (senior manager, TNK-BP, regional, Russian, translation). The company in Nizhnevartovsk was restructured, splitting off the oil-producing units. Many more assets were acquired at auction: Orenburg, Onarco, Sidanco, Orenburg-Geologiya, Kondpetroleum, Chernogorneft, etc. (middle manager, TNK-BP, regional, Russian, translation). Although the company acquired assets aggressively, its approach to employees was softer than that of neighbouring Yukos. 'The company did a lot to avoid social unrest' (ibid.).

TNK significantly improved working conditions for the oil workers by upgrading shift-worker accommodation on the oilfields, which were located up to 300 km away from the city. Living conditions had been appalling – accommodation in old railway wagons with several men sharing a room. New brick-built hostels were constructed with maximum two people per room, hot showers, mini sports halls, televisions and refrigerators: 'Either you arrive back from work to a place where you haven't even got a place to dry your working clothes out, or you live in a three-star hotel, well three-and-a-half stars – of course your performance is going to be better!' (senior manager, TNK-BP, Regional, Russian, translation). Payment of salaries and improved working conditions significantly increased employee motivation.

The TNK-BP joint venture was set up in June 2003. One of the terms of the deal was that BP appointed the CEO, who should have a clear set of delegations to be able to run the company. However, BP's power was substantially reduced: before the deal was done the charter was changed, they registered the company very quietly, which made those powers that BP thought it had negotiated, illegal (top manager, TNK-BP, Western). Many of the Russian staff thought, 'this is going to be another example where the Russians sell out as shareholders to BP and then they still run the company' (top manager, TNK-BP, Western). However, BP had learnt its lesson from the Sidanco experience: in Russia you need a Russian partner, but you also have to have control. A difficult situation, with the CEO, Dudley, only able to exercise control via the veto, lasted until June 2004 when it was resolved to the benefit of BP, giving them back the level of control originally anticipated.

An important factor for the success of the JV was the extent to which the two prime movers in TNK, Khan and Vekselberg, would cooperate. They were very powerful figures in the organisation, used to 'just calling up and telling people what to do' (top manager, TNK-BP, Western). However, their ability to control the organisation was reduced both by the new governance system and the new organisational structure, which had 'lots of span-breakers, you know Russian and BP heritage, or independent expatriates, or just independent Russians, all through the structure, so it's designed to create lots of checks and balances' (ibid.). The span-breakers were placed in key positions throughout the organisation to break the span of control of the TNK managers. However, given the limited number of such span-breakers it was impossible to extend this system to any great extent to the regions. Therefore there was centralised financial control: 'You have to have the ability to influence contracting or influence the amount of money the subsidiary may get, based on the fact that they are or not performing well, or implementing technology well' (top manager, TNK-BP, Western).

A major issue for BP as a respected multinational was how to deal with the bribery and corruption in Russia. The size and importance of the company gave it leverage in this respect, and it also seemed that top TNK managers were becoming more aware of the importance of clamping down on such issues. Vekselberg himself was involved in developing an anti-bribery and corruption initiative within the World Economic Forum sub-committee of energy, oil and mining.

In Sidanco a considerable amount of change was promoted by organisational restructuring, breaking down the functional silos and establishing a structure designed around the common company goal of profitability. There were significant structural changes in the trading and downstream functions. The old system of 'each to his own' (middle manager, Yukos, Russian, translation) was replaced by coordination across factories and across functions. Export and domestic sales departments, which had previously competed against each other and had been located on different floors, were combined into one trading unit. A new accounting function was set up, based on an optimisation model, and an analytical group was created. 'It was a great leap forward' (ibid.)

The biggest changes in TNK-BP were initiated in HSE. For instance, refinery plant managers were made responsible for performance of the contractors, who did much of the dangerous work on the site. They had to stop work if they were found to be violating regulations: 'Now it is rather good to watch how they work. They have all purchased good quality wood, you look at them – they have good safety harnesses which can be clipped in place, and not just a piece of rope to tie themselves on with' (middle manager, TNK-BP, regional, Russian, translation).

Resource reconfiguration also involved office changes. In Sidanco the move towards a more open organisation was mirrored in the move to new open-plan offices:

> We were in a Soviet building. Beautiful old building but it had the traditional Soviet structure. Long halls, doors. Nobody knows who works . . . I walk in, I go through doors and find people I didn't even know existed. So I said 'That's going to stop'. So we moved into a new building and it was open-plan. And I thought people were going to have a stroke. It lasted about six months and at the end of that they said, this is actually fun, we kind of like this, it's open. (top manager, TNK-BP, Western)

Attention was paid to ergonomics and high-quality equipment was installed, all of which proved popular with the staff. The same process occurred in TNK-BP, who moved from their Soviet-style offices spread around Moscow into one central prestigious location at the end of 2004.

Dynamic Capabilities – Resource Divestment

The predominant activity of TNK was acquisition of resources rather than divestment. But early on there were many redundancies to reduce costs. The oilfield services were separated out from oil production and some were sold, but most remained as subsidiary companies. The issue of what to do with these remained for TNK-BP.

At the end of 2004 there was still confusion in TNK-BP about what should happen to oilfield services. Whilst the company wanted to sell these non-core activities, the lack of competitors would have created local monopolies. Lack of clear direction on this issue was associated by many people with BP's slow decision-making.

Dynamic Capabilities – Resource Creation

The focus in TNK was on company turnaround and introducing Western business practices rather than the creation of resources. In TNK-BP the focus was still to a large extent on introducing and embedding Western business techniques and bringing all aspects of the company up to Western operating standards. The creation of the technology block, however, was an important step in resolving the lack of technical expertise.

Dynamic Capabilities – Resource Integration

TNK had been very aggressive in acquiring and reconfiguring assets, which were then integrated into a saleable entity. 'It was ruthlessly efficient in terms of taking over other assets, acquiring assets cheaply, turning them around' (top manager, TNK-BP, Western). From a starting point of multiple businesses a strong TNK corporate identity was formed: 'TNK is a company that is really a confederation of Russian oil companies and state departments, and they've created an identity and an intense loyalty' (top manager, TNK-BP, Western).

Resource integration was a major issue for TNK-BP and included conflicts of interest between the partners, operational and cultural integration, the language issue, the differences between the TNK and BP approaches, the conflict between expatriates and locals and, finally, managing the synergies.

The main conflict of interest between TNK and BP was that TNK were interested in short-term gain – in particular maximising the value of company within the three years they were tied into the venture – whereas BP were interested in long-term value creation.

> They've been in a massive hurry those guys [TNK]. Suddenly they need to start managing an oil company. German Khan? For God's sake. They haven't got patience to do that. They just go out and shoot someone. . . . And they [BP] gloss over it all the time, which is their duty. Because I think they went into it with open eyes, I think they knew the 50/50 would be difficult. (investment bank executive, Western).

An instance of the kind of conflicts that arose was a disagreement over BP secondees. TNK managers did not want the expense of the secondees – they wanted to maximise the value of the company and monetise their share by exiting from the JV as soon as possible: 'and so things like voting on bringing in secondees was blocked, everything that sort of made sense was blocked and they were trying to make a point' (top manager, TNK-BP, Western). The only way for BP to resolve such issues in the first year was to escalate it to the board, to a smaller group of owners.

The conflict of interests were obvious also to outsiders:

> I was at a dinner with Dudley and his senior people, German Khan . . . and it was on . . . HSE issues. And . . . they were on different planets . . . very, very different, not only just from a cultural perspective but also . . . They know that they're the natural sellers and these guys are the natural buyers, and they are thinking, why do we need to be spending all this money on upgrading health, safety and environment? . . . I mean they said, 'you just want to jack up the costs and lower the short-term profit'. (investment bank executive, Western)

Operational integration of the two companies included a major project at the end of 2004 to reorganise the legal entities into one holding. The large number of different legal entities made communication very difficult; often information was lost, or reached its destination in a very distorted form:

> Even just to launch a project is very difficult, because there are dozens of companies, thousands of people, and you have to embrace them all. And it is a big problem, especially when it is a large number of legal entities which each have their own legal issues, with whom you have to communicate in a certain way, not in the way we do here within the corporate centre, but by writing letters, fulfilling certain procedures connected with the fact that it is another legal entity and has its own board of directors. (middle manager, TNK-BP, Russian, translation)

Operational integration also involved the standardisation of procedures. The large Samotlor oilfield represented one TNK-BP business unit, which was divided into different performance units. In the first year of the JV, the endeavour was to standardise the operations of the performance units: 'We work real hard at coming up with a somewhat standardised organisation among all the different performance units because standardisation allows the benchmarking to occur' (top manager, TNK-BP, regional, Western).

Building an integrated corporate culture represented a critical success factor for the JV (top manager, TNK-BP, Western). The challenge of merging the two company cultures was underestimated by BP: 'I think people were shocked, I think people had no idea that this was going to be as difficult as it was. There were immediately power struggles set up, there were immediately ideas of trying to drive people out, make life very difficult for people' (top manager, TNK-BP, Western). The problem was not just the culture clash between Russians and the West, but also the culture clash between an aggressive entrepreneurial company and a mature 'establishment' company:

> Most people would assume that this is a big cross-border merger and it's Russian culture and international cultures together, that's actually not the biggest challenge. . . . The biggest challenge . . . is the combination of an entrepreneurial

owner/founder set who basically self-managed and directed the company on all matters, combined with a big large public corporation that has many, many reporting requirements and transparency requirements and financial assurances and enterprise-wide risk assurance processes and all the Sarbanes Oxley[4] direction. (top manager, TNK-BP, Western)

The conflict at the top between the two partners was 'translated downwards into the organisation and there was definitely a Them and Us situation' (middle manager, TNK-BP, Russian, translation). However, this situation was mitigated by the fact that around 40 per cent of the people in head office were new recruits, coming from outside the two companies. 'So the pure *tankisti*[5] [TNK employees] were in the minority. A large wave of outsiders came in, who had no past' (ibid.).

Within a relatively short period of time, however, even the TNK employees began to take a positive attitude towards the changes being introduced, 'even Khan himself, which was a big surprise for me. Well externally, at least, he changed' (middle manager, TNK-BP, Russian, translation). Significant progress had been made on cultural integration after the first two years: 'I actually think they've just done an incredible job in the last two years. This company is two years old and the conversations they're having, the sophistication of the conversations are just fantastic considering the fact . . . you've got these two cultures that came together' (top manager, TNK-BP, Western).

The language barrier represented a major constraint on integration. Multinational companies normally expect local employees to speak English if they want to develop a career. The stated TNK-BP policy was different:

> We have committed to becoming a bilingual organisation in which English or Russian will be spoken as a given business situation requires. And that means that in the majority of cases, certainly out in the regions, Russian will be the language of choice and our expatriates will have to learn Russian. (top manager, TNK-BP, Western)

The gulf between desire and reality was, however, huge. Expatriates, faced with a challenging job in a new environment, simply did not have the time or energy to learn a difficult language as well.

> Coming in never having worked in Russia, probably the language is my biggest challenge. The people that I work with closely on a day-in day-out basis, there's one Russian national that speaks English, everybody else I work through a translator, so that's a definite challenge. . . . I've been trying [to learn Russian] but at the end of the day I just don't have the energy. The days are long. (top manager, TNK-BP, regional, Western)

The Russian employees, on the other hand, found it difficult to understand why after 18 months in Russia, most expatriates still could not speak Russian. 'That is a huge barrier between us. History dictated that few people in Russia spoke English' (middle manager, TNK-BP, regional, Russian, translation). People in the regions were understandably baffled by the fact that when there was just one expatriate permanently based there, that they should be expected to speak English, the attitude of the expatriates being one of 'these damned Russians just don't want to speak English' (ibid.). Incentives to learn the language were offered to only about 30 executives in the form of personal bonuses linked to language proficiency targets.

TNK and BP had different approaches to life and to doing business. The following anecdote was quoted as an example of the contrast between the Russian rogues and the English gentlemen:

> There's an anecdote about Chepaev, the war hero . . . Chepaev returns from a trip and he tells Petya, his adjutant, 'Petya, I was playing cards with an English gentleman – can you believe it, he was sitting there and said "I've got 21". So I said "show me your cards". He almost got offended at me: "We have got our English word of honour, gentleman's word of honour and if I said that I've got 21, I've got 21, I don't have to show my cards"'. Chepaev said, 'Petya you wouldn't believe the run of luck I had after that'. (consultant, Western)

This gulf in mentality led to a certain amount of discontent. The Russian employees were very sensitive to the fact that the expatriates believed themselves to be superior: 'I frequently have the feeling that Westerners, when they talk, it is as if they are saying: "We have come to you, bringing you civilisation.". . . So where were we before? Still primitive? Did bears walk on the streets?' (middle manager, TNK-BP, regional, Russian, translation). However, a view from head office was rather different, and recognised that each company had different strengths to bring to the joint venture that needed to be utilised:

> You cannot import everything from BP or you cannot resist forever trying to do things the way TNK has always done things. . . . It's a little give and take going on. It could have been done in a different way by simply importing everything BP is doing everywhere in the world – but I wouldn't bet on the success of that. And I think this is a very specific country with rather peculiar ways of doing things and rather peculiar mentality – not only of the local managers but of the authorities. Insisting on having it the BP way or no way wouldn't be right. And there is no such insistence. I mean I think when you go to 50/50 alliance there has to be a clear understanding that there will be always a striving to strike a balance. (senior manager, TNK-BP, Russian/Western)

However, the balance did not seem to have been struck in the oil regions. There the discontent was aggravated by difficulty for local employees to identify any real technological benefit that BP had brought:

> Our mentality is to believe in fairy tales. Our eternal hope is that somewhere abroad there will be some kind of miracle which we have never had here . . . I remember the first meetings here. . . . Now BP is going to overwhelm us with Western technology. And then there was such a huge disappointment. (middle manager, TNK-BP, regional, Russian, translation)

TNK had already implemented a lot of new Western technology and achieved significant success in increasing oil production, and therefore BP had little to add:

> TNK . . . were starting to get recognition in the oil patch for good management, good internal management and good results and innovativeness in technology. It was they, for example, who established the existence of the so-called Ryabchik horizon in Samotlor, which turns out to be an untouched horizon of oil that Soviets had not recognised and had drilled right through. So now that BP formed its joint venture with AAR, and TNK has become TNK-BP, they are going to town on this opportunity. But BP did not discover it, they simply walked into it. (energy consultant, Western)

In addition to the disappointment over BP's technological contribution, relationships with the Technology Block in the head office, which was where the majority of the expatriates were based, were poor. 'Is it the mentality or the fault of the management – it is difficult to say. I am simply saying that as of today I believe we have not developed a decent relationship with the Technology Block' (middle manager, TNK-BP, regional, Russian, translation). This view contrasted rather sharply with the one from head office described above where the dissemination of knowledge via working groups was judged to be successful.

One of the most sensitive issues in the JV was the clash between expatriates and locals: 'The biggest frustration is the level of trust between Russians and expatriates . . . mostly of the expatriates towards Russians. There is a missionary attitude from some of the expatriates. "Learn from me". . . . "F*** you", that's what I want to say when I hear that' (senior manager, TNK-BP, Russian/Western). The missionary attitude was particularly frustrating when adopted by employees perceived to be 'second-rate'. It was also a source of great discontent among locals that the expatriates had salaries three times higher than they would back home, a car with a chauffeur, $10 000 for an apartment each month and VIP treatment at the airport. The gulf between local and expatriate conditions was enormous (ibid.). On the other hand one Russian employee felt that the reaction of the Russian employees towards expatriates was a little unfair because he had seen the real benefits of Western experience: 'I saw examples when this really paid off and when the experience and knowledge being brought into the country by Westerners . . . is extremely valuable, and there is no price tag attached to that, it's invaluable' (middle manager, TNK-BP, Russian, translation). Over time, greater mutual understanding was reached: 'People began to listen to each other, to understand each other and to recognise that, in spite of the fact that they were different, they could learn something from each other' (middle manager, TNK-BP, Russian, translation).

Learning from each other was important to achieve synergies from the joint venture. External experts viewed the JV as having great potential: 'This is a very powerful partnership, to have BP behind you, which clearly has political leverage and has direct access to Putin or has done on occasions' (newspaper correspondent, Western). BP also brought access to cheaper foreign capital, management expertise, production technology and management systems. In principle a key source of synergy in the JV was the combination of the Western business experience of BP with the local knowledge of TNK: 'And what can the Russian side contribute to this company? Above all, knowledge of Russian reality' (top manager, TNK-BP, Russian, translation). The company was largely dependent on the Russian partners' ability to manage relationships.

> I think it's a very unique blend here because I don't believe that if this were a BP company we would be able to operate in the way that we do today. The reason why it's good, a company like this would be subject to a lot of pressures in the regions from governors and from law enforcement and other things. And if it were all run by mainly foreigners, things would happen out there and pressures would be put on the company that would be extremely difficult to foresee and react to. And by having good Russian partners who know that that's going to happen, know how to make sure it doesn't happen, can have relationships here in the centre in Moscow that can say, there's a problem out there that's not in the best interests of the country, things can be taken care of. (top manager, TNK-BP, Western)

Synergies were potentially available also from combining the entrepreneurial style of TNK with the corporate systems of BP. The concern of any big corporate was how to foster entrepreneurship within a bureaucratic structure. The intention of the new joint venture was not to extinguish the entrepreneurial spirit, but to foster it:

> There are too strong personalities involved to squash. And obviously you don't want to squash all of them . . . The art of it all is getting the blend, I mean that's the key, that's the trick. If you just squash it then you've lost some of the benefits, or if you just let it run you've lost some of the benefits of the corporate. (top manager, TNK-BP, Western)

The ideal was to capture the best of both cultures, integrate them and come up with a different culture that would be a source of competitive advantage both in Russia and internationally (ibid.)

Operational Capabilities

In TNK, significant strides were made in production capability helped by Western expertise. Two major technological breakthroughs substantially increased oil production at very low cost (middle manager, TNK-BP, regional, Russian, translation). The implementation of the supervising system brought tangible benefits in terms of increased efficiency.

A key capability was the ability to present a good story to the Western investment community. 'Kukes was . . . the face to the external world. He had good contacts because of his experience in the US' (top manager, Western oil company, Western). Kukes also helped the organisation to develop capabilities in marketing and retail – a strong brand was developed and revolutionary Western-style petrol stations began to appear. However, he did not manage to bring TNK completely up to Western standards: 'There was a lot he did not manage to do . . . It was a period of time when all these Western values were not much in demand. They were not necessary to increase competitiveness, to secure market success' (top manager, TNK-BP, Russian, translation). But enough progress had been made on expanding and turning around the company, setting up the basic organisational structure and controls and increasing oil production to make the company attractive to a Western investor. Other operational capabilities around transparency, corporate governance, HR and HSE had not been developed.

The arrival of BP boosted the development of operational capabilities. One contribution was the concept that a looser system of control, giving employees greater empowerment within certain boundary conditions, could be more effective than a strict top-down system of control. 'And what I was trying to convince people of was, I'm not against control, . . . but there's procedures and process and systems that you can build that give people an enormous amount of opportunity to use their creative spirit and with boundary conditions' (Top Manager, TNK-BP, Western).

The development of an open communication system was another significant contribution: 'TNK-BP is very open. For example, a presentation was made to employees going on a two-year placement – they were told everything – all about the strategy, what was happening in E&P and refining, details of capital expenditure and costs in detail' (middle manager, TNK-BP, Russian, translation).

BP boosted HR capability from its traditional low standing in Soviet organisations:

What is 'personnel'? Traditionally in the Soviet Union, 'personnel' were the people who sit there and deal with hiring and firing people and determine any benefits. But now, with the arrival of BP and Western people, extremely interesting . . . things are happening in HR, in particular unbelievable opportunities for training have been created and promoted. (top manager, TNK-BP, Russian, translation).

Many HR initiatives were undertaken, including a new performance management system: 'The performance management system is rather unique to TNK-BP in the Russian industry . . . it aligns goals, objectives, performance, remuneration, personnel policy, in one large cycle' (senior manager, TNK-BP, Russian/Western).

The newest and most difficult functional area for Russian employees was HSE: The BP 'trademark' is health, safety and environment. These questions are no longer remembered just at the end, but people have started to talk about them constantly (middle manager, TNK-BP, regional, Russian, translation). HSE is of fundamental importance for oil and petrochemical companies and therefore the development of this operational capability was particularly urgent as very little attention was paid to such matters in the typical Soviet enterprise.

Project management skills were practically non-existent in TNK. With BP's arrival a project and engineering group was developed and Western project managers were allocated to projects that were already running. One of the major successes was turning around the construction of the vacuum gasoil plant construction in the Ryazan refinery:

It hadn't been executed. They spent over $300 million and hadn't really delivered anything, and it was slipping a year at a time. It needed either to be put back on the tracks or the board was just going to drop it, you couldn't continue to see the leakage. [The TNK guys] didn't know how to run a project . . . They had no idea. They know that now. (top manager, TNK-BP, Western)

The organisation was expected to improve efficiency in all areas. In the Ryazan refinery, instructions had been received to reduce the plant turn-around time[6] from 60 days to 35 days. The 35-day target derived from international best practice (middle manager, TNK-BP, regional, Russian, translation). Across the board the organisation was being challenged to perform to Western standards, to build the necessary capability to compete.

So all facets of trying to build capability, waiting for the cavalry to come over the hill five years from now. I don't know how long it would take for us to really get a cycle and get these people up and running . . . What I think BP or TNK-BP really wants is a really powerful organisation, technically competent, strong and capable of taking on anything. (top manager, TNK-BP, Western)

Many new processes and systems were being put in place, but they needed time to be embedded: 'It is very difficult to create processes, they are still ineffective . . . for the time being they are still like a foam, if I can use that comparison, the waves are still breaking . . . so there are no clearly defined working processes yet, a lot of things are still at the stage of development' (middle manager, TNK-BP, Russian, translation).

A significant amount of progress in a short period of time (18 months) had been made in building operational capabilities in knowledge sharing, HR, HSE and project management to secure short-term survival in a market economy. The encouragement of creativity and the delegation of authority within established boundaries was likely to contribute to the strategic flexibility required for long-term survival in an unstable environment.

ORGANISATIONAL TRANSFORMATION

Efficiency and Robustness

After the chaos of the time of troubles TNK brought order: 'They brought stability . . . they brought work. The units began to be started up again . . . not just started up again, but also to be improved . . . our specialists began to use their brains, it became interesting again' (middle manager, TNK-BP, regional, Russian, translation).

Although TNK was beginning to be recognised for good management, they were still no match for Yukos: 'They [TNK] were a higher cost producer, no question about that' (energy consultant, Western). Nevertheless, significant cost economies had been made. In Nizhnevartovsk, for instance, as a result of the tendering process, costs fell by 40 per cent, equivalent to about $10 million, over a period of six months (middle manager, TNK-BP, Regional Russian, translation). Drilling efficiency also improved: 'The wells took less time to drill . . . the cost of wells . . . decreased significantly. At the same time, the quality of work increased significantly' (ibid.).

TNK's aggressive, top-down management style had generated rapid results:

> TNK was entirely different, and the respect for human beings was very low. It was: 'If you don't like it, f*** you, get the f*** out of here, now', that type of an attitude . . . I think experience demonstrates that it's not the most efficient model. I didn't find the TNK system . . . horrible . . . In many, many, many respects it was terrific and you were trying to get something done. You'd much quicker do it with TNK than with Lukoil, but maybe not with Yukos. Yukos maybe was a bit smarter than that. (senior manager, TNK-BP, Russian/Western)

TNK's key achievement was to monetise their success by selling a 50 per cent share of the company to BP. BP was able to provide a further boost to the progress TNK had made in increasing efficiency:

> By their own admission they [TNK] never worked those assets terribly well. And of course BP will. . . . The kind of portfolio they've got in Russia is not like the kind of portfolio they have elsewhere, but they remembered the Amoco guys.[7] They remembered the onshore knackered properties that they had, and I think all those people were dragged along and are working hard. (investment bank executive, Western).

BP thus had the capability to improve the performance of the company and further drive down costs:

> [TNK-BP] have an agenda to be as low cost as they can be, now that's driven by BP – I think TNK thought they had gone as far as they could in terms of running a business with the few scattered oilmen they brought in. But they needed somebody who would run the business properly, so along comes BP. (investment bank executive, Western)

A senior Yukos representative was of the view that TNK-BP would very quickly catch up and even overtake Yukos' erstwhile pre-eminent position in the Russian oil industry:

> TNK-BP . . . will change very quickly . . . In the next year or two TNK-BP will catch us up, maybe even overtake us on a whole raft [of measures]. They will simply go through the same thing as Yukos, but via the hands of BP. I think that as a rather large group from BP transferred to TNK, everything will happen rather more quickly, in a rather more structured way. It will be quicker simply because a whole element of the debate simply will not arise, because the order will come from senior managers to do it in such and such a way. (senior manager, Yukos, Russian, translation)

BP could leverage its previous experience of successful development of organisational capability in Sidanco:

> If you look at the qualifications of people who worked in Sidanco, they are higher than those working in Yukos. When you talk to people from Sidanco, they talk about business, and they do business, and focus on results. And when you talk to older people in Yukos, they are interested in how to do something to survive, not to be fired, and to receive a bonus. Different interests, different priorities. (top manager, Yukos, Russian, translation)

Evidence of the success of BP's intervention was already available with a 14 per cent growth in oil production: 'and that's all because new people have taken over assets and have started running them differently' (investment bank executive, Western). Efficiency derived not just from applying new technology to drive down costs, but also from the introduction of new business systems and procedures, creating the threshold operational capabilities that were needed for survival in a market economy. Work was still needed in this respect in the regions:

> I think that probably [the challenge] is to move into the regions, because I think that in the corporate office we are now in reasonably good form . . . Whereas in the regions little has changed, and there are a mass of problems ranging from the social problems, linked with the low salary levels, all the social . . . the living conditions, etc. – all of that is like a delayed reaction bomb. The management structure of the companies, the people who run the companies – all of that is very very far behind. (middle manager, TNK-BP, Russian, translation)

The progress that TNK-BP had made in increasing efficiency and developing operational capabilities needed to be continued in the regions in order to increase the robustness of the organisation as a whole.

Responsiveness and Strategic Flexibility

The strategic flexibility of TNK was manifested in the entrepreneurial flair of the TMT. Their readiness to solve problems with a fresh approach signalled their strategic flexibility. However, strategic flexibility in TNK was confined to the TMT. Their top-down leadership style did not encourage flexibility within the organisation.

The acquisition of knowledge and expertise from BP was likely to develop human capital with both operational efficiency and strategic flexibility. The influence of BP was seen as beneficial not just for the company, but even for the country as a whole: 'The more companies like TNK-BP we have in the country the better for the country, I'm absolutely convinced of that' (middle manager, TNK-BP, Russian, translation). The fact that Russian managers were used to change was also of importance, given the instability of the environment: 'People have experience of change and they have learnt how to work in times of change. This is very important because the situation will change' (middle manager, TNK-BP, Russian, translation).

The flexibility, entrepreneurial approach and knowledge of how to manage Russian reality of the TNK managers were coupled with the experience BP had of operating in many different countries across the world and of adapting to political and social change. Furthermore, BP's encouragement of decision-making at all levels increased the flexibility of the organisation: 'It can react more quickly to changes, it becomes more adaptable' (ibid.).

Given the political and economic significance of the Russian oil industry, it was very important to maintain good relationships with the government: 'When our shareholders signed the agreement with BP, President Putin was standing behind them. This demonstrated that our company was sub-servient. TNK-BP did not pass through any "no entry" signs, did not engender any opposition. None of our managers said that he wanted to become the President of Russia' (senior manager, TNK-BP, regional, Russian, translation). However, dealing with the authorities was becoming ever more complex. Flexibility was required to manage the shifting location of power:

> [Other centres of power] over time are also very relevant and may be able to mess up your business without actually getting onto the sort of radar screen of the main group of power brokers in the country. So you need to have as many of these folks on board as possible, . . . or at least connected with and have some influence and understanding of them and from them of your business. (top manager, TNK-BP, Western)

BP's international standing and experience of dealing with governments and authorities in different countries of the world was beneficial in this respect, as were the relationship skills of the Russian partners: 'You do need well-connected and informed and successful Russian partners . . . Doing business in Russia is complicated, complex, you can argue that having Russian partners complicates things, but that's a necessary prerequisite, you just have to kind of swallow that' (ibid.). A slight concern was that perhaps BP would not be flexible enough to deal with the complexity of operations in Russia: 'The question is whether Bob Dudley has the . . . well, there's no doubt that he has the leadership skills, the question is . . . is he adaptable enough to the Russian scene to be able to be effective in dealing with what is after all and has to be a Russian structure?' (energy consultant, Western).

In summary, the combined strengths of BP and the Russian partners indicated significant synergy could be achieved in terms of responsiveness to changes in the environment. The gradual empowerment of the organisation initiated by BP would increase the overall strategic flexibility of the organisation.

Performance and Competitive Advantage

The TNK managers had brought about remarkable changes: 'These people [TNK TMT], they've done the lot, and they will stay in the history as heroes. They will stay in the history of those people who changed the face of Russia' (middle manager, TNK-BP, Russian, translation). They had made a breakthrough in image and quality when they introduced the new look, Western-style gasoline stations:

> If you remember that period – our Soviet gas stations were awful – then suddenly there appear these unbelievable white-as-snow, white and blue gas stations. Everyone was amazed. That was a significant breakthrough – the customers were absolutely delighted. We simply developed the brand. Of course it was Kukes' [CEO, TNK] idea and he brought it from America. (top manager, TNK-BP, Russian, translation)

By most other performance criteria, however, TNK was outperformed by Yukos: 'And I think it worked, it worked in many kind of directions. Clearly not as well as Yukos, because when we were comparing ourselves to Yukos we would always be losers. . . . In terms of production growth, cost control, you know all the kind of fundamental measurements' (senior manager, TNK-BP, Russian/Western). Nevertheless, given their starting point, they had made a lot of progress. Coming late to the privatisation process they had acquired the rump assets: 'The overall process that TNK has made is really impressive from where they started and now they're really getting things into place. The Samotlor field is an ageing field and quite a difficult one' (headhunter, Western).

By selling a 50 per cent shareholding to BP the TNK managers demonstrated the success of their strategy of monetising their investment: 'Look at the outcome. What did TNK do? TNK merged. It's a unique transaction. No one will ever repeat that transaction . . . well don't ever say never, but in the near future I don't think any Russian oil company will repeat that kind of performance' (senior manager, TNK-BP, Russian/Western).

By the end of 2004, TNK-BP had taken over the lead position from Yukos in terms of production growth. (Yukos had been in a state of collapse since Khodorkovsky's arrest in 2003.)

> This company has grown its production over the course of the last 12 months by whatever, 12 per cent or 13 per cent, and I think the target was 14 per cent. Have you seen it elsewhere? No. We are the best in Russia and I think we are among the very best performers in the industry overall . . . in terms of production growth, cost management, because it's not just pure production. It's very much balanced against EBITDA target, cost containment and stuff like that. (ibid.)

The sustainability of this competitive advantage would be a function of the degree to which BP continued to empower the organisation and encourage flexibility.

> I've got to try to create capability where they think for themselves, and they're going to build this . . . and I am going to support them. So when I see them take some initiative I'm going to be there. 'Yes? You want a billion dollars? You really think you've got a programme? Here it is.' I'm going to help them manage it. I've got a whole group that's going to help them manage it . . . it's a big vote of

confidence for thinking for yourself. A sustainable future is only from trying to unlock that natural capability. (top manager, TNK-BP, Western)

CONCLUSION

TNK came later than the other Russian oil companies to the privatisation process and acquired an inauspicious collection of assets. However in a short period of five years, from the time AAR took over the assets in 1998 to the time of the sale of a 50 per cent holding to BP in 2003, they succeeded in developing some of the key operational capabilities for survival in a market economy. The arrival of BP in a 50/50 JV in 2003 brought fresh impetus to the process of organisational transformation. The combination of BP's international knowledge and expertise with TNK's local knowledge and entrepreneurial flair was already moving TNK-BP into prime position in the Russian oil industry by 2004.

Tables 5.1 and 5.2 above provided an overview of TNK's and TNK-BP's organisational transformation, showing the interrelationships between the TMT, administrative heritage, organisational learning and organisational capability. A further data display in Table 5.3 presents a conceptually ordered summary (Miles and Huberman, 1994) of the evidence of organisational transformation in TNK and TNK-BP in terms of efficiency and robustness; responsiveness and strategic flexibility; and performance and competitive advantage.

Table 5.3   Conceptually ordered data display of TNK and TNK-BP organisational transformation

Construct	Evidence – TNK	Evidence – TNK-BP
Efficiency and robustness	• Stabilisation and turnaround Introduction of some **operational capabilities**: finance, production, marketing, PR • Costs reduced but still higher than Yukos • Rapid implementation of change, but not as efficient as Yukos • Attractive to Western investor	• Introduction of **operational capabilities**: transparency, corporate governance, HR, finance, production systems, marketing, PR, knowledge sharing • Further cost reduction • 14% increase in oil production • Industry consensus that TNK-BP has potential to become leading oil company

Table 5.3   (continued)

Construct	Evidence – TNK	Evidence – TNK-BP
		• Increased **robustness** in the context of a market economy • Move to empower organisation • Operational capabilities not fully **embedded,** especially in regions
Responsiveness and strategic flexibility	• **Strategic flexibility** vested in TMT – entrepreneurial flair	• BP international experience plus TNK adaptability and local knowledge increases **strategic flexibility**. • Putin's support important in context of 'reversion to state control' • Moves to **empower** organisation
Performance and competitive advantage	• Breakthrough in image and quality in retail • Increased oil production and reduced costs, but lagging Yukos	• **Competitive advantage** – leading production growth of 12–14% in 2004. Strong cost and EBITDA performance • Empowered organisation likely to lead to **sustainable competitive advantage**

NOTES

1. TNK – Tyumenskaya Neftyanaya Kompaniya or Tyumen Oil Company.
2. A kind of heavy fuel oil specific to the Russian market.
3. BP Office in UK.
4. The Sarbanes Oxley Act is a US law enacted in 2002 following a number of accounting scandals. It is associated with increasing the complexity of financial and accounting disclosure.
5. Tankisti is a Russian word for 'tank-driver'. It is a play on words (TNK=TANK) which reflects the aggressive nature of the TNK people.
6. Turnaround time is the time a plant is non-operational and undergoing maintenance.
7. BP acquired Amoco in 1998. Amoco owned many depleted oilfields in the USA.

6. Lukoil and Surgutneftegaz case studies

INTRODUCTION

Chapters 4 and 5 presented case studies of the organisational transformation of Yukos and TNK/TNK-BP (Western-style companies). This chapter presents contrasting case studies of Surgutneftegaz and Lukoil (Soviet-style companies), which demonstrated little organisational transformation.

Lukoil was the first vertically integrated oil company to be created after the collapse of the Soviet Union. It was set up in 1991 in accordance with a blueprint developed by the then First Deputy Minister of the USSR Oil Industry, Vagit Alekperov. Alekperov then became the Lukoil President. Lukoil did not take part in the 'loans for shares' deal. Alekperov and other members of the management team had significant shareholdings in the company.

Surgutneftegaz was set up in 1992, but retained the General Director who had been in place since 1984, Vladimir Bogdanov. In the 1995 loans for shares deal the Surgutneftegaz pension fund acquired 40.16 per cent of Surgutneftegaz, making Surgutneftegaz management (Bogdanov) de facto sole owner of the company.

TOP MANAGEMENT TEAM

This section reviews the Lukoil and Surgutneftegaz TMTs, describing key personalities and the characteristics and management style of the teams.

Alekperov, General Director of Lukoil, was an oilman, so was therefore very much an insider, having spent his whole career in the oil industry.

> Everyone acknowledges that Lukoil, as distinct from practically all other Russian firms, was created by production people who came from a good school in life. Mr Alekperov progressed from a rank-and-file driller to the First Deputy Minister of the USSR Oil Industry, after which he headed up this company. Of course we are proud. (senior manager, Lukoil, Russian, translation)

His employees were very proud of him and of the company he had put together: 'Alekperov was a very good motivator of people, a man who saw an opportunity and grabbed it' (investment bank executive, Western). He had started his career in oil in Azerbaijan and still had strong connections there:

> Lukoil . . . really began with an oil general, a so-called oil general from the Soviet era. In Surgut it was Bogdanov, in the case of Lukoil it was Vagit Alekperov, who really rose up through the ranks of the Azerbaijan oil industry during the Soviet era. And he has used his Caspian connections very astutely to expand Lukoil's horizons. But it's really a case of the original managers taking over control of the company during the privatisation process. (energy consultant, Western)

With his political connections Alekperov was perceived to have a strong position of influence:

> Well they're all part of a big club in a way, because I think the Russian political system can influence what the Russian oil companies are able to do domestically. So whether there's sort of a strong bond which someone like Alekperov, who's ex-government, or whether the bond is a bit weaker but it's commercially proven, the bonds are still there . . . So it's a network of people that used to have good relations and they've developed them commercially. (energy consultant, Western)

The acquisition by Lukoil of the Getty Oil network of gasoline stations in the US was popular with the Russian government:

> From the government's point of view the Russian flag has been firmly planted on the East Coast of the United States. That meant a lot, because in the 'shadow governor' or 'shadow minister' mentality that seems to exist at the high levels of Lukoil, that kind of nationalistic or ministerial portfolio is very, very important. So they haven't broken away from that . . . Alekperov was Deputy Minister of Oil and Gas in the old days, so he still has an attachment to the importance of that thing. And I'm sure if there was a way to have a new national oil company created he would love to be the person in charge. (consultant, Western)

However Alekperov's popularity with Putin seemed to have waned somewhat: 'He was publicly slapped on the wrist a couple of years back. . . . There was some really visible falling out with Putin and Vagit Alekperov' (headhunter, Western). With the reversion to state control of the oil industry, Putin's new favourites were Miller, head of Gazprom, and Bogdanchikov, head of Rosneft, the two main state gas and oil concerns.

The Lukoil TMT consisted only of Russian managers, most of whom had a background in the oil industry, either in production or in the ministry. In other words they were mostly insiders who had been associated with the oil industry for a long time: 'There's been practically no turnover of management personnel since the early 90s, they are all the old guard, or very closely associated to the old guard' (energy consultant, Western). Within Lukoil itself the oil industry background of the top managers was regarded positively:

> By background Maganov is an oilman, as is Alekperov, they both had an oil education . . . Kukurov – the main finance man – he also worked in that team in Western Siberia. Mr Tarasov – a new man – he used to be a specialist in foreign trade . . . so Tarasov is a new man, but all the rest of the team came earlier – for example Kozirev, he came from the Ministry. (senior manager, Lukoil, Russian, translation)

Two managers were more recent recruits from the outside. Matytsyn, in charge of accounting, had come from KPMG, who were Lukoil's accountants from 1991. Gaidamaka, in charge of strategy and investor relations, was an analyst in Morgan Stanley, covering Lukoil (investment bank executive, Western). Gaidamaka had some Western experience (newspaper correspondent, Western). However, there seemed to be no desire to have foreigners working there (investment bank executive, Western). Lukoil was therefore very much a Russian company. As one senior Lukoil manager expressed it, 'In our company, thank goodness, Mr Alekperov [CEO] is not an American' (senior manager, Lukoil, Russian, translation). Although there were no expatriates on the management team, two Westerners had been appointed as independent board members: Richard Matzke from Chevron and Mark Mobius from Templeton Asset Management (consultant, Western). It was doubtful, however, what power they could wield against the other 10 board members: 'You really wonder how much influence they can have on the board' (investment bank executive, Western)

Apart from Alekperov himself, a Western expert considered that none of the management team were very strong: 'You look at the Lukoil board, they are very good at running their bit of the business in most cases – but would you trust all of them to direct the strategy of a business? No, you wouldn't' (investment bank executive, Western). There was little evidence of an entrepreneurial orientation in the management team as such; however, Alekperov could be described as entrepreneurial in that he took the initiative to form and head up Lukoil.

> There are older people clearly, who have proved quite entrepreneurial and adaptive as well, who were already active in the Soviet period but have been able to emerge . . . those who are here now are there partly because they have had all the attributes that have been necessary also for survival in a very complex and rapid evolution from Soviet to post-Soviet times. And Alekperov survived in the Soviet system, but has been able to survive in this one and probably only been able to keep his company together because he has a mixture of those old and new attributes. (newspaper correspondent, Western)

Survival was one thing, but change was another and Lukoil's management style had changed little from Soviet days:

> Old Soviet style is Lukoil, that's clear, old Soviet style. . . . It's a ministry. Very slow moving, . . . everybody sits in their positions for years and years and years. The document flow determines . . . the result. . . . People are thinking each piece of paper has the weight. . . . They are allergic to any drastic changes. They are very proud of . . . the Soviet oil industry legacy . . . and they're preserving it. (senior manager, TNK-BP, Russian/Western)

The company offices also looked like a ministry. They had a brand new building, as impressive from the outside as the new TNK-BP or Yukos buildings. But inside it was a maze of endless corridors and closed doors [Personal observation].

Although Alekperov had a strong position in Lukoil, the heads of the regional subsidiaries were also rather powerful: 'Situations where you have very strong regional leaders, such as the case with Lukoil, where you have key regional leaders calling the shots and then basically a really weak corporate head office that loosely controls these various princes' (headhunter, Western). Lukoil had multiple competing influences within the organisation. The Lukoil subsidiaries were referred to as 'baronies' operating in a feudal system, with 'a lot of dividing and conquering going on' (newspaper correspondent, Western).

> What plays against them [Lukoil] is . . . that it is still a very complex series of competing baronies, much more than the other more tightly integrated companies, and that's going to be a challenge in the next few years. . . . He [Alekperov] sort of pulls it all together, but he's not got total control. I think there's quite a lot of sharing of responsibility and power. (ibid.)

On balance, respondents described the company as highly decentralised, which fitted with the concept of baronies: 'It's very, very decentralised, no matter what the company would have you believe, essentially it's run as a fiefdom which is not optimal' (investment bank executive, Western). The decentralised nature of the business, together with its size and complexity, meant that the process of introducing change was slower:

> This process [of introducing Western business practices], considering the size of the company, is not moving as fast as, say, in smaller companies, simply because Lukoil's business is not structured in such a vertical way as, for example, TNK's business, where there was German Khan, whose word was everyone's command. . . . In Lukoil . . . the situation is rather different, i.e. the structure is less centralised due to the way it was set up and correspondingly the introduction of centralised mechanisms for economic models is much slower. (middle manager, Lukoil, Russian, translation)

On the other hand another respondent suggested that decision-making was still very centralised: 'you do get the feeling that the decision making is very centralised still at the top' (headhunter, Western). A possible explanation for this apparent dichotomy of views was that Lukoil was decentralised, in that it consisted of many different baronies, but within each barony decision-making was centralised. Another explanation was that when Lukoil was first set up there was an excessive degree of centralisation. However, as managers developed who could be trusted, they were given more freedom: 'As soon as a strong manager appeared, who ran the business well and had a good management system, the empire gave him a piece and no longer interfered (middle manager, Lukoil, Russian, translation).

Lukoil was a patriarchal company that looked after its employees, engendering intense loyalty:

> No one ever leaves Lukoil . . . very patriarchal company . . . At the beginning I thought that it was horrible, it was bloody horrible. Now I'm reconsidering. There are a lot of good things in the Soviet style, certainly in terms of how you deal with people and how you develop people and how you embed into people love for their company, for their profession. And there is a lot of it in Lukoil. (senior manager, TNK-BP, Russian/Western)

Workers in the regions were offered a good social package:

> We construct the compensation package so that a large part of it is made up of social benefits. I would say for that the average worker . . . the social benefits represent up to 30 per cent of the salary – that is schools, nurseries, insurance, paid holidays, annual bonuses, which are progressive depending on length of service. In other words the system helps to retain people. (middle manager, Lukoil, Russian, translation)

In summary, Lukoil was a complex organisation with competing power bases in the regions. The TMT was homogeneous, all-Russian and consisted mainly of oilmen (insiders). There was little evidence of an entrepreneurial orientation. The management style was described as Soviet or ministry style, i.e. highly bureaucratic. Its patriarchal approach engendered high employee loyalty.

Bogdanov, General Director of Surgutneftegaz was, according to respondents, in total control of Surgutneftegaz. He was the only decision-maker: 'Surgut . . . is strictly centralised – completely . . . the guy there, Bogdanov, runs everything – operations and strategy and investment – he's a guy who is 'Mr Everything' (middle-manager, Lukoil, Russian, translation). The only listing under 'Management Team' on the Surgutneftegaz website was Bogdanov (Surgutneftegaz, 2005). 'Just reading the press is revealing. Whereas around 100 different names may be mentioned in different articles about Lukoil, when it comes to Surgutneftegaz there is reference only to Bogdanov, and possibly his press secretary' (middle manager, Lukoil, Russian, translation). The only way to obtain a meeting with Surgutneftegaz was to send a fax to Bogdanov himself with an official request [Personal observation]. Nothing could be done without his say so. 'It's just the most extraordinary company. It's a one man show' (top manager, Western oil company, Western). Surgutneftegaz was described as a dictatorship: 'Surgut is opaque . . . Soviet style. It is run as a tight ship – it is a dictatorship – an extreme case of a Russian oil company' (top manager, Western oil company, Western). The head office was in Surgut, not in Moscow, as were the other companies', and all decisions were made there (headhunter, Western).

Bogdanov as an individual was likeable, quiet, introverted and interested in technology (top manager, Western oil company, Western). He took pride in his oil background and was very well technically informed: 'He is very technically focused . . . but much more so than actually most Western oilmen . . . [who have] people to worry about the horizontal wells' (ibid.). Bogdanov was an oil industry insider and came across as a benevolent technocrat with no apparent entrepreneurial orientation. He corresponded closely to the image of a Soviet Red Director:

> It's a more Soviet company, it's run by a guy who doesn't answer to anyone really, it's got a Red Director . . . This is the mentality of the people who worked in the Russian or Soviet oil and gas industry all their life. People like Bogdanov do . . . take pride in a well-run business, in a well-run oil rig. (newspaper correspondent, Russian/Western)

His leadership style was patriarchal. Whereas Yukos and TNK/TNK-BP had been keen to divest non-core activities and reduce their social obligations, Surgutneftegaz was quite the opposite. Bogdanov wanted to protect the interests and benefits of the workers:

> The approaches of the two companies are obviously dramatically different in regards to compensation and social benefits. Yukos paid more but had fewer social benefits. Surgut pays less and . . . sets up as many state structures that they're able, to take care of anyone near the company from cradle to grave. So for . . . people who grew up in Soviet times this is an incredibly comfortable situation, because in many ways Bogdanov has taken place of the state. (headhunter, Western)

This meant that employees were intensely loyal to the company because 'This social package, the benefits that they get along with their cash salary, is so good that it really keeps people there' (headhunter, Western). A Yukos manager gave a rather uncomplimentary description of Bogdanov in this regard:

> For Bogdanov it is very important that 'I am a good man and I do not care how much money I spend . . ., the main thing is that I am a good man'. It is a quite different approach. I think that we should not be compared with this. If you have one person who is so strange, should all others be strange as well? And in the whole country no one [no company] is building flats [for the workers] – it is only Bogdanov who is acting in this way. Well that's his decision. (top manager, Yukos, Russian, translation)

Bogdanov's motives were quite different from those of the financial managers of Yukos and TNK. He was not interested in cost efficiency and profit: 'I'm not sure Bogdanov is really after money that much. He may be driven by other incentives like seeing his company growing, producing, employing people' (senior manager, TNK-BP, Russian, translation). He was very keen to protect and develop the region where the company was based: 'He feels a huge responsibility for the people and his workers. And therefore he's very reluctant to do anything that puts their livelihood at risk' (investment bank executive, Western). He was concerned for the long term: 'Surgutneftegaz does not want to increase production – they don't want to "rape and ravage" the oilfields, as they call it. He finds it easier to manage his town that way. He is seen as caring for you and your grandchildren' (top manager, Yukos, Western). Bogdanov exhibited far more loyalty to his employees than to his minority shareholders: 'They're not there to serve shareholders really, they're there to serve themselves. . . . The shareholder comes last (investment bank executive, Western). Bogdanov ensured that dividends would be as small as possible, for example by financing the construction plan for the following year out of post-tax profit (consultant, Western).

Surgutneftegaz was a very 'closed' organisation. It was extremely difficult to arrange meetings there and every request had to be made officially to Bogdanov by fax. To penetrate Surgutneftegaz one had to 'play this game. . . . They have their set procedures' (headhunter, Western). Access was difficult for correspondents – 'the shutters slammed down' (newspaper correspondent, Western) – and for investor organisations: 'They're very difficult in general . . . Bogdanov . . . he's come to the conclusion . . . that there's no benefit from . . . having any kind of a serious interaction with the capital market' (investment bank executive, Western). Given this attitude it was not surprising that the researcher failed to gain direct access to the company. Research on Western management issues would not have been of interest as Surgutneftegaz was still operating in the traditional Soviet way.

In summary, Surgutneftegaz was run as a one-man band by an oil indus-try insider with no entrepreneurial orientation. His management style was patriarchal and he preferred protecting the interests of the employees and region to making profits.

All respondents identified a clear distinction between two types of company, the ones which have retained much of their Soviet heritage (Soviet-style) and the ones which have transformed towards a Western model (Western-style):

> There is a clear division in the oil industry – the traditional companies and the non-traditional companies. The first category – the traditional ones – you can probably put Surgut and Lukoil in that one. . . . Basically the people who head up the companies are from the oil sector. The oil sector has not applied any man-agement principles or management instruments – or they are only introduced gradually, when they are ready for it. Then you have TNK-BP, Yukos – people came from a completely different sphere, they came from business or finance where there were completely different standards and approaches. This is what determines the difference. And probably above all in terms of speed. (top manager, Yukos, Russian, translation)

The overall objectives of the two different types of company were very different:

> There is a big distinction between Alekperov and Bogdanov on the one hand, who were Red Directors, oilmen, and had a long-term, very Russia-focused view, and Khodorkovsky and Friedman and Vekselberg, who were basically investor merchant bankers, [for whom] this was a short- to medium-term investment proposition, which turned into an unanticipatedly attractive cash cow. But they always had the logic of ultimately preparing for future sale. (newspaper corre-spondent, Western)

The management approach of the companies run by insider oilmen was based on the old Soviet way of doing things: 'simply, people had always done things that way, and they were not used to doing things in a new way' (senior manager, Russian oil company, Russian, translation). But in com-panies where there were outsider financial owners (e.g. Yukos, TNK) a commercial approach was taken and Western business techniques were introduced.

To summarise, Lukoil and Surgutneftegaz were traditional 'Soviet-style' companies, run by oilmen, or 'Red Directors', who were insiders in the industry and retained to a large extent their traditional ways of doing busi-ness. Yukos and TNK were the more innovative 'Western-style' companies, run by financiers, who were outsiders to the oil industry and who were introducing Western ways of doing business. The Soviet-style companies were characterised by homogeneity and lack of innovation, whereas the Western-style companies were characterised by heterogeneity and an entrepreneurial approach.

ADMINISTRATIVE HERITAGE

The general characteristics of the administrative heritage of the Soviet oil industry have been described in Chapter 2. The management characteristics of Surgutneftegaz and Lukoil described above closely correspond to that heritage. No evidence was found of Surgutneftegaz breaking with its administrative heritage or leveraging that heritage to bring about change. Limited evidence was found in Lukoil as described below.

Break with Administrative Heritage

In Lukoil, administrative heritage was recognised as being a brake on the introduction of new Western business techniques: 'If [people] have spent half their working life working under one system, they find it rather difficult to understand people who come along and start to break that all up and change it. But nevertheless, progress is being made' (middle manager, Lukoil, Russian, translation). It took time for people to accept change. For example, the introduction of financial KPIs had started two years previously, but they were only now just beginning to be understood and used:

> You had already submitted your report long ago – that's it, the project is completed, everything should be working. Inertia. Inertia prevents this . . . And the absence of economic thinking . . . The corporate culture is industrial – people are more comfortable with production indices rather than financial ones. (ibid)

A new bonus system, linked to KPIs, promised to speed up acceptance:

> Now is the turning point in this whole story, because we introduced these KPIs, we measured them, communicated them, collected information, and now the time is coming to link them to compensation . . . moving from a lot of hot air to really concrete things . . . bonuses. Now, suddenly, people are beginning to see these KPIs in a completely different way. (ibid.)

Leverage Administrative Heritage

In Lukoil, the implementation of new business techniques was helped by the command-and-control heritage – people were used to taking orders:

> I think there is no resistance [to the new systems]. The level of discipline . . . in our company is very high – implementation discipline . . . All obey, all say 'Yes Sir', like in the army. There is a lack of understanding . . . of course – for completely understandable reasons – [from] people, who have grown up in a system for 20 years. (middle manager, Lukoil, Russian, translation)

People could implement, without actually understanding what it was they were implementing.

Summary of TMT and Administrative Heritage

The TMTs of the Soviet-style companies were homogeneous, conservative and consisted of insiders. This determined the nature of their relationship with their administrative heritage. Since they were situated inside the heritage, their bounded rationality meant that they could not readily see the need to change. Lukoil was beginning to move very slowly towards an understanding of the value of moving towards a Western model, but Surgutneftegaz made a virtue of its Soviet heritage and showed no inclination to transform its organisation.

ORGANISATIONAL LEARNING

In Lukoil, there was some evidence of an attempt to break with administrative heritage, therefore there was some organisational learning. In Surgutneftegaz there was no attempt to break with the administrative heritage, therefore there was no effective organisational learning with respect to Western management skills, although there was evidence of the acquisition of technical skills.

Absorptive Capacity

Because both Lukoil and Surgutneftegaz were still anchored in their Soviet administrative heritage, their absorptive capacity was limited. Both were run by oilmen with no experience of Western business practice. This limited their ability to conceive of different ways of doing things:

> Bogdanov is an oilman, Alekperov is an oilman. I mean, find me an oil person who has been out, got his hands dirty, actually pumped the oil, lived in West Siberia, that understands succession issues, that understands organisational management, that understands even numbers and performance. I mean it's pretty rare, and yet these are the profiles of the people at the very top. . . . And so if that's the type of profile you have at the top, I think instilling that type of change is very difficult because I think even realising that that type of change is needed . . . will take a lot of effort. (headhunter, Western)

Their focus was on technology and their experience of management was rooted in the Soviet planned economy:

> Simply if, for example, the directors of Surgut and Lukoil were to get a general picture of proper management – you see they have never ever studied it – they probably studied technology. Management was only ever something on top, without any special rules. . . . This is where the cultural problem comes in. They normally don't want to learn. (top manager, Yukos, Russian, translation)

> The managers of these companies were successful under the old system – they became General Directors – therefore they see no need to learn: If it's your company, which you inherited by being a General Director, then you're less willing to listen – people like Bogdanov and many of the board of Lukoil, who are probably narrow-minded about these things. (investment bank executive, Western)

The same problem – one of pride – is linked to the reluctance of these companies to bring in foreign expertise. Lukoil and Surgut 'look at their companies as their heritage and they don't want foreign companies wrecking it' (ibid.)

Absorptive capacity is determined by the prior experience of the organisation. Lukoil and Surgutneftegaz were both, therefore, constrained by their background as oil professionals in the Soviet system. Thus the tendency of the Soviet-style companies was to promote traditional Soviet ways, and only very slowly to start learning about and introducing Western management concepts.

Knowledge Acquisition

Of all the Russian oil companies, Lukoil was the most active internationally and 20 per cent of the company's assets were located abroad. The ostensible objective of acquiring the Getty Oil gasoline stations in the USA was to gain experience of business in the West: 'To be honest, we needed to try out the Western market, to get experience, to master technology. So this [Getty acquisition] was a route to gaining Western experience and Western technology' (senior manager, Lukoil, Russian, translation). However, it was perceived by the Western oil industry and financial community as a bad investment, and was possibly related more to PR and national pride than to learning.

Lukoil did not have many foreigners working in the company: 'A sense we didn't get was that there was any genuine desire to have foreigners working there' (investment bank executive, Western). In fact there seemed to be even an aversion to employing foreign expertise:

To be honest I just don't understand what they are doing in Yukos and TNK, when the top managers are foreigners. . . . Of course specialists can bring experience, knowledge, but it is really totally unnecessary to remove a whole level of managers and replace them with Americans or English people. . . . This implies that our own local staff aren't good enough. But that is not the case. . . . For me personally, I do not approve of this. (senior manager, Lukoil, Russian, translation)

However, it was recognised that some of the Russian managers were too fixed in their ways to change and needed to be replaced, but with Russians with Western experience, not with Westerners:

Many people who are working today are former Soviet enterprise directors. Of course it is not always easy to move them onto the track of market thinking. It is necessary to gradually replace them with new managers, but that will require 3–5 years for the process to be complete. . . . We are talking about new people who already developed under the conditions of a market economy. (senior manager, Lukoil, Russian, translation)

However, a more positive attitude was taken towards foreign consultants such as McKinsey, KPMG and ParisBas (energy consultant, Western). Alekperov also visited Western oil companies seeking advice on how to create an integrated oil company.

Knowledge acquisition via training and development of employees took several forms. 'Dozens of people study every year in Western business schools'[1] (senior manager, Lukoil, Russian, translation) and there were also links with Russian business schools. With the sale of 7.5 per cent of Lukoil to Conoco-Phillips it had been agreed that an exchange programme would be set up for 20–25 senior managers from each side (senior manager, Lukoil, Russian, translation). A management training programme for middle and senior managers was developed that included courses at various Moscow institutes. In June 2004, a programme was launched to develop high potential managers destined to become directors of enterprises or top managers in the company. This 18-month programme was set up by MGIMO (Moscow State Institute of International Relations) and UOP (a US technology and process provider). Nine people were studying in the US on the programme (ibid.).

Surgutneftegaz, however, had no interest in learning about Western management techniques. They employed no Western specialists and used no consultants or oil service companies. However, they were actively involved in acquisition of technical knowledge:

Surgut . . . Bogdanov . . . doesn't like to have the foreign oil service company personnel on his fields. But on the other hand . . . they have a lot of infrastructure set up and capacity to assess all the technologies, and they send a lot of people to the States. And they go about it very differently, but they've had some success, and they definitely buy a lot of the foreign service companies' technology and products. They are much more secretive and reluctant to have, for example, the personnel on their fields. (investment bank executive, Western)

Whilst the other Russian oil companies were securing the services of companies like Halliburton and Schlumberger, Surgutneftegaz was developing its own 'me too' technology. They sent their own specialists overseas to learn how to drill multilateral wells and then they reproduced the technique back in Siberia (top manager, Western oil company, Western). There was a strong desire to be self-sufficient: 'The head of the company is an engineer, and as an engineer he understands what the engineering principles are and does want to be self-sufficient. And has his own institute for doing all the design' (consultant, Western).

Knowledge Internalisation

No information was available on knowledge internalisation for either company.

Knowledge Dissemination

In Lukoil cross-functional working groups were used to disseminate best practice. They involved specialists from different areas and levels whose expertise was required on a particular project (middle manager, Lukoil, Russian, translation). However, the existence of corporate silos, that restricted the transfer of knowledge, was recognised as being a problem: 'Of course there is [resistance to sharing knowledge] – this is an absolutely normal process – corporate silos' (ibid).

Although transfer of knowledge might happen in head office, it was less likely in the regions. Knowledge sharing was generally poor in Russian organisations:

It's definitely feudal – I think Russian companies in general . . . are traditionally very secretive, people don't share information. So the idea of what we learnt from the US, kind of being disseminated across the workforce is not really part of that approach, and so . . . my assumption is that there would be quite a lot of brakes on that process. There may be more at Lukoil than some of the others. (newspaper correspondent, Western)

There was also some dissemination of best practice in Lukoil via professional skills competitions, which were held in different locations. Around

30 people would be involved in these events, which provided an opportunity for exchanging experiences and networking. At the senior management level, meetings were held every quarter at different locations (senior manager, Lukoil, Russian, translation).

In Surgutneftegaz since there was little knowledge acquisition, knowledge dissemination was only relevant with respect to the technical expertise acquired abroad and brought back for development as 'me too' technology in the company.

The dissemination of knowledge in traditional Russian companies such as Lukoil and Surgutneftegaz was inefficient: 'They are not very efficient. We see great silos within the Russian companies we deal with. Often in some of our dealings we've been acting as the communicator between, almost within their organisation, trying to get the different bits to talk together' (top manager, Western oil company, Western). A major limitation on the dissemination of knowledge was the difficulty young managers had in re-integrating into the system and utilising knowledge and experience gained in training and development:

> The older guys have come through the Soviet times – to change their mentality is difficult. They're the guys in charge and they've got a lot of the youngsters coming through who want to change but they've got respect for their elders and the way things have been done there, and change doesn't happen as quickly as everybody would like. You've got those old processes in place and it's very difficult. (consultant, Western)

The system was not conducive to knowledge transfer up the hierarchy. Furthermore, older managers were likely to cling to their positions of power regardless of whether they were the best-equipped for the job: 'You have people that are still holding onto their positions . . . [whose] skills might be better utilised in other functions, but because of issues of power and authority . . . skills are not being utilised in the right way' (headhunter, Western).

Summary of Organisational Learning

Since the absorptive capacity of the Soviet-style companies was low there was little evidence of organisational learning. Lukoil was starting to acquire Western management skills, but the process was constrained by the Soviet administrative heritage. Surgutneftegaz remained firmly within the Soviet heritage and was interested only in acquiring technical knowledge.

ORGANISATIONAL CAPABILITIES

Dynamic Capabilities – Resource Reconfiguration

Lukoil was the first Russian oil company to introduce a corporate governance system, but apart from this it had generally been slow to reconfigure its resources and improve performance:

> Very early he [Alekperov] took steps to sell Lukoil shares to Western shareholders. . . . They were the first to really try to go with more transparent corporate governance; they were the first to present their accounts in US GAAP standards, so they were the cat's pyjamas as far as the foreign investor community was concerned. Right through about 1998, and then at that point somebody started to ask the question, well gee they're transparent they're wonderful, but what the hell do they actually do? High-cost producers. (energy consultant, Western)

The early promise began to fade as Lukoil fell behind its competitors in efficiency. However, some changes were being made to increase efficiency, albeit more slowly than their competitors Yukos and TNK. 'People here are adequate . . . they are studying . . . they are mastering modern technology. . . . Perhaps not at such a rapid pace, no such radical transformations have taken place, but perhaps that's not such a bad thing' (middle manager, Lukoil, Russian, translation).

Lukoil had started to try to move from a production to a profit orientation. A cost reduction programme was introduced: 'This, for the time being, does not involve getting rid of people. Costs are being reduced by optimising procurement, in the first instance, that is materials and energy, optimising logistics, and avoiding any unnecessary expenditure' (senior manager, Lukoil, Russian, translation). A reason given for not cutting employees was that Lukoil was expanding its operations, both in the upstream and downstream, and could not afford to lose people (senior manager, Lukoil, Russian, translation).

New business planning systems were being introduced and a major change was planned for intercompany relationships, with a move away from transfer pricing to market pricing:

> There have been a lot of things, we tried different types of management, forms of business organisation. All the time we were gaining experience. Now we are preparing to move to a new business model next year. That will involve a lot of work. We are moving away from transfer pricing and processing . . . to a normal form of business organisation where the oil production unit will sell its oil to our refineries at market prices. (middle manager, Lukoil, Russian, translation)

In summary, Lukoil's initial popularity with investors had faded because the introduction of Western business concepts was too slow, compared with their competitors.

Surgutneftegaz was regionally focused in Western Siberia, primarily engaged in the upstream business and with one refinery in Kirishi, European Russia. 'They seem to be very content with themselves in their region, in their development' (consultant, Western). There was no evidence of reconfiguration of resources.

Dynamic Capabilities – Resource Divestment

Lukoil had already undertaken some actions to sell off the oil service companies and the work was continuing. Transportation had been hived off and maintenance and construction had been separated out into independent companies: 'We hived off . . . an army of people, subdivisions, for which a market was beginning to appear in Russia' (senior manager, Lukoil, Russian, translation). In the refineries there was also discussion about selling off waste treatment facilities since they served the municipality, the refinery and other manufacturing plants: 'So we are trying to ensure that a minimum number of specialists remain in the refineries, who deal with technology and production – this is our work' (ibid.). Lukoil was thus making considerable progress in selling off non-core activities.

Surgutneftegaz made no resource divestments and had no intention of hiving off oilfield services:

> I'm pretty sure that the drilling rigs they're doing it with will be Surgutneftegaz drilling rigs and the pipeline contractor that comes along will be a Surgutneftegaz pipeline contractor. And they are, as far as I can tell, not going away from that model at all . . . Surgutneftegaz . . . they do everything themselves . . . very much following a model of 'This will be an old-style integrated company with all of the activities managed by Surgutneftegaz'. (top manager, Western oil company, Western)

Dynamic Capabilities – Resource Creation

The long-term vision of Alekperov was to become a world-class international company on a par with the Western majors and to diversify Lukoil's portfolio to have a significant amount of production outside Russia (energy consultant, Western). Lukoil had been active in acquiring assets abroad, including oil interests in the Caspian, refineries in Eastern Europe and the Getty gasoline stations in the USA. To describe the latter acquisition in positive terms, it was a learning experience, but in negative terms it was a bad investment. It was mooted by the international oil community that Lukoil had made the move for reasons of national pride rather than on the basis of sound commercial logic. 'Lukoil has taken some slightly curious international investments, like the petrol stations in the US that were more like prestige than actual industrial logic' (newspaper correspondent, Western).

As well as international acquisitions and expansion of their reserve base, Lukoil was also creating new resources in the downstream. In 2003/4 they had brought on stream several major units including hydrocracking in Perm and reforming in Nizhny Novgorod (senior manager, Lukoil, Russian, translation). In addition a programme had almost been finalised for increasing the depth of refining by 2014 to allow them to compete on the European market with new grades of oil products corresponding to European standards: 'In this way we will take the lead, outstrip the development of events in Russia' (ibid.).

In Surgutneftegaz there was no evidence of resource creation apart from copying Western technology.

Dynamic Capabilities – Resource Integration

Strong efforts were being made to integrate and coordinate the activities of Lukoil (newspaper correspondent, Western). There were some first indications that the influence of the fiefdoms was on the wane as more efficient coordination processes were introduced: 'I turned very positive on their stock when . . . in the space of six months I was exposed to four different parts of very senior management and they all told me the same thing. And that spanned international activities – West Siberia, . . . head office strategy, . . . and Perm' (consultant, Western). Communication, at least at the top management level, seemed to be improving.

In Surgutneftegaz no evidence was found of resource integration.

Operational Capabilities

Lukoil had started to make improvements in many of the functional areas, particularly in the finance and business planning areas. US GAAP accounting had been introduced and other economic evaluation systems had been put in place:

> [The Lukoil finance team] would tell you about a year ago . . . we have the best . . . well and production metrics in the industry, we know exactly what's being produced. We now have proper accounting systems so we know exactly what's capital and what's maintenance. We can't put both together, or we're not yet in a position where we can put both together, so they can't allocate capital spending against the results that a production manager achieves. Now that's the gap they're closing. (investment bank executive, Western)

Efforts were being made to evaluate the performance of all the business units: 'We are checking everything, calculating efficiency, calculating profitability of projects from the point of view of return on capital employed' (middle manager, Lukoil, Russian, translation). But there was still lack of clarity on the real economic value of each part of the value chain: 'Our company is at the stage of reaching understanding . . . exactly what value is added by this or that business unit in the value chain' (ibid.). This was linked to a move from transfer to market pricing.

Another key initiative was the introduction of a business planning and budgeting process focusing on economic performance indicators rather than the traditional cost-based approach. This was making slow progress.

> The process [of moving to an economic model] is now under way. . . . This year we put together budgets with our subsidiaries. This is the first individualised approach to evaluating projects, before it was a cost approach. The logic of the directors of the factories consisted of, if we gave them 50 million, they should spend it all, or they would get less next time. You can imagine with such a logic no one ever thought about KPIs. Now the situation is changing a little, but not as fast as we would wish, but we are putting in the maximum effort, taking into consideration the reality of working in this company. . . . This year we can say that the first signs of progress are there, when people really understood that they had to put together business plans, that they had to do them properly. (middle manager, Lukoil, Russian, translation)

Apart from the limited training described above, there was little evidence of progress on HR. The HR director had come from the Ministry of Defence: 'He is a general, who has certain ways of doing things . . . so everything is very clearly formulated, all is systematised, everything works' (senior manager, Lukoil, Russian, translation). However, an HR director from a ministry seems unlikely to bring much in the way of modern Western thinking on HR management.

Lukoil was also increasing production efficiency, but much more slowly than Yukos.

> In terms of modern reservoir management Yukos and Sibneft[2] are just miles ahead. But I think [Lukoil] have brought their costs down by doing some of the easy things. . . . But to then get to the much harder stuff . . . that's the difference between the $2.50 [Lukoil] and the $1.50 [Yukos lifting costs]. (investment bank executive, Western)

Lukoil's costs were higher than their competitors although there was no geological advantage among the Russian oil companies: 'That's not the defining factor. It's how the people are managing' (investment bank executive, Western).

Efficient communications and information management are a key aspect of operational capability. However, Lukoil did not have good, or even basic, management information systems, partly due to the silos created by the fiefdoms (investment bank executive, Western). The email system was underdeveloped: 'In Lukoil they don't even have documents circulating by email, what more can I say? You have to get each piece of paper signed and show it' (senior manager, Yukos, Regional, Russian, translation). There was a general lack of the normal type of communications infrastructure that would be expected in a Western company.

In summary, Lukoil was making rather slow progress in developing the operational capabilities required for survival in a market economy.

Surgut had a good reputation for the way it ran its business and the local town: 'It runs Surgut extremely well . . . neat town and clean good airport and so on' (top manager, Western oil company, Western). By looking after the community it endeared itself to the Kremlin:

> Surgut has all the way through been fairly consistently cautious and loyal and patriotic and Russia focused. And Putin has mentioned it a couple of times as a sort of good example of how companies should be focused on Russia, reinvesting, providing facilities in the community and so on. . . . Surgut is essentially a Soviet company town. . . . And certainly when you go round the plant, I mean there's been a lot of investment and they're very proud of it. (newspaper correspondent, Western)

Bogdanov is regarded by Western experts as a manager doing a good job in running his business in the traditional Soviet way. 'They've always done things the old fashioned way, and that has brought them success up to a point' (top manager, TNK-BP, Western, translation). Their technical skills were respected in the Western community: 'Surgutneftegaz is a company that we have a lot of respect for in terms of what they achieve technically' (top manager, Western oil company, Western). However, a rather different view was expressed by one of their Russian competitors, who explained that the Surgutneftegaz capability in producing oil was much inferior to theirs:

> You can see [from the data] that Yukos drills very few wells, but our wells are very effective, we get more than 140 tonnes per well. By comparison, let's take Surgut, their average flow rate per well is even below 20 tonnes, i.e. to obtain what Yukos gets by drilling one well, Surgut would have to drill more than seven to get the same effect. Therefore this might be an explanation of why they drill more. (senior manager, Yukos, regional, Russian, translation)

Another criticism of the operational capabilities of Surgut related to the lack of incentivisation of his people: 'That's the other thing . . . that

Bogdanov struggled with so badly. He may not have many bad people but he certainly doesn't incentivise the good people to out-perform and get rid of the bad that he has, because he has this kind of grandfather-figure kind of approach to life' (investment bank executive, Western).

Although Surgut had a good reputation with respect to technical performance, nevertheless they were a more inefficient and higher-cost operator than their competitors. There was no evidence of the introduction of any Western processes relating to HR, finance, marketing, PR or HSE.

Summary of Organisational Capabilities

By comparison with the Western-style companies, there was little evidence of dynamic capabilities or the development of operational capabilities in the Soviet-style companies. Lukoil had made some progress, but was still at the early stages of introducing new business systems and functions. Surgutneftegaz had introduced no Western operational capabilities. The development of organisational capabilities in the Soviet companies was constrained by the failure of their TMTs to break with administrative heritage and the reduced level of organisational learning in consequence.

ORGANISATIONAL TRANSFORMATION

Efficiency and Robustness

Yukos had overtaken Lukoil in performance: 'Yukos . . . overtook us in efficiency . . . they had significantly lower costs. . . . They did a lot in the area of oil production' (senior manager, Lukoil, Russian, translation). The view of Western investors was that Lukoil was held back by the insider nature of the management team:

> Look at TNK-BP, 14 per cent growth this year, and that's all because new people have taken over assets and have started running them differently. So if new people took over Lukoil you'd probably see quite a strong production growth because people would look at it and say, well we can do this differently. (investment bank executive, Western)

The rate of transformation in Lukoil was far slower than in Yukos and TNK/TNK-BP with the result that it lost its pre-eminent position in the Russian oil industry.

In 2001, Surgutneftegaz was still performing quite well and it was a favourite with investors: 'This Red Director turned out to be much more effective than a lot of the young bankers who came into the oil industry like Khodorkovsky' (newspaper correspondent, Russian/Western). However, they soon began to trail behind as the new business systems and processes put in place in the other companies began to take effect. By 2003, their costs were significantly above those of their competitors:

> [Surgut's cost per barrel is] about $4.50, so they are definitely higher than Lukoil, certainly way higher than Sibneft or Yukos. . . . When you look at the numbers they're not at all a good operator. They grow their output, but I think they grow their output by throwing maximum amounts of money at it. (investment bank executive, Western)

This was confirmed in a presentation made by a representative from Surgut:

> And he was extremely proud of how many metres they drilled each year. And he said, well we drill the most and that's really great. Then he showed another slide which showed how much additional production they had based on drilling and Surgut was the last, and those who had drilled the least were on the top. (consultant, Western)

The company had recently acquired a production licence in a new area – Talakan. This was felt to be a test for Surgutneftegaz to see whether they were really as inefficient as they seemed, or whether it was just a factor of the difficult nature of the oilfields in Surgut.

> But the Talakan licence is the thing that will let us know in five years' time whether Surgut is congenitally inefficient or whether actually it's as efficient as you could be in the specific environmental conditions of the Surgutneftegaz area, heavily depleted area . . . I am slightly dubious. . . . That's one company that does not seem to have gone through a too radical transformation. (investment bank executive, Western)

To summarise, Surgutneftegaz was considerably less efficient than its competitors and showed no evidence of organisational transformation.

Responsiveness and Strategic Flexibility

The entrepreneurial characteristics of Alekperov were described above and it was explained how he had been able to survive and prosper not just in the Soviet system, but also in the transition context. This was evidence of his personal strategic flexibility. However, there was no evidence of strategic flexibility elsewhere in the organisation.

Ostensibly Lukoil's international assets should have provided an element of strategic flexibility; however, their poor capability in evaluating acquisitions and their lack of operational capabilities meant that they were unlikely to be able to compete in the international market against the Western oil majors.

In Surgutneftegaz, no evidence was found of responsiveness and strategic flexibility.

Performance and Competitive Advantage

Lukoil's portfolio balance in terms of exploration, production, the downstream and international assets was believed to be a potential source of competitive advantage:

> They have been quite effective in . . . getting that . . . right balance between finding new and exploiting, but not over-exploiting, the existing reserves, and thinking about international networks, refining, distribution networks outside as well as within Russia. And certainly that kind of international ambition . . . ties into the new sort of Russian economic diplomacy. (newspaper correspondent, Western)

However, in terms of oil production Lukoil had been overtaken by Yukos in 2002: 'Lukoil . . . *had* been the leader for many years in Russia. By . . . about the third quarter of 2002 Yukos had outstripped Lukoil in terms of daily production. And that's because Lukoil production was stagnant or changing very, very slowly, whereas Yukos had been increasing at this incredible rate' (top manager, TNK-BP, Western). It was also lagging in cost efficiency, although its costs were still much lower than the international oil majors:

> In their upstream, their [the Russian oil majors'] financial performance has been remarkable. I mean their production costs have been driven down, including Lukoil. Yukos and Sibneft are quite well known, $1.50 to $1.80 per barrel in cash production costs. Lukoil has driven their equivalent to below $2.50 and I mean you don't see any of the [Western] majors at that level. (investment bank executive, Western)

It was only the collapse of Yukos in 2003/04 that gave Lukoil the chance to re-exert its position of pre-eminence by the third quarter of 2004: 'Today, going on the results of nine months, everything is indicating that Lukoil is in a leading position . . . in terms of cost reduction and increased efficiency' (senior manager, Lukoil, Russian, translation).

Lukoil's position had been turned to advantage by the collapse of Yukos, but TNK-BP was the new threat and they were already declaring that they were in leadership position by the end of 2004. Pride might be the key in future to unlocking Lukoil's organisational transformation: 'I think Lukoil is getting there, but it's getting there at its own pace. And it's getting there through a combination of peer pressure or peer embarrassment' (investment bank executive, Western). Lukoil was effectively being pulled along by the successes of its competitors. However, robustness in a market economy was not the sole criterion for success in the Russian oil industry:

> And taking a view of a shareholder is not the only view to take . . . Lukoil, they're inefficient . . . My views have changed for Lukoil in particular . . . Understanding their philosophy. They are statesmen. They have a bigger view of the world. And the fact that I don't share it or most of the Western investors don't share it, doesn't mean that they are wrong. (senior manager, TNK-BP, Russian/Western)

Furthermore, the 'reversion to state control' in Russia had reinforced the importance of close alignment with the state: 'The Russian press today acknowledges that Lukoil is considered to be . . . the most loyal company with respect to state policy regarding taxation' (senior manager, Lukoil, Russian, translation). Good relationships with the Kremlin were a source of competitive advantage for Lukoil. Although relations had cooled at one stage between Putin and Alekperov, they seemed to have returned to normal:

> Mr Putin met our President on more than one occasion. He visited units in the North Caspian. Our President accompanied him. There have been a large number of business meetings . . . in the Kremlin, which were broadcast on TV, in the newspapers. The loyalty of the company to the state was also demonstrated by the deal with Conoco-Phillips[3] when they received the approval of the highest positioned person in the state. (senior manager, Lukoil, Russian, translation)

Surgutneftegaz had no competitive advantage in the context of a market economy. However, it is important to consider competitive advantage in terms of a Russian external context, characterised by a 'reversion to state control':

> Bogdanov has been consistently very, very cautious, conservative about his political relationships, keeping a low profile, paying his taxes, staying out of trouble. And evidently ploughing a good deal of it back into the local communities. He is now being hailed as a model. And competitive advantage Russian style is not simply a matter of profitability and cost control it's a matter of minding your political fences. (energy consultant, Western)

The big question was whether Surgutneftegaz's Soviet-style business model was sustainable:

> They're best of friends with the state . . . But . . . in the long term, is that sustainable? – I think not. But it depends . . . on the direction the country takes. If

the authorities continue to make life difficult for progressive companies like Yukos, then Surgut is in good shape. *If* market forces are allowed to run their course . . . then companies like Surgut have a very limited future. (senior manager, TNK-BP, Western)

A significant limiting factor on their growth and sustainability was the depleted nature of their oilfields in Surgut. 'They do have a relatively small and very concentrated resource base in that area of Siberia. So . . . in let's say a ten-year view they clearly are going to have to start thinking about expansion unless they are going to wither up and die in a 20-year cycle' (newspaper correspondent, Western).

In summary, Surgutneftegaz had no competitive advantage by market economy indicators. However, the acceptability of its business model to the Kremlin had increased its competitive advantage in the context of reversion to state control. There were doubts, however, about the long-term sustainability of their competitive advantage given the need to secure access to new fields and the uncertainty in the external environment as to whether a move back towards the market economy would occur at some stage.

For all Russian oil companies, good relationships with the Kremlin were critical: 'So the real question of the future of the industry is not on reserves, it's on managing the political risk in regards to managing the relationship with the ruling dictator' (headhunter, Western). But regardless of political climate all the companies would sooner or later be competing for capital to explore for and exploit new reserves: 'Directionally they're on the same route because they realise that they're going to compete for capital. And capital is a function of many things . . . like corporate governance, . . . transparency. . . . Matching up to their international peers has become more and more important to them' (consultant, Western).

The question remains, however, as to what business model is right for Russia, whether now or in the future. Some respondents kept an open mind as to whether the business model of the Soviet-style organisations was better or worse for the Russian context:

Is it a bad process, yes? But it's a bad process from which perspective? With which goal in mind do you call that inefficient? Maybe they have a different goal. And by their goal it's not inefficient, it's perfectly efficient, they can perfectly justify it. Investing into a field where BP would never invest, is it good or bad, is it bad from the process of financial investor, bad from the process of the region, bad from the process of a country, bad from the process of macro-economic development, GDP growth, is that bad? I'm not so sure. What's the alternative? Expatriate the earnings? . . . I'd be very careful in kind of framing. (senior manager, TNK-BP, Russian/Western)

Summary of Organisational Transformation

Of the Soviet-style companies Lukoil was the most advanced, but had lost its former leadership position to Yukos. Lower efficiency meant reduced robustness in the conditions of a market economy. Furthermore, strategic flexibility was vested only in Alekperov himself. Surgutneftegaz had not transformed at all towards a Western market orientation. Its oil production was inefficient and costs were high, indicating the company was less robust than its competitors in conditions of a market economy. There was no evidence of responsiveness or strategic flexibility. Both companies lacked any source of competitive advantage in terms of competing in a market economy; however, their good relations with the Kremlin gave competitive advantage in the 'reversion to state control' scenario.

NOTES

1. One of the interviewees had done an Executive MBA at the London Business School.
2. One of the other integrated Russian oil majors.
3. In 2004 7.5 per cent of Lukoil shares remaining in government hands were sold to Conoco-Phillips.

7. Leadership, administrative heritage and absorptive capacity

This chapter presents a cross-case comparison which forms the basis for a theoretical framework explaining the role of the TMT in breaking with and leveraging administrative heritage to increase absorptive capacity. This broadly corresponds to Stage I of the integrative theoretical framework – 'Break with the Past' (see Chapter 3).

Previous studies of transition economies have shown that enterprise transformation is hindered because changes in organisational structures and subsystems were not accompanied by parallel changes in the inherited organisational values and beliefs (Clark and Soulsby, 1995). In other words managerial learning goes beyond the acquisition of new techniques or single-loop learning and must extend to double-loop learning and the redefinition of the tasks, and the goals and values that they reflect (Child and Czegledy, 1996). The key task for managers in such circumstances is to break with past values that no longer support the organisation in its new environment. In drawing on the empirical data from the study of the Russian oil industry this chapter therefore focuses on three specific areas. First I explain the characteristics of the top management team that promote the break with the past – an entrepreneurial approach, heterogeneity of the team and the presence of 'outsiders' (non-traditional managers). Second I describe the dual approach of the TMT in dealing with the past or what I term the administrative heritage, defined as a configuration of assets and capabilities, a set of routines and a distribution of managerial responsibilities and influence. The TMT on the one hand breaks with the administrative heritage to promote new behaviours and on the other hand leverages aspects of the heritage, in particular the command-and-control management style, to accelerate the rate of change. Third, I explain how the break with administrative heritage increases absorptive capacity, or the firm's ability to value, assimilate and apply new knowledge. Absorptive capacity is a prerequisite for organisational learning and organisational transformation. The key question addressed in this chapter is:

> How does the top management team of a company in a transition economy break with the organisation's administrative heritage in order to increase absorptive capacity?

CROSS-CASE COMPARISON

Two data displays are provided to facilitate understanding. A cross-case display (Table 7.1) compares the four oil companies with respect to the TMT, its relationship with administrative heritage and the development of absorptive capacity. The companies are grouped in pairs: the Western-style companies and the Soviet-style companies. An in-case data display (Table 7.2) illustrates the development of absorptive capacity in Yukos using the paradigm approach[1] – organising the data into three elements, the conditions, the actions/interactions and the consequences (Strauss and Corbin, 1998).

Top Management Team

Both Yukos and TNK were characterised by a strong entrepreneurial orientation (Table 7.1, rows 1 and 2). In a play on words (TNK – TANK), a number of respondents compared TNK managers with tank crews in the army: 'because it was really a very aggressive company in the positive sense of the word' (middle manager, TNK-BP, regional, Russian, translation).

The shareholders and the top managers, frequently combining both roles, were mainly young, self-made men – billionaires before the age of 40 (Table 7.1, row 2). Mikhail Khodorkovsky, CEO of Yukos, was highly dynamic and encouraged innovation throughout the organisation (Table 7.2, row 1). One employee maintained Yukos was more like a business school, the way training and new projects were encouraged. The management team was characterised by drive, enthusiasm and a great willingness to learn. TNK's managers exhibited the same characteristics, especially German Khan: 'He could take anything which seemed like a bad business and ignite it all over again' (middle manager, TNK-BP, Russian/Western). Both Yukos and TNK TMTs comprised a mix of young financial managers, such as Khodorkovsky and Khan, and oil professionals. A number of expatriates in senior executive positions brought oil industry and Western business expertise. In TNK the CEO, Simon Kukes, was an American citizen of Russian extraction with an oil industry background. With the arrival of BP in 2003 to form the JV the heterogeneity increased further. In 2004 there were 14 people on the TNK-BP management committee, seven BP, six Alpha/Access Renova (owners of TNK), and one independent, ex-Chevron. The President and CEO was from BP.

The heterogeneity of the Western-style TMTs contrasted with the homogeneity of the Soviet-style ones. Surgutneftegaz represented the extreme case – Vladimir Bogdanov exerted total patriarchal control over the privatised company just as he had done as a so-called 'Red Director' in the Soviet

Table 7.1 Cross-case display: TMT, administrative heritage and absorptive capacity[2]

	Western-style organisations		Soviet-style organisations	
	Yukos	TNK/TNK-BP	Lukoil	Surgutneftegaz
TMT				
1 TMT characteristics	Heterogeneous, outsiders, young and inexperienced, entrepreneurial, Russian/ Westerners	Heterogeneous, outsiders, young and experienced, entrepreneurial and conservative, Russian/ Westerners	Homogeneous, insiders, older and experienced, Russians	Homogeneous (one man), insiders, experienced, conservative, Russians
2 CEO/director	Khodorkovsky – charismatic, financial manager. Ex-Komsomol. Entrepreneur	Khan – TNK, financial manager Vekselberg – TNK, financial manager Entrepreneurs Kukes – Russian born, Western CEO Dudley – ex Amoco/BP, Western Oil Multinational	Alekperov – oilman USSR Deputy Minister for Oil & Gas	Bogdanov – oilman Career in Surgut
2 CEO/director background	1963 – born Moscow (Age 42) Mendeleev Institute of Chemical Technology Deputy Head Komsomol 1986 – first business – private café 1988 – import/export business 1989 – Bank Menatep	Khan: 1962 – born Kiev (Age 41) Moscow Institute of Steel and Alloys 1989 co-founded Alfa-Eco, commodity trading To 1998 – manager in Alfa Group, a financial industrial conglomerate 2000 – Deputy Chairman TNK	1950 – born Azerbaijan (Age 55) Azerbaijan Institute of Oil and Chemistry To 1979 – Caspian oil fields To 1984 – Siberian oil fields 1984 – Gen. Director Kogalymnefaz 1990 – Deputy/Acting Minister of Fuel and	1951 – born Siberia (Age 54) Tyumen Industrial Institute 1973 – started as technician in Siberian oil fields Rose to deputy general director and general director

	1996 – First VP Yukos	2003 – Executive Director TNK-BP	Energy 1991 – President Lukoil	Surgutneftegaz
	Oil industry experience: 9 years	Oil industry experience: 7 years	Oil industry experience: 35 years	Oil industry experience: 34 years
2 Ownership/ control	Oligarch: Khodorkovsky	Oligarchs: Vekselberg, Aven, Friedman Later 50% BP	Industry bureaucrat: Alekperov	Industry bureaucrat: Bogdanov
Administrative Heritage				
4 Break administrative heritage	Remove blockers; incentives; expatriates; strategic alliances; learning on the job; training; project teams; success; job rotation; success; restructuring; promotion of young managers with CEO support.	TNK: replace blockers; new managers; centralised management; expatriates TNK-BP: openness; incentives; move to empowerment; working groups; success; Russian consultant; restructuring; training; expatriates	Future link with bonus system	No evidence
5 Leverage administrative heritage	Command-and-control; Pride	Command-and-control	Command-and-control	No evidence
6 Absorptive Capacity	TMT drive; promote innovation vs experience; critical mass of Western expertise	TNK: TMT drive; open up minds; TNK-BP: ready and willing to change; soak up like sponge; critical mass of Western expertise	Little: constrained by tradition, oil background and pride	None: constrained by tradition, oil background and pride

Note: ² Data provided is as 2005.

153

Table 7.2 Data display of creation of absorptive capacity – Yukos

Paradigm	Findings	Examples
Conditions (1995–2003)	1–2 **TMT heterogeneous, entrepreneurial, outsiders** • TMT absorptive capacity high, unbounded by Soviet oil industry rationality	They are a team of people with great professionalism, motivated not only by money, but with a huge desire for learning and self-development. (middle manager, Russian)
	• Organisation constrained by 3 **Soviet administrative heritage** • Low absorptive capacity	It required time to overcome the psychological resistance, because . . . [the oil industry] has its own traditions. There are people who have worked for years and years, who are used to certain ways of working. (senior, manager, Russian)
Actions/ interactions	4 **TMT break with administrative heritage** • Promote move to market economy • Acquire Western knowledge • Training • Remove blockers • Rotate managers • Promote young managers • Favour analysis over experience • Project teams • Incentives/bonus system • Early successes	A commission was sent there which established that the team there was a dyed-in-the-wool, ossified team which had been working together for years and years. They had their own internal objectives, but not the objectives of the company. Therefore the management of the company took the decision to replace the local management. (senior manager, regional, Russian)
	5 **TMT leverage administrative heritage** • Top-down leadership to implement change • Respect for hierarchy to support young managers backed by TMT • Relate oil production increases to early Russian inventions	It's like Stalin, big father and all that. It's intrinsic in the Russian oil industry because it's very macho, it's army style. You have to obey the commands. (middle manager, Russian)
Consequences	6 **Absorptive capacity** of organisation increases enabling	I make it clear to people that for me your experience is not the

Table 7.2   (continued)

Paradigm	Findings	Examples
	organisational learning (acquisition, assimilation, transformation and exploitation of knowledge)	principle matter. The principal thing is your ability to analyse, to substantiate . . . to defend your point of view. (senior manager, regional, Russian)

era. In Lukoil's TMT, oil industry backgrounds predominated and there had been little team turnover since privatisation: 'Lukoil . . . was created by production people who came from a good school in life. Mr Alekperov progressed from a rank-and-file driller to the First Deputy Minister of the USSR Oil Industry . . . Of course we are proud' (senior manager, Lukoil, Russian, translation).

There were significant differences in the age, tenure and education of the Western-style and Soviet-style companies. The Western-style managers were largely younger (early 40s in 2005), had a short tenure in the oil industry (less than 10 years) and did not have an educational background in the oil industry. In contrast the Soviet-style companies were run by oilmen in their mid-50s with 35 years' experience in the oil industry and an oil industry education (see Table 7.1, rows 1 and 2).

However one thing both the Western-style and Soviet-style managers had in common was a command-and-control approach to leadership (Tables 7.1 and 7.2, row 5) 'Khodorkovsky was a puppet master . . . he has strings attached to every part, every little manager there . . . keeping things very tight' (middle manager, Yukos, Russian). The 60 000 TNK employees were used to taking orders from the 10 to 15 people who effectively ran the company. German Khan was a key control figure: 'You only had to say: "German said . . .", and everyone's mouths dropped open' (middle manager, TNK-BP, Russian). Surgutneftegaz was described as 'a dictatorship – an extreme case of a Russian oil company' (top manager, Western oil company, Western). Lukoil's leadership style was also top-down, however the company was more decentralised, comprising a series of 'fiefdoms' or 'baronies' in the regions.

The characteristics of the TMTs of the Western-style and Soviet-style companies are quite distinct. The former are characterised by an entrepreneurial orientation, a predominance of 'outsiders' and heterogeneity. The latter are largely homogenous, insiders and experienced only in the Soviet oil industry. The Western-style TMTs could see the need for the introduction of Western management techniques: 'These people [TNK TMT] . . . realised that they needed to be thinking . . . West.' (middle manager, TNK-BP, Russian). The Soviet-style companies were less inclined to change: '[Surgutneftegaz and Lukoil] Simply people had always done things that way, and they were not used to doing things in a new way' (senior manager, Russian oil company, Russian, translation). Due to their heterogeneity and experience outside the oil industry, the TMTs of the Western-style companies had a broader set of experiences on which to draw to recognise, interpret and internalise new knowledge, creating a stronger absorptive capacity. The role of an 'enlightened' top management was key to overcoming the lack of experience and knowledge of operating in a market economy.

Break with Administrative Heritage

Both the literature (for instance Kornai, 1992; Elenkov, 1998; Naumov and Puffer, 2000) and the findings demonstrate that the Soviet administrative heritage was characterised by organisational routines totally unsuited to a market economy (Table 7.2, row 3). There was a focus on production volumes, rather then profit and on cost-based economics rather than profit-based. In fact there was no cult of making money and 'manager' was a dirty word. 'The word "manager", traditionally for a Russian person, it's a kind of incomprehensible word. Of course it's not a swear word, but all the same, people are disparaging about it, because "manager" – no one understands what it is.' (top manager, TNK-BP, Russian, translation). Production volumes were understated in order to achieve plan, whereas in the West employees would have incentives to achieve stretch targets. There was a high level of job security and employment came with a large package of social amenities (accommodation, kindergartens, holidays, healthcare, etc.) which led to high immobility of labour. Organisational silos discouraged knowledge sharing. The rigid hierarchy, with the boss as 'father figure', contributed to the 'knowledge is power' syndrome and there was a pronounced blame culture: 'In Russia there's a tremendous opportunity for somebody to say no . . . if somebody was to say yes . . . you look around and you look over your shoulder and, have I done the right thing, and if I'm wrong will I be fired? (top manager, Western oil company, Western).

Recognising the need to break with this administrative heritage (Tables 7.1 and 7.2, row 4), both Yukos and TNK forced through a number of initiatives in their organisations using a top-down approach. The first priority for TNK was to stop theft, increase efficiency and introduce new Western methods: 'You need the old managers in place, you can't replace them all . . . but some of them just don't have the financial or the managerial understanding to work in the new system, and some of their interests . . . aren't completely aligned with the shareholders. And therefore I go for centralised management' (senior manager, TNK, Western). In TNK, cash flow analysis was driven down to level of subsidiaries in the regions who were instructed to make investment decisions based not on criteria of 'How do I increase production 5 per cent this year?' but 'How do I put in place higher IRR projects?' (senior manager, TNK, Western). Managers who, nevertheless, persisted in their old behaviours were removed. For example the whole management team of a Yukos subsidiary was replaced.

Incentive systems were introduced to motivate changes in behaviours. 'The incentivisation . . . was aligned with the programme of change. . . . It's complicated in Russia . . . The Soviet history in that sector . . . generated behaviours that were absolutely 180 degrees out of phase with what I needed' (top manager, BP, Western).

Expatriates played a key role in breaking the administrative heritage. 'Learning on the job', under the tutelage of the Western expatriates, was an important part of staff development. In the oil fields an expatriate would systematically shoot down any arguments from the locals: 'And in the end they had to give in, they had to accept that he was right. . . . He drove through this programme' (middle manager, TNK-BP, Russian, translation). Formal training programmes were used extensively to introduce Western management skills and to encourage people to think 'out of the box' and overcome the tendency to adopt an attitude of 'that won't work here'. Putting people together to work on projects was another way to break down the barriers. Experimentation was encouraged and a new business climate, promoted by the TMT, encouraged people to learn by their mistakes, rather than fear retribution.

BP's openness was particularly shocking for managers brought up in the Soviet system and used to business being conducted behind closed doors: 'Suddenly – wham! – everyone starts to live by new rules, even to the extent that all office doors are open (top manager, TNK-BP, Russian, translation). BP managers also tried to empower the organisation by encouraging employees to develop ideas, make decisions and take the initiative. However this was not easy, because people were used to being punished for stepping out of line: 'Many . . . were turning off their brains the day they walked in. . . . So we're going to give them the opportunity to turn it back on. Now that's another problem because in the Soviet period every initiative was punished' (top manager, BP, Western).

Initially the attempt to involve Russian managers in defining projects for working groups met with incredulity and silence. In one instance, managers were given a day-and-a half in a hotel conference room to come up with suggestions, at the end of which they had to make a presentation to the CEO and the head of the Technology Division: 'So the pressure cooker was in place. . . . And they did it' (top manager, TNK-BP, Western). The success of such working groups was helpful in persuading others to change, as was the success in terms of increased oil production and lower costs: 'We had some early successes, we had things that worked and they saw behaviours change and they saw people perform, given the right set of circumstances and processes' (top manager, TNK-BP, Western).

With the use of new technology and new methods the production of oil compared to the previous year grew by about 12 per cent in one of the regional production subsidiaries of TNK-BP: 'It is obvious that this is only welcomed and is supported in all ways possible' (middle manager, TNK-BP, regional, Russian, translation). In Sidanco, a Russian management consultant was helpful in persuading people to change. He had his own successful company in the 1990s and later moved into international consultancy and academia. 'And he was able to bring the connection: 'Wait a minute, this isn't from the moon, this actually works in Russia, and I've done it' (top manager, BP, Western).

Difficulties of breaking with administrative heritage were magnified by the existence of organisational silos – each part of the organisation hoarding knowledge. In Yukos managers were rotated from one subsidiary to another to enable them to network and gain understanding of other parts of the operation, 'starting to knock down the walls that were . . . put up by the Soviet traditions' (consultant, Western). Change was further promoted by organisational restructuring, breaking down the functional silos and establishing a structure designed around the common company goal of profitability. For example, the old system of 'each to his own', whereby, for instance, factories were run independently, or export and domestic sales departments competed with each other, was redesigned and new systems established, for instance an accounting function based on an optimisation model for oil products: 'It was a great leap forward' (middle manager, Yukos, Russian, translation).

In Yukos, young high-fliers, who had undergone extensive postgraduate training under the tutelage of expatriates, were fast-tracked to positions of authority in the regions. One of these was promoted as deputy to the head geologist in an oil producing subsidiary at the age of 26: 'Probably in the whole history of Russia there hadn't been this kind of thing where the senior geologist was 26 years old' (senior manager, Yukos, regional, Russian, translation). Strong backing directly from Khodorkovsky enabled these young managers to overcome the resistance of local managers.

In summary, the TMTs of the Western-style companies achieved a break with administrative heritage via a combination of measures, summarised in Tables 7.1 and 7.2, which were driven through via top-down management.

The situation was quite different in the Soviet-style companies (Table 7.1, row 4). Surgutneftegaz at the extreme, demonstrated no break with administrative heritage. In Lukoil, administrative heritage was recognised as a significant brake on the introduction of new Western business techniques: 'If [people] have spent half their working life working under one system, they find it rather difficult to understand people who come along and start to break that all up and change it' (middle manager, Lukoil, Russian, translation).

The introduction of financial KPIs had started two years previously in Lukoil, but they were only now just beginning to be understood and used because managers were finding it difficult to move away from a production to a financial focus: 'The corporate culture is industrial' (ibid.). It was hoped that the introduction of a new bonus system might help to increase progress. However, compared to the measures being undertaken by the Western-style companies, little was being done in Lukoil. There was a much lower intensity of training, very few expatriates and silos were a severe problem.

The Western-style companies used an authoritarian management style to break with the administrative heritage (Tables 7.1 and 7.2, row 5): 'The buy-in in TNK was an executive order. That's the Russian style, more a military style, and very much TNK style' (senior manager, TNK-BP, Russian/ Western). Managers whose views were not aligned with the objectives of the new TMT were replaced. In the Soviet-style companies the managers were themselves a part of the administrative heritage of the oil companies. They were unable to foster the absorptive capacity of the organisation: 'If that's the type of profile you have at the top [oilmen], instilling . . .change is very difficult because even realising that . . . change is needed will take a lot of effort' (headhunter, Western). The managers of these companies had been successful under the old system – therefore they saw no need to change. Thus the tendency of the Soviet-style companies was to promote traditional Soviet ways, and only very slowly to start introducing new Western management concepts.

Leverage Administrative Heritage

The section above demonstrated how the Western-style TMTs broke with the administrative heritage. However in certain key respects they preserved critical aspects of the heritage which were helpful for the implementation of change. Above all they were able to leverage the command-and-control aspects of the administrative heritage (Tables 7.1 and 7.2, row 5): 'The buy-in in TNK was an executive order' (senior manager, TNK-BP, Russian/Western). BP managers soon realised the benefits of adopting a similar approach, at least in the short term, in order to ensure rapid implementation. It was acknowledged by BP that the organisation was at a stage of development which still required 'supervision', for instance coercion was still required to implement new safety regulations. Therefore although BP managers were trying to introduce Western styles of management, encouraging decision-making and accountability in the organisation, they also recognised that there was still a role for top-down management in some areas. Familiarity of employees with this management style was utilised to achieve rapid implementation of organisational change: 'That's very powerful because once the group decide to do something, they implement – it's one of the strengths of the Russian culture' (top manager, TNK-BP, Western). This manager gave the example of a well evaluation tracking system that was implemented in three months in Russia whereas it had taken much longer, or was still not implemented, in other parts of BP. The same phenomenon of rapid implementation was found in Yukos where decisions were not permitted to be delayed by more than 24 hours.

Administrative heritage was also leveraged with respect to hierarchy and respect for authority. Young high-fliers had the protection of Khodorkovsky and his team: 'All the managers who were above us, including the general director had quite clearly been given orders how to behave towards us' (senior manager, Yukos, regional, Russian, translation). Another important aspect of the administrative heritage was Russian pride in their scientific and technical achievements. Attempts were made not just to destroy the old and bring in the new, but also integrate the new with the old: 'The good things are always kept' (top manager, Yukos, Russian, translation). The new approach to oil production was justified by relating it to prior Russian scientific studies: 'That method, by the way, was invented by your Russian guy. That equation you are using is by that Russian guy; it's not American, it's you guys' (middle manager, Yukos, Russian).

In Lukoil the same command-and-control system was used to implement new business techniques – people were used to taking orders: 'The level of discipline . . . in the company is very high, implementation discipline . . . All obey, all say "Yes Sir", like in the army.' (middle manager, Lukoil, Russian, translation).

Absorptive Capacity

I have described above how the Western-style TMTs managed to both break with and leverage the administrative heritage. Because the TMTs themselves were not a part of the administrative heritage, they had a fresh approach and could see the value of adopting Western techniques, facilitating the emergence of a new dominant logic within the organisation – the

market-oriented logic. '[TNK] have no history . . . They have no traditions . . . they view problems with a fresh approach.' (middle manager,
TNK-BP, Russian, translation). This enabled them, in turn, to increase the
absorptive capacity (Tables 7.1 and 7.2, row 6) of the organisation. The
openness to new ideas of the TMT had a positive effect on the rest of
the organisation: 'TNK had some very high quality people . . . it's the way
you open up your mind to a different view. And that happens . . . I've seen
some critical cases, initially that they were considered really diehards. And
after a few months of talking it out they would convert on both sides
(senior manager, TNK-BP, Russian/Western).

Once managers began to understand how a new routine or process could
help them: 'They will just soak it up like a sponge' (top manager, TNK-BP,
regional, Western).

Of importance for increasing the absorptive capacity of the organisations was the availability of a critical mass of people within the organisation familiar with Western techniques: 'Without the kind of people who
know in practice how a Western company operates, it is very difficult to
transform a Russian company, because it is just not realistic to think you
can do it just by relying on textbooks' (middle manager, TNK-BP, Russian,
translation). By the time the TNK-BP JV was created the organisation
already understood the importance of Western management techniques to
improve performance. The organisation was ready for further innovations:
'TNK started to transform itself quite quickly, because the things that BP
brought were desired and expected by many people' (middle manager,
TNK-BP, Russian, translation).

Table 7.2 summarises the process of development of absorptive capacity
in Yukos with illustrative quotations.

Above I have demonstrated how the Western-style companies increased
the absorptive capacity of their organisations by breaking with the administrative heritage. This was not the case in the Soviet-style companies.
Because both Lukoil and Surgutneftegaz were still anchored in their Soviet
administrative heritage their absorptive capacity was limited. Both were
run by oilmen with no experience of Western business practice. This
limited their ability to conceive of different ways of doing things:
'Instilling that type of change is very difficult because I think even realising that that type of change is needed . . . will take a lot of effort' (headhunter, Western). The managers of these companies were successful under
the old system – they became General Directors – therefore they saw no
need to learn. They were 'less willing to listen [and] narrow-minded about
these things (top manager, Yukos, Russian, translation). The reluctance of
these companies to bring in foreign expertise was also linked to pride in
their past.

CONCLUSIONS

The objective of this chapter was to explain how the TMT can break with the organisation's administrative heritage in order to increase absorptive capacity. On the basis of the cross-case analysis of four Russian oil companies presented above a theoretical framework (Figure 7.1) was developed to explain this process.

The TMT characteristics of the Western-style companies were critical for breaking with administrative heritage and establishing a new dominant logic of the organisation. To the extent that the TMT was new, the pre-existing dominant logic (the Soviet administrative heritage) was no longer supported by the TMT's values and actions and thus changed. To the extent that the TMT was heterogeneous, its absorptive capacity was high and it was thus able to entertain a wider range of ideas, to assimilate external innovations and to develop new capabilities, thus facilitating the emergence of a new dominant logic within the organisation – the market-oriented logic. The TMT was thus able to break with the administrative heritage, thereby also increasing the absorptive capacity of the organisation and enabling learning.

Furthermore, by adopting a top-down management style the TMT could leverage one aspect of the Soviet heritage which was beneficial for

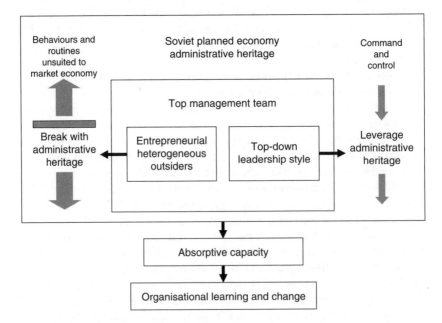

Figure 7.1   TMT, administrative heritage and absorptive capacity

implementation – the command-and-control system. The TMTs of Yukos and TNK/TNK-BP thus both broke with administrative heritage to increase absorptive capacity and leveraged administrative heritage for rapid implementation of change. In contrast the two Soviet-style companies, whose TMTs were characterised by homogeneity, conservatism and insiders, did not break with the administrative heritage and therefore did not create absorptive capacity. The basis for the theoretical framework is described in more detail below, linking the findings with the literature.

The administrative heritage of all the organisations was characterised by rigid hierarchy, lack of innovation, a blame culture, lack of knowledge sharing, an antipathy to Western business methods and no focus on profitability. The 'dominant logic' was that of the Soviet system. However, many of the top managers in the Western-style companies came from *outside* the organisations, either from an entrepreneurial or a Western business background. They were therefore not constrained by bounded rationality and limited cognition (Simon, 1955; Tripsas and Gavetti, 2000) or by path dependency and the 'stickiness' of the historical and administrative heritage (Teece et al., 1997). Furthermore, the TMTs of the Western-style companies were characterised by an entrepreneurial approach and heterogeneity, typically the characteristics which are associated with organisational change (Lawrence, 1997; Clark and Soulsby, 2007). The outsider managers were aware of the need to adapt to a changing environment and they were able to diffuse that understanding down through the organisation with their top-down style. This confirms Filatotchev et al.'s (2003) proposition that organisations privatised through divestment to strategic investors (outsiders) are likely to have higher learning capacity. A strong infusion of Western managers helped the organisations to interpret Western management information, thus broadening the frames of reference and increasing the absorptive capacity of the organisations.

The Soviet-style TMTs, on the other hand, were characterised by conservatism and homogeneity. They did not have outsiders with radically differing skills and mindsets from the 'dominant logic' of the organisation. These TMTs themselves did not have any absorptive capacity, being unable to see the relevance of new knowledge or the need to break with administrative heritage.

The entrepreneurial approach of the Western-style TMTs, together with the diversity of backgrounds, experience, age and tenure, enabled them to break with the administrative heritage, providing support for Hodgkinson and Sparrow's (2002) theory that heterogeneity in the TMT results in a lower level of investment in the prevailing strategy and a lower likelihood of cognitive inertia. The role of an 'enlightened' top management in the Western-style companies was key to overcoming the lack of experience and knowledge of operating in a market economy. The absorptive capacity of the TMTs was high, facilitating the emergence of a new dominant logic within the organisation – the market-oriented logic. The role of these TMTs was therefore akin to the one described by Cohen and Levinthal (1990) for conditions of rapid and uncertain change, where absorptive capacity is a function of the individual standing at the interface of the firm and the external environment. By mediating the influences of the external environment the TMTs were able to circumvent the constraints of history, existing structure, power and politics within their organisations (Pettigrew, 1997; Pettigrew et al., 2001). Past experience became irrelevant and the capability of people to think, analyse and make decisions was fostered.

On the other hand, the role of history, existing structure, power and politics within the Soviet-style organisations constrained change. These managers exemplified the limiting effects of managerial cognition and bounded rationality. Because there was no change in management in these companies they were subject to path dependency and the 'stickiness' of historical and administrative heritage. The managers were situated within this heritage and their views and actions were constrained by it. Absorptive capacity is determined by the prior experience of the organisation. However these managers had been successful under the old system – therefore they saw no need to change. Thus the Soviet-style companies continued in their traditional Soviet ways, and introduced Western management concepts only very slowly.

Paradoxically, acceptance of the changes introduced by the TMTs of the Western-style companies was assisted by the 'servility and a heads-down mentality' (Kornai, 1992: 121) of managers in the Soviet planned economy. The CEO's endorsement is particularly important in Russia with its strong paternalistic traditions. (Gurkov and Maital, 2001). Russian organisations were characterised by a command-and-control approach, manifested in authoritarianism, obedience to authority, the use of coercive power, and an emphasis on rank and status (Kets de Vries, 2001). Russian leaders have typically been highly directive, strong leaders with centralised decision-making and a rigid hierarchy (McCarthy et al., 2005). Russian employees were used to carrying out orders. The army metaphor (*tankisti* – tank crews), used to describe the TNK/TNK-BP top managers, was a reflection of this type of organisation. The managers in both Yukos and TNK/TNK-BP, in adopting an authoritarian top-down style, leveraged this aspect of the administrative heritage to accelerate the pace of change.

Organisational learning is vital for companies in a transition environment that must adapt to new ways of doing business. The absorptive capacity of the Russian oil companies was initially limited by their experience in a different economic system. The actions of the TMTs, that had a high absorptive capacity due to their diversity of experience and entrepreneurial approach, meant that they were able to provide the initial impetus for organisational learning. Standing at the interface of the firm and the external environment they were able to understand the importance of new ways of thinking and acting and to pass on that understanding to the rest of the organisation. Furthermore the effect of the TMT breaking with administrative heritage meant that managers came to understand that their prior learning and frames of reference were not only no longer valid, but also would not be tolerated in the strict top-down management environment. Those managers who were unable to adapt were removed. The use of expatriates and young managers, trained in Western business techniques, helped other managers to gain understanding and become more amenable to different ways of doing things. Breaking with the administrative heritage increased the absorptive capacity of the organisation by making prior knowledge obsolete and acknowledging the necessity to acquire new knowledge relevant to market conditions via the process of organisational learning. Since the Soviet-style companies had failed to break with their administrative heritage they exhibited no evidence of absorptive capacity.

This chapter has examined the first stage of organisational transformation – break with the past. This served to enhance the absorptive capacity of the Western-style organisations as a result of the actions of the TMT. This enhanced absorptive capacity created the basis for the second stage of organisational transformation – the initiation of organisational learning, which is described in the next chapter.

NOTE

1. See Appendix Methodology for more information on the paradigm approach.

8. Organisational learning and the development of organisational capabilities

This chapter builds on the discussions in Chapters 3 and 7 using a cross-case analysis to explain how the theoretical concepts advanced in the organisational learning literature help explain enterprise transformation in transition economies. On the basis of iteration between the literature and the grounded case analysis I propose a theoretical framework for organisational learning in organisations facing major external change.

How do organisations faced with radical external change learn how to survive and prosper under a new set of circumstances? A call to link the study of organisational change with learning theory (Hendry, 1996) has been answered by studies utilising organisational learning perspectives to explore this question in both joint ventures (for instance, Lyles and Salk, 1996) and domestically-owned firms (Newman, 2000; Uhlenbruck et al., 2003). Suggested causes of lack of learning include weak 'absorptive capacity' (Lyles and Salk, 1996), lack of managerial knowledge (Child and Czegledy, 1996), organisational cultures that inhibit knowledge sharing (Michailova and Husted, 2003) and cognitive barriers to recognising and implementing new organisational routines (Newman, 2000). However, these studies still do not provide a detailed understanding of the processes by which organisational learning leads to the development of organisational capabilities.

This chapter investigates these issues in the Russian oil industry exploring the variations between the companies and their causes. On this basis, I propose a theoretical framework explaining a two-stage process of organisational transformation, the first stage being the development of operational capabilities via exploitation learning and the second stage being the development of strategic flexibility via exploration learning. This model corresponds to Stages II and III of the integrative framework described in Chapter 3. In this chapter the focus is on organisational learning, whereas Chapter 9 will elaborate on the concept of dynamic capabilities. Both are interrelated and are relevant for stages II and III of organisational transformation. The key question addressed in this chapter is:

How do the concepts of exploitation and exploration learning help us to understand the processes by which an organisation in a transition economy develops the operational capabilities required for short-term survival and the strategic flexibility required for sustainable competitive advantage?

CROSS-CASE COMPARISON

This section describes the process of organisational learning within the four Russian oil companies in two sections: exploitation learning and exploration learning. The break with administrative heritage and the creation of absorptive capacity was covered in Chapter 7. The data display in Table 8.1 provides a cross-case comparison of the four companies with respect to organisational learning and the development of operational capabilities and strategic flexibility. For the Western-style companies it includes an indication of the timing of each stage and links this with the development of absorptive capacity.

Exploitation Learning

For the Western-style organisations, developing the absorptive capacity of the organisation by breaking with the administrative heritage prepared the ground for the first stage of organisational learning – exploitation learning. (See Table 8.1 for a cross-case data display and Table 8.2 for a data display using the paradigm approach to explain exploitation learning in Yukos). Exploitation learning (Tables 8.1 and 8.2, row 2) involved the acquisition of Western knowledge to increase production and efficiency. Expatriates were a key source of knowledge. Basic Western petroleum engineering principles, acquired via an alliance with a Western oil services company, enabled Yukos to 'catch a lot of low hanging fruit' in terms of a rapid increase in oil production (senior manager, TNK-BP, Western).

Training was important in both Western-styles companies. 'Right from the beginning, Khodorkovsky (CEO, Yukos) set the target – 100 per cent training' (middle manager, TNK-BP, Russian, translation). Khodorkovsky encouraged employees to select and exploit Western management practices: 'When I looked at all the Western methods I selected the best, and also the ones which could be implemented in the company' (middle manager, TNK-BP, Russian, translation). Relationships were established with leading Western business schools and a masters programme in petroleum engineering, co-organised by Heriot-Watt University, was set up in Tomsk, Siberia. The young specialists graduating from this course, the so-called

Table 8.1 Cross-case comparison of organisational learning and the development of organisational capabilities

	Western-style organisations		Soviet-style organisations	
	Yukos	TNK (TNK-BP)	Lukoil	Surgutneftegaz
1 Absorptive capacity (see Chapter 7)	**Stage 1** • TMT drive • Top-down management • Promote innovation versus experience • Early successes • Crisis stabilisation (1995–2001) **Stage 2** • Move to participatory leadership • Empower • Encourage innovation (2002–03)	**Stage 1 (TNK)** • TMT drive • Top-down management • Early successes • Crisis stabilisation (1995–2003) **Stage 2 (TNK-BP)** • Train to think out of the box • Empower • Encourage innovation (2003–05)	• Little • Constrained by tradition, oil background and pride • Few Western employees	• None • Constrained by tradition, oil background and pride • Soviet-style management • No Western employees
2 Exploitation learning	• Western expertise via alliances • Expatriates • Russians with Western experience • Visit Western companies • Training in Russia and abroad	**TNK** • Western expertise via alliances • Expatriates • Russians with Western experience • Training (1998–2003)	• Acquire foreign assets • Few Western employees (none on TMT) • Western consultants • Management training • Cross-functional working groups	• No Western employees • Technical training in West • Copy Western technology • No alliances • No Western

		TNK-BP		
	• Learn by doing • Job rotation • Project teams • Break down silos (1998-2003)	• Many expatriates • Access to BP knowledge • Training • Mutual secondees • Rotating regional master-classes • Learn by doing • Job rotation • Project teams • Working groups (2003-05)	• BUT silos and resistance to information sharing	management techniques
3 Operational capabilities	• HR • Finance • Technology • Production • Marketing • Corporate governance • PR and investor relations • Planning • Business processes (1998-2003)	**TNK** • Finance • Technology • Production • PR • Marketing **TNK-BP** • HR • Planning • Project management • HSE • Corporate governance	*In process of implementation:* • Finance • Planning • Project evaluation • Business processes • Limited HR	• No Western functional capabilities • Technology based • Soviet-style social support

Table 8.1 (continued)

	Western-style organisations		Soviet-style organisations	
	Yukos	TNK (TNK-BP)	Lukoil	Surgutneftegaz
4 Exploration learning	• Learn by mistakes • Encourage innovation • Begin to delegate decision-making (2002–03)	• Business processes (1998-2003) **TNK-BP** • learn by doing • Project teams • Job rotation • Learning by mistakes • Working groups • Change agents • Encourage participation and innovation (2003–05)	Not applicable	Not applicable
5 Strategic Flexibility	• Evidence of innovation in oil production • Still largely vested in TMT, but CEO failed to adapt to new political environment (2003)	• In process of development – focus still on exploitation learning (2003–05)	Not applicable	Not applicable

'Heriot-Watters', completed their training in the Yukos technical centre in Moscow and were then sent out to the regions in senior positions. On the collapse of Yukos, many of these young managers were recruited by TNK-BP. TNK-BP had the additional advantage of many expatriates and BP secondees providing expertise.

In contrast, Surgutneftegaz had little interest in learning about Western management techniques. They employed no expatriates and did not utilise Western oil service companies. However they did send their specialists to the USA to learn about technology, then developed a 'me too' version themselves. Yet, this approach did not create the direct interfaces that would be required to effectively transfer tacit knowledge.

Lukoil engaged in the acquisition of both technology and Western management techniques. Of all the Russian oil companies Lukoil was the most active internationally and 20 per cent of their assets were located abroad, however respondents believed this was more for status reasons than for learning. They did not perceive the need to employ expatriates: 'To be honest I just don't understand what they are doing in Yukos and TNK, when the top managers are foreigners. . . . I do not approve of this' (senior manager, Lukoil, Russian, translation). However the Lukoil leadership recognised that some managers were too fixed in their ways to change and needed to be replaced: 'It is not always easy to move them onto the track of market thinking. It is necessary to gradually replace them with new managers' (senior manager, Lukoil, Russian, translation). Some Lukoil managers were sent on business training courses, but concern was voiced about the extent to which any newly trained managers would be accepted back into suitable positions in the organisation. However a manager from head office was of the view that 'All bright individuals who work well . . . all progress, they are in demand, regardless of their rank (middle manager, Lukoil, Russian, translation). The reality was probably that parts of the organisation (for example, the head office) were much more amenable to young managers with Western training than others (for example, the regions).

Thus, the two Soviet-style oil companies differed in their approach to learning. Lukoil was more open to Western management skills than Surgutneftegaz, but still lagged far behind the Western-style companies. Surgutneftegaz, and to a lesser extent Lukoil, failed to create conditions that would lead to unlearning of existing routines, which would be a precondition for learning new practices (Newman, 2000). The primary cause was the inability of the TMT to envisage major change or to identify and implement radically different routines.

Learning by doing was important in Yukos and TNK/TNK-BP for internalisation of knowledge. In Yukos, there was a policy of job rotation so that

Table 8.2   Data display of exploitation learning – Yukos

Paradigm	Findings	Examples
Conditions	**1998–2003 Move to market** • Low oil production and 1998 financial crisis in Russia provides impetus for organisational learning	The Russian oil industry now is very, very different from what it was a decade ago . . . There's no question that they are basically now quite commercially focused. . . . There's also been a number of policy changes that have allowed that supplier response to occur, like the devaluation of the rouble, certain kinds of tax reform, . . . legal reforms and so forth . . . it's been sufficient to allow the industry to completely change and revolutionise itself already. (energy consultant, Western)
	TMT • Heterogeneous, entrepreneurial, outsiders • Top-down management style	Khodorkovsky was lucky with his management team. They are a team of people with great professionalism, motivated not only by money, but with a huge desire for learning and self-development. (middle manager, Yukos, Russian)
	Break with administrative heritage • Replace blockers • New managers with CEO support • Strategic alliances • Training • Quick successes • Learn by mistakes • Project teams • Incentives	I came here, aged 26, and became deputy to the head geologist. This had never happened before. Probably in the whole history of Russia there hadn't been this kind of thing where the senior geologist was 26 years old. (senior manager, Yukos, regional, Russian)
	1 Increase absorptive capacity • TMT drive • Top-down management • Promote innovation versus experience • Early successes • Crisis stabilisation	Khodorkovsky . . . advocated innovations . . . he promoted the 'Western' direction of development. And if he had not propounded and created this culture, Yukos would not have changed – I can say that unequivocally. (top manager, Yukos, Russian)

Table 8.2 (continued)

Paradigm	Findings	Examples
Actions/ Interactions	2 **Exploitation learning** • Western expertise via alliances • Expatriates • Russians with Western experience • Visit Western companies • Training in Russia and abroad • Learn by doing • Job rotation • Project teams • Break down silos	The brilliant thing was Khodorkovsky, he hired maybe . . . two dozen . . . expats. Let's say he pays them $1 million a year cash compensation, that's 25 million a year. And the technology that they brought, I mean there was so many multiples of that. I mean he just got it at a steal. (Investment Bank executive, Western) In Yukos we divided personal development into 5 areas: development on the job, development through business projects, development through learning from others etc. So development was a broad process. And training courses they are the least important, because training courses are not the most developmental. The most developmental are business projects. (middle manager, TNK-BP, Russian)
Consequences	3 **Operational capabilities** developed, e.g. HR, finance, production	We are growing about 2 times faster than the industry as a whole. . . . We succeeded in 2–3 years in building a new management system and a new technological system. . . . We began to change, earlier than others, the system which used to exist in Soviet times. (senior manager, Yukos, Russian)

managers could gain experience in different environments. Demonstrable success from the application of Western techniques was another key way for specialists to internalise knowledge: 'If I'm doing it one way and you can't demonstrate to me how . . . you're proposing it's going to be better, why should I change?' (top manager, TNK-BP, regional, Western).

The different methods of knowledge internalisation in the Western-style companies helped employees to overcome the lack of organisational and technical skills required for survival in the different context of the market economy (Swaan, 1997). Learning by doing was a way of acquiring some of the tacit knowledge associated with these capabilities (Meyer and Møller, 1998).

The spread of exploitation learning into the regions presented problems for all companies due to geographic spread and multiple entities. Yukos employed 100 000 people over a large geographical area from European Russia and the Baltics to Eastern Siberia. The problems were magnified by the existence of organisational silos: 'one of the features of Yukos is in every function, in every department, people have a rather narrow perspective' (top manager, Yukos, Western). One way of breaking down these barriers and transferring knowledge was to encourage a culture where communication and open discussion became a part of life: 'If you have a set of common goals . . . and the culture of discussing things, then I think it works towards just trying to work out mutual acceptable solutions' (middle manager, Yukos, Russian). In Yukos there was a policy of rotating directors' meetings around different sites. And in TNK-BP, so-called 'masterclasses' were organised at centres of excellence: 'But it is not direct training, but indirect learning, more like professional networking, linked with the implementation of innovations' (middle manager, TNK-BP, Russian). Change agents, such as the Heriot Watters in Yukos, were also used to disseminate new ideas. In TNK-BP, six technology working groups were set up and given substantial support. The Corrosion working group made a case for, and received, $1 billion over five years for a corrosion management project. Similar working groups were used in functions such as human resources and planning.

In Lukoil, there were various ways of disseminating best practice. Professional skills competitions were held in different locations. Senior management meetings were held every quarter, visiting factories and discussing problems across the different business divisions. Knowledge was also shared via cross-functional working groups. However corporate silos were a strong brake on knowledge sharing across the company. The powerful regional companies – the 'fiefdoms' – resisted sharing information. The process of knowledge dissemination was therefore slow and perceived as painful for those involved.

Organisational learning in the Western-style companies was exploitation learning since it involved refinement, choice, production efficiency, selection, implementation and execution in relation to business techniques and processes which were already in existence in Western companies. The effect of this exploitation learning was a significant improvement in operational capabilities (Tables 8.1 and 8.2, row 3). Yukos, in particular, developed many of the basic operational capabilities required for success in a market economy. Russian competitors readily acknowledged that Yukos were ahead of their peers in developing Western capabilities: 'Everyone agrees that they [Yukos] made a significant breakthrough from the point of view of establishing a normal ... corporation by Western standards' (top manager, TNK-BP, Russian). TNK had also made significant strides in production capability, public relations and marketing. A strong retail brand was developed and Western-style petrol stations began to appear.

The Soviet-style companies had made significantly less progress in developing operational capabilities, which was consistent with their reduced level of exploitation learning. Lukoil had started to make improvements in some of the functional areas, particularly in finance and business planning. However progress was slow. The technical skills of Surgutneftegaz were respected by the Western community but there was no evidence of the introduction of any Western processes relating to HR, finance, marketing, public relations or health and safety. Surgutneftegaz increased their oil production, yet this output growth was achieved by drilling more oil wells, rather than improvements in efficiency. Thus, their growth path resembles more closely 'extensive growth' strategies employed in the early days of the Soviet Union than the 'intensive growth' employed by resource-scarce market economies (Lavigne, 1999).

Exploration Learning

The operational capabilities created by exploitation learning would enable survival in the market economy, yet they would not equip the companies to attain sustainable competitive advantage in a volatile environment. This requires higher levels of learning, namely exploration learning (Table 8.1, row 4). In the time period under study, the main focus for the companies was on developing the operational capabilities for survival in a market economy. This subsection describes some of the early signs of exploration learning in the Western-style companies, however there was much less evidence of this type of learning. Nevertheless both Western-style companies had started to make progress in developing exploration learning by changing internal structures and cultures such as to encourage experimentation.

Yukos' predominantly authoritarian management style, which was used to break with administrative heritage and introduce exploitation learning, nevertheless imposed restrictions on the ability of the organisation to develop its own unique capabilities rather than just copying best practice from elsewhere. This, prima facie, would appear to confirm the incompatibility of exploitation and exploration learning. However, there was some evidence that Yukos was moving towards a more participatory management style, encouraging risk-taking and innovation. Some employees were trusted and supported: 'I was given total and absolute support.' (middle manager, TNK-BP, Russian, translation). An example of successful innovation in Yukos was the establishment of a new database which could prioritise wells for maintenance. This innovation was a contributing factor to the dramatic growth in oil production. One expatriate in the organisation was, however, rather scathing about the innovation capacity of the organisation: 'There weren't many ideas coming up – creativity and innovation has been killed by the former system' (top manager, Yukos, Western). Although Yukos fostered innovation, there was some doubt about how successful they were at encouraging people to come up with breakthrough ideas: 'that really does just happen at the top' (investment bank executive, Western).

With the creation of TNK-BP in 2003, the large numbers of expatriates and Russians with Western experience contributed to a critical mass of knowledge and experience within the organisation. One significant contribution of BP in terms of organisational processes and systems was the idea that a looser system of control could be more effective than a strict authoritarian system. Establishing boundary conditions and then allowing people the freedom to innovate within those conditions was important for exploration learning. In Yukos, too, there were signs of an environment that encouraged innovation: 'Management put absolutely no brake, absolutely none, on any innovations'. (middle manager, TNK-BP, Russian, translation). Employees were encouraged to come up with new ideas and projects. Even mistakes were permitted if some learning derived from them, which presented a radical departure from the blame culture of the Soviet system where knowledge sharing was discouraged. However, as mentioned above, innovation was not encouraged in all parts of the organization.

Since TNK had lagged Yukos in the development of operational capabilities, the main focus of TNK-BP was on bringing the company up to Western operating standards. However several respondents recognised the considerable innovation potential of Russian managers. Additionally, BP had experience of operating in many different countries, adapting to political and social changes. They were used to delegating authority down through the organisation, enabling decision-making at all levels. Thus BP's experience and leadership style encouraged exploration learning. Sustainable competitive advantage would depend on BP succeeding in pushing through changes in terms of empowering the organisation and encouraging strategic flexibility (Table 8.1, row 5): 'We've got to try to create capability, where they think for themselves. . . . A sustainable future is only from trying to unlock that natural capability' (top manager, TNK-BP, Western).

The Western-style companies were both moving towards an early stage of exploration learning, which was needed for the development of strategic flexibility to adapt to changes in the environment. The gradual change from the authoritarian management style which had originally prevailed in Yukos and TNK, to a more participatory style, encouraged innovation and experimentation. In contrast, there was no evidence of exploration learning in the Soviet-style companies, which were either still in the early stages of exploitation learning (Lukoil) or not engaging in organisational learning at all (Surgutneftegaz).

CONCLUSIONS

On the basis of iteration between the literature and the grounded case studies (presented in Chapters 4–6) I develop a new framework for organisational learning in transition economies (Figure 8.1). The role of the TMT varies at different stages of enterprise transformation. In the first stage of transformation into an exploitation learning organisation, an authoritarian approach forces a break with the administrative heritage. Exploitation learning leads to the development of operational capabilities for survival

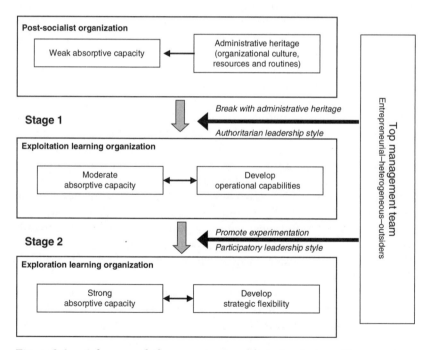

Figure 8.1   A framework for organisational learning in transition economies

in a market economy. In the second stage of transformation into an exploration learning organisation, a more participatory leadership style fosters experimentation and risk taking. Exploration learning facilitates strategic flexibility permitting development of new indigenous capabilities that support sustained competitive advantage.

The cross-case analysis of the Western-style companies (Yukos and TNK/BP) shows that TMTs play a pivotal role in organisational learning processes. Top managers who came from outside the organisation were able to break with the administrative heritage, which was characterised on the one hand by rigid hierarchy, lack of innovation, and a blame culture, and on the other by an antipathy to Western business methods and a lack of focus on profitability. Top managers located outside this heritage were more able to overcome path dependency. They did not have vested interests tied to existing structures and they were not affected by cognitive inertia. Their entrepreneurial approach enabled them to do things differently. These characteristics resemble features observed in other turbulent contexts, which show that short tenure and heterogeneity of the TMT assist organisational change (Lawrence, 1997; Clark and Soulsby, 2005) and improve organisational performance in turbulent environments (Keck, 1997).

The role of the TMT varies at different stages of enterprise transformation. In the first stage, the TMTs in the Western companies largely used an authoritarian approach to overcome the dominant logic of the organisation. Acceptance of the changes was assisted by the fact that the general characteristic of managers in the Soviet planned economy was one of 'servility and a heads-down mentality' (Kornai, 1992: 121). The break with the administrative heritage, enforced by the TMT, provided the necessary conditions to initiate organisational learning. Without the impetus from a management with radically differing skills and mindsets from the 'dominant logic' of the organisation, the organisation would not be capable of absorbing and utilising knowledge, simply because members would not recognise the relevance of that knowledge. The TMT were aware of the need to adapt to a changing environment and they were able to diffuse that understanding down through the organisation. This confirms Filatotchev et al.'s (2003) proposition that organisations privatised through sale to strategic investors ('outsiders') are more likely to have higher learning and absorptive capacity.

In the first stage of organisational learning the emphasis was on exploitation learning (March, 1991) or adaptive (survival) learning (Senge, 1990). This was required to 'cope' with the new conditions of a market economy. Knowledge was acquired, assimilated and disseminated throughout the organisation. The scope of acquisition and implementation of new routines was extensive and the change involved was radical.

However, unlike Newman (2000), who suggested this was exploration learning, I maintain that, although change was radical, this learning was still at the level of exploitation learning, since it involved the acquisition and implementation of operational capabilities already in existence in Western companies.

In the second stage of organisational learning, there were signs in both Western-style organisations of a move towards exploration (March, 1991). This was facilitated by a change in the management style of the TMT. By the end of 2002, the Yukos TMT was beginning to mature towards a more participatory style of leadership, encouraging innovation, risk-taking and decision-making and fostering a climate for exploration learning. TNK at that time was not so far advanced as Yukos in the development of operational capabilities, having come later to the privatisation process. The main focus for the new TNK/BP JV, formed in 2003, was on exploitation learning to achieve Western operating standards. However, BP's participatory management style and encouragement of innovation and risk-taking implied that exploration learning would gradually be developed. This transition from exploitation to exploration learning in the Western-style companies could be considered to be an example of punctuated equilibrium, whereby a long period of exploitation learning is followed by a short burst of exploration learning (see Burgelman's empirical study of Intel 2002). This would imply that the sought-after balance between the two types of learning for organisational success (March 1991) is achieved via the sequential allocation of attention rather than by a simultaneous ambidextrous approach (see Gupta et al., 2006 for a discussion of this issue).

Whereas the break with administrative heritage had created moderate absorptive capacity enabling organisational learning to take place in the first place, subsequent exploitation learning further increased the absorptive capacity of the organisations. Strong absorptive capacity, fostered also by the encouragement of experimentation, seemed likely to enable the development of entirely new capabilities such as to provide the strategic flexibility (Hitt et al. 1998) to adapt to the turbulent conditions of a transition economy. This is important for such companies because of the need for new business models appropriate for emerging economy contexts (London and Hart, 2004; Prahalad, 2004).

The Soviet-style companies provide a sharp contrast (theoretical replication). Surgutneftegaz developed technical capabilities, but neglected business capabilities. It continued to operate Soviet-style and exhibited no organisational transformation. In Lukoil there was some evidence of exploitation learning and the development of operational capabilities, but the process was constrained by a homogenous, traditional TMT that did not tackle the Soviet administrative heritage. The characteristics of the TMT and their ability to break with the administrative heritage therefore determine whether or not, and at what pace, organisational learning takes place.

This chapter has expanded on the integrative framework presented in Chapter 3, with a particular focus on organisational learning (exploitation and exploration) and the development of operational capabilities and strategic flexibility. The next chapter will explain the linkages between organisational learning and dynamic capabilities.

9. Organisational learning and dynamic capabilities

In this chapter I develop a theoretical framework that explains the linkages between organisational learning and dynamic capabilities and how they affect organisational transformation. It takes the framework developed in Chapter 8 a step further by introducing the intermediary concept of dynamic capabilities between organisational learning and organisational capability outcomes. It broadly corresponds to Stages II and III of the integrative framework presented in Chapter 3.

Organisational learning (Shrivastava, 1983; Fiol and Lyles, 1985) and the development of dynamic capabilities (Teece et al., 1997; Eisenhardt and Martin, 2000; Helfat et al., 2006) have become of pivotal interest to organisation scholars as well as management practice. However, the dynamics of these processes as well as their impact on organisational performance remain poorly understood. This is a particular concern for organisations facing radical change in their external environment, which thus have to accelerate their learning and the reconfiguration of their resources (Newman, 2000; Fey and Denison, 2003). Moreover, organisational learning may be subject to contextual influences that have rarely been analysed in previous research (Tsui et al., 2004; March, 2005; Meyer, 2007).

In this chapter, on the basis of the empirical research, I explain how exploitation learning is linked to the deployment function of dynamic capabilities, involving the reconfiguration, divestment, creation and integration of resources to provide the operational capabilities required to survive in the market economy in the short term. On the other hand, exploration learning relates to the search and selection function of dynamic capabilities, involving search, monitoring, reacting and creation to generate the strategic flexibility required for sustainable competitive advantage vis-à-vis their Western peers. In explaining these relationships I make two main contributions. First I build understanding of the relationships between organisational learning and dynamic capabilities, and second I explain how these affect organisational transformation in organisations in transition economies. The two companies that successfully engaged in organisational learning developed dynamic capabilities, that enabled them to lead the modernisation of the industry in a volatile market environment.

The theoretical perspectives on organisational learning and dynamic capabilities as they relate to organisational transformation in transition economies were presented in Chapter 3. This chapter presents the findings from the empirical research on the four Russian oil companies, using data displays to assist understanding. On the basis of the empirical research I propose a new conceptual framework to explain the links between organisational learning, dynamic capabilities and organisational transformation, linking the findings back to the literature. The key question addressed in this chapter is:

> How does the linkage between organisational learning and dynamic capabilities help us to understand the processes by which an organisation in a transition economy develops the operational capabilities required for short term survival and the strategic flexibility required for sustainable competitive advantage?

CROSS-CASE COMPARISON

I discuss the case evidence in two steps. First I explore dynamic capabilities in terms of resource reconfiguration, divestment, and integration (Teece et al., 1997). This, together with the information on exploitation learning in the preceding chapter, illustrates how the Western-style companies were able to create operational capabilities which fitted them for short-term survival in a market economy. This discussion is supported by in-case and cross-case data displays in Tables 9.1 and 9.2.

Second, I present evidence search and selection and resource creation, the dynamic capabilities which are supported by the exploration learning described in Chapter 8. The cross-case data display in Table 9.3 illustrates the linkage between exploration learning and the search and selection function of dynamic capabilities for Yukos and TNK/BP. The distinction between the two concepts of exploration learning and the search and select function of dynamic capabilities becomes rather blurred. Indeed, as Zollo and Winter (2002) point out, organisational learning forms both a part of the dynamic capabilities of organisations and contributes to them. I demonstrate how these interlinked processes had the potential to develop strategic flexibility and sustainable competitive advantage for the Western-style companies. In all respects the Soviet-style companies provide a contrast, thus representing theoretical replication.

Exploitation Learning and Deployment

Details of exploitation learning were provided in Chapter 8. This organisational learning provided the Western-style companies with the necessary knowledge of a Western business model to be able to reconfigure resources (Table 9.1 and 9.2, row 4) to bring systems, processes and routines in line with those required for success in a market economy: 'The restructuring was complex – on all fronts. This was both restructuring of human assets, for example training, development and classification, and it was restructuring of the material assets, and as well the improvement of business processes and reporting systems' (senior manager, Yukos, Russian, translation). But not all the new systems were fully embedded in the organisations, for instance the Hay grading system: 'The results were not always used correctly' (top manager, Yukos, Russian, translation).

Restructuring and the introduction of new business systems was most difficult in the regions. Radical action was undertaken if managers persisted in their old behaviours. Whole management teams were replaced, for example in Yukos' Samara subsidiary. This job rotation helped 'to knock down the walls that were . . . put up by the Soviet traditions' (consultant, Western).

Physical assets were also reconfigured – basic hygiene factors were improved, whether via new, well-appointed, open-plan offices, or improved working conditions for shift-workers on the oilfields: 'Either you arrive back from work to a place where you haven't even got a place to dry your working clothes out, or you live in a "three-star hotel" – of course your performance is going to be better!' (senior manager, TNK-BP, regional, Russian, translation).

Lukoil showed some evidence of restructuring and introduction of new business systems, albeit slower than in the Western-style companies: 'People here are adequate . . . they are mastering modern technology. . . . Perhaps not at such a rapid pace, no such radical transformations have taken place' (middle manager, Lukoil, Russian, translation). No substantial restructuring happened in Surgutneftegaz.

Resource divestment (Tables 9.1 and 9.2, row 5) included transferring social assets, such as kindergartens and farms, to local authorities, hiving off non-core activities such as maintenance and transport, and removing employees who were not prepared to adapt to the new Western business practices: 'Many people had to change their approach totally – both their relationship to work and their relationships with other people – this is not always easy. Some couldn't take it, some could not make the transition. And that happened quite often' (senior manager, Yukos, Russian, translation).

Resource integration (Tables 9.1 and 9.2, row 6) in the Western-style companies involved integrating various subcultures, aligning people behind common goals, improving telecommunications, integrating operations, and, for TNK-BP, managing the synergies between the two companies. Integration of subcultures was challenging, for instance: 'There are two

Table 9.1 Data display of exploitation learning, dynamic capabilities (deployment) and operational capabilities – TNK-BP

Paradigm	Findings	Examples
Conditions	• TNK initiates organisational transformation • TNK-BP JV established 2003 • Significant influx of Western expertise from BP • BP acquires control and exerts influence on the JV • Operational and cultural integration commences	'The first trick, before . . . decentralised initiatives, is rigid centralisation, strict control of cash flows, transparency in operations, and . . . driving international management techniques top-down through the company.' (Senior manager, TNK, Western) 'I [TNK] achieved a lot . . . I were rather successful, developing rapidly. And I only need you [BP] for your technology and technical skills. And then suddenly – wham! – everyone starts to live by new rules, even to the extent that all office doors are open.' (Top Manager, TNK-BP, Russian, translation)
Actions/ Interactions	**Exploitation learning** (Chapter 8) 1 • *Knowledge acquisition* – many expatriates, secondees and Russians with BP experience, Yukos specialists (Heriot-Watters), technology block expertise, supplement tertiary education, work shadowing, fewer training programmes than Yukos, focus on upstream not downstream 2 • *Knowledge internalisation* – learn by doing, involvement in projects, finding cultural key, demonstrable success. 3 • *Knowledge dissemination* – masterclasses/	'Without the kind of people, who know in practice how a Western company works, changing a Russian company is very difficult, because it is not realistic to think that you can do everything just by reading the text books . . . There needs to be a critical mass of people who are prepared to change the company' (Middle Manager, TNK-BP, Russian, translation.) '. . . Learn as you go . . . various people got involved and they try to understand what exactly they were supposed to be doing in their section of work.' (Senior Manager, TNK-BP, Russian/Western, translation) 'I think that the company resolves the problem [of transfer of best practice] by transferring top managers . . . from time to time from one sector to another [laughter]. He goes from one division to

	networking, job rotation, publication of best practice, working groups, focus on communication, change agents	another. He is just about being recognised there, when he has to start learning things here.' (Senior Manager, TNK-BP, Regional, Russian, translation)

Dynamic capabilities (deployment)

4 • *Resource reconfiguration* – resolve charter issues to give BP control, span breakers, clamp-down on corruption, organisational restructuring/remove silos, HSE regulations, open plan offices

'. . . Lots of span-breakers, you know Russian and BP heritage, or independent expatriates, or just independent Russians, all through the structure, so it's designed to create lots of checks and balances.' (Top Manager, TNK-BP, Western)

5 • *Resource divestment* – no evidence, considering divestment of oilfield services

6 • *Resource integration* – resolve partner conflicts, operational and cultural integration, language training, deal with different management styles, expatriates vs. locals, synergies

'I work real hard at coming up with a somewhat of a standardised organisation among all the different performance units because standardisation allows the benchmarking to occur.' (Top Manager, TNK-BP, Regional, Western)

Consequences 7 • **Operational capabilities** developed for survival in market economy – increasing empowerment, knowledge sharing, HR, HSE, project management

'What is "personnel"? Traditionally in the Soviet Union "personnel" were the people who sit there and deal with hiring and firing people and determine any benefits. But now, with the arrival of BP and Western people, extremely interesting . . . things are happening in HR.' (Top Manager, TNK-BP, Russian, translation)

Table 9.2   Cross-case display: exploitation learning and dynamic capabilities (deployment)

	Western-style		Soviet-style	
	Yukos	TNK/TNK-BP	Lukoil	Surgutneftegaz
1 Exploitation learning Knowledge Acquisition	Western expertise via alliances, expatriates, Russians with Western experience, visit Western companies • 100% training in Russia and abroad	**TNK** • Western expertise (technology and management) via alliances, expatriates, Russians with Western experience • Some training **TNK-BP** • Many expatriates • BP knowledge • Training • Secondees	• Acquire Western assets • Few Western employees (none on TMT) • Western consultants • Some management training in Russia and abroad	• Technical specialists trained in West • Copy Western technology • No alliances • No acquisition of Western management skills
2 Knowledge Internalisation	Learn by doing • Learn by mistakes • Job rotation	**TNK** • No evidence **TNK-BP** • Learn by doing • Project teams • Job rotation • Learning by mistakes	• No evidence	• No evidence
3 Knowledge dissemination	Project teams • Communication • Break down silos • ICT including email • Databases • Data systematisation	**TNK** • Top-down **TNK-BP** • Rotating regional masterclasses • Publishing improvement projects	• Some sharing best practice • Cross-functional working groups • BUT silos and resistance to information sharing	• No evidence

		• Working groups • Change agents		
4 Dynamic Capabilities Reconfigure resources	Resolution of debts • Consolidate legal entities • Organisational restructuring • Rapidly establish new business systems • Not all embedded • Introduce corporate governance • Replace blockers • Job rotation • Break down silos	**TNK** • Acquire and consolidate assets • Restructuring • Pay off debts. • Replace blockers • Set up controls • Upgrade facilities **TNK-BP** • BP gain control • Span breakers • Clamp-down on corruption • Remove silos • Introduce HSE regulations • Open plan offices	• Sell shares to Western shareholders • Introduce corporate governance • Initiate cost reduction programme • Slowly introduce new business systems	• No evidence
5 Divest resources	• Remove non-aligned employees • Transfer social assets • Hive off non-core activities	**TNK** • Remove non-aligned employees • Transfer social assets **TNK-BP** • No evidence • Considering divestment of oilfield services	• Some divestment of non-core assets	• No evidence
6 Integrate resources	• Integrate sub-cultures • Align behind common goals • Improve telecoms • Integration not uniform across company	**TNK** • Integrate acquired entities **TNK-BP** • resolve partner conflicts • Operational and cultural integration • Language training	• Attempt to integrate and coordinate company activities across fiefdoms	• No evidence

Table 9.2 (continued)

	Western-style		Soviet-style	
	Yukos	TNK/TNK-BP	Lukoil	Surgutneftegaz
		• Expatriate *vs.* local issues • Manage synergies		
7 Operational Capabilities	• HR, finance, technology, production, marketing, corporate governance, PR and investor relations, planning, systematic business processes	**TNK** • Finance, technology, production, marketing, PR **TNK-BP** • HR empowerment, knowledge management, project management, HSE, corporate governance, systematic business processes	• Slow implementation: finance, planning, project evaluation, business processes • Limited HR • Poor knowledge management and ICT	• No Western functional capabilities, technology based, Soviet-style social support
8 Short-term survival	• Leading oil company in terms of move to a **Western operating model** **Robust** in context of a market economy • Some signs of **empowering** organisation • Operational capabilities not completely **embedded**	**TNK** • Rapid change, but less efficient than Yukos • Attract Western investor **TNK-BP** • Reduce costs • Potential to become leading oil company • Increasingly **robust** in market economy • BP encourage empowerment • Operational capabilities not fully **embedded**	• Lost leadership position on oil production first to Yukos and then TNK-BP • Higher cost of production meant **reduced efficiency and robustness**	• Costs high compared to competitors • Inefficient drilling/oil production • **Less efficient and robust** than competitors

different formations of people in this industry. There are the old oil men with their good relationships and large production experience, and there is the young generation which does not have any significant production experience, but they do have current [business] knowledge. Now, if these people of the old formation start to sabotage . . .' (top manager, Yukos, Russian, translation). Conservatism predominated in the regions. However even there the culture had changed, because managers were in constant communication with the Moscow office, helped by improved telecommunications. The availability of company telephone and email directories, quite normal for Western companies, was a huge step forward. Job rotation had also been a key factor in promoting a common culture and in sharing knowledge.

TNK-BP had to resolve a conflict of interest between the two partners: the TNK shareholders were interested in short-term gain – maximising the company value within the three years they were tied into the venture – whereas BP were interested in long-term value creation. The conflict at the top was translated downwards into the organisation, but was mitigated by recruiting 40 per cent of the people in head office from outside the two companies: 'A large wave of outsiders came in, who had no past' (middle manager, TNK-BP, Russian, translation). Each company had different assets to bring to the joint venture: 'You cannot import everything from BP or you cannot resist forever trying to do things the way TNK has always done things. It's a little give and take going on' (senior manager, TNK-BP, Russian/Western).

In Lukoil there was some evidence of resource integration and coordination, however this was significantly hampered by the resistance to change of the more conservative elements in the organisation and of the strong subsidiaries (so-called 'fiefdoms').

The Western-style companies thus used exploitation learning to develop dynamic capabilities that enabled the (re-)deployment of resources, which in turn provided the operational capabilities (Tables 9.1 and 9.2, row 7) that secured survival in a market economy: 'I succeeded in 2–3 years in building a new management system and a new technological system. This is a complex integrated system which allows us to achieve results. I began to change, earlier than others, the system which used to exist in Soviet times' (senior manager, Yukos, Russian, translation). Russian competitors and Western observers acknowledged that Yukos were leading in developing Western capabilities: 'Everyone agrees that they [Yukos] made a significant breakthrough from the point of view of establishing a normal . . . corporation by Western standards' (top manager, TNK-BP, Russian, translation).

TNK had also made progress, particularly in production capability, however. 'They were a higher cost producer [than Yukos], no question about that' (energy consultant, Western). They also lagged Yukos because they did not place the same emphasis on Western values: 'There was a lot he [CEO TNK] did not manage to do. . . . It was a period of time when all these Western values were not much in demand' (top manager, TNK-BP, Russian, translation). But enough progress had been made on turning around the company, setting up organisational controls and increasing oil production to make the company attractive to a Western investor. Once BP arrived, the focus changed to introducing systematic business processes and improving competencies in HR, marketing etc.: 'So all facets of trying to build capability, waiting for the cavalry to come over the hill five years from now' (top manager, TNK-BP, Western). Many new processes and systems were being put in place, but as in Yukos, they still needed time to be embedded: 'It is very difficult to create processes, they are still ineffective . . . for the time being they are still like a foam . . . the waves are still breaking' (middle manager, TNK-BP, Russian, translation).

The development of Western operational capabilities was much slower in Lukoil: 'Now the situation is changing a little, but not as fast as I would wish, but we are putting in the maximum effort, taking into consideration the reality of working in this company. . . . This year [2004] I can say that the first signs of progress are there . . .' (middle manager, Lukoil, Russian, translation). Due to the lack of exploitation learning, Lukoil lost its position as the leading Russian oil company: 'Yukos . . . overtook us in efficiency . . . they had significantly lower costs' (senior manager, Lukoil, Russian, translation). Surgutneftegaz failed to develop new operational capabilities, apart from adapting certain Western technologies. Their growth in oil production was achieved at high cost: 'You can see [from the data] that Yukos drills very few wells, but the wells are very effective, I get more than 140 tonnes per well. By comparison, let's take Surgut, their average flow rate per well is even below 20 tonnes, i.e. to obtain what Yukos gets by drilling one well, Surgut would have to drill more than seven to get the same effect' (senior manager, Yukos, regional, Russian, translation). 'They're not at all a good operator, they grow their output . . . by throwing maximum amounts of money at it' (investment bank executive, Western).

Exploration Learning and Search and Selection

After the initial development of operational capabilities to survive in a market economy, the Western-style firms moved on to exploration learning and the development of dynamic capabilities for search, selection and resource creation in order to develop the strategic flexibility required for sustainable long-term advantage (see cross-case display for Yukos and TNK-BP in Table 9.3).

Table 9.3   Exploration learning and dynamic capabilities (search and selection and resource creation) – Yukos and TNK-BP

	Western-style	
	Yukos	TNK/TNK-BP
1 Exploration Learning Search, risk taking, experimentation, discovery and innovation	• Encourage innovation and experimentation • Begin to delegate decision-making • Project teams to develop ideas • Learn by mistakes	**TNK** • No evidence **TNK-BP** • Project teams • Working groups • Learn by mistakes • Encourage participation and innovation
2 Dynamic Capabilities Search and selection Resource creation	• Systems and routines established for encouraging innovation • Fund projects • Orientate bonus system to new projects • Competitions for ideas • New training centres • Sponsor upcoming managers	**TNK** • No evidence **TNK-BP** • Creation of technology block • Setting up systems and routines to encourage innovation • Leadership development • Competitions for ideas
3 Strategic Flexibility	• Innovation in oil production • Continuous adaptation to changes in unstable environment • **Strategic flexibility** still vested mainly in the TMT, although signs of organisational empowerment	**TNK** • **Strategic flexibility** vested only in the TMT – entrepreneurial flair **TNK-BP** • In process of development – focus still on operational capability • Combination of BP knowledge and experience with Russian adaptability and ability to manage relationships with sources of power has potential for **strategic flexibility** • Blessing of Putin means organisation has some protection from hostile environmental trends such as reversion to state control

Table 9.3   (continued)

| | Western-style | |
	Yukos	TNK/TNK-BP
		• Organisation beginning to be **empowered**
4 Performance and Competitive Advantage	• Successful strategy to be leading Russian oil company by growth, operating costs, capex efficiency, marketing approach, market capitalisation • Oil production growing by 18-20% pa • Operating costs below Western oil majors • Profits higher than Western oil majors • Leading on corporate governance, HR, training and development • Clear **competitive advantage** in the industry • However failed to adapt to change in political climate – reversion to state control	**TNK** • Breakthrough in image and quality in retail • Significant progress in increasing oil production and reducing costs, but lagging behind Yukos **TNK-BP** • **Competitive advantage** – production growth of 12-14% in 2004 – best in Russia • Strong cost and EBITDA performance • Empowering organisation

As was explained in Chapter 8, exploration learning (Table 9.3, row 1) includes search, risk-taking, experimentation, discovery and innovation. Similarly dynamic capabilities involve routines for search and selection and creation of resources (Table 9.3, row 2). All of these were present in Yukos and were beginning to be evident in TNK-BP with the arrival of the Western partner. Yukos actively encouraged employees to come up with new ideas: 'After about a year I realised that Yukos was not like a company, but more like a business school where the challenge was to see what innovations and projects you could introduce to get access to the pot of money available for this' (middle manager, Yukos, Russian, translation). The bonus system was oriented towards the introduction of new projects or innovations, rather than normal measures of operating efficiency. There were many opportunities to experiment: 'Yukos always had money available to try the things out that they wanted to' (top manager, Yukos, Russian, translation). One example of successful innovation mentioned in Chapter 8 was the introduction of a new system for prioritising well maintenance which contributed to the dramatic growth in oil production: 'In 2002 we were increasing [production] in significant volumes . . . about 300 thousand barrels per day – the same as an average-sized oil company. . . . And this was all in addition to what we were producing in one year!' (senior manager, Yukos, regional, Russian, translation). While highly progressive by Russian standards, the innovation did not reach the levels that Western managers would have liked to see: 'There weren't many ideas coming up – creativity and innovation has been killed by the former system' (top manager, Yukos, Western).

Exploration learning, coupled with the search and selection function of dynamic capabilities, enabled Yukos to develop a certain amount of strategic flexibility (Table 9.3, row 3): 'The company was simply characterised by innovation. And the concept of innovation includes flexibility, openness to new things and being prepared – all of this exists' (top manager, Yukos, Russian, translation). The company was the benchmark for success (Table 9.3, row 4) 'If you look back to the time when TNK-BP was formed a year ago, just over a year ago, the norm for success in Russia was unquestionably Yukos – unquestionably' (top manager, TNK-BP, Western). However two factors were possibly responsible for the fact that this competitive advantage was not sustainable. First, the high political profile of the industry meant that a certain strategic agility was required to keep pace with changes in the political environment. 'It is an extremely specific thing, oil. It is always politics. Conditions in the country were changing, they were changing depending on each period. The company had different strategic goals and tasks. . . . Therefore to say that there is one key criterion for survival . . . at each concrete period of time they might have been completely different things' (senior manager, Yukos, Russian, translation). In 2003, however, Khodorkovsky, the CEO, failed to adjust his behaviour to changes in the political climate, and indeed, professed a wish to stand against President Putin in the next presidential elections. Second, Yukos was heavily reliant on Khodorkovsky's leadership – although he was beginning to encourage decision-making lower down in the organisation, this was still at an early stage. Therefore the organisation as a whole lacked strategic flexibility. 'Only the top management team has the capability to react to changes in the environment. It will take a long time for the organisation to develop such that lower parts of the organisation will be able to react and take decisions in accordance with changes in the environment' (top manager, Yukos, Western).

TNK-BP lagged Yukos in exploration learning and search and selection capabilities (Table 9.3, rows 1 and 2) because their focus was still on exploitation learning, deployment and the development of operational capabilities. However, BP brought an empowering management style, encouraging managers to innovate and take decisions within a control framework: 'There's procedures and process and systems that you can build that give people an enormous amount of opportunity to use their creative spirit and with boundary conditions' (top manager, TNK-BP, Western). BP managers tried to create a climate conducive to innovation and risk-taking: 'We've got to try to create capability where they think for themselves . . . and we are going to support them: "Yes? You want a billion dollars? You really think you've got a programme? Here it is." It's a big vote of confidence for thinking for yourself. A sustainable future is only from trying to unlock that natural capability' (top manager, TNK-BP, Western).

Benefits were potentially available from combining the entrepreneurial style of TNK with the corporate systems of BP. The intention was not to extinguish the entrepreneurial spirit, but to foster it: 'There are too strong personalities involved to squash. And obviously you don't want to squash all of them. . . . The art of it all is getting the blend, I mean that's . . . the trick. If you just squash it then you've lost some of the benefits, or if you just let it run you've lost some of the benefits of the corporate' (top manager, TNK-BP, Western). The flexibility, entrepreneurial approach and knowledge of how to manage Russian reality of the TNK managers was to be coupled with the BP experience of operating in different countries across the world and of adapting to political and social change. (Table 9.3, row 3) BP's skill in managing political relationships contrasted with Yukos' downfall: 'When the shareholders signed the agreement with BP, President Putin was standing behind them . . . TNK-BP did not pass through any 'no entry' signs, did not engender any opposition. None of the managers said that he wanted to become the President of Russia' (senior manager, TNK-BP, regional, Russian, translation). In summary, the combined strengths of BP and the Russian partners indicated significant synergy could be achieved in terms of responsiveness to changes in the environment. The gradual empowerment (Table 9.3, row 4) of the organisation initiated by BP would increase the search and selection function and strategic flexibility of the organisation.

In conclusion it should be stressed that the strong political dimension to the Russian oil industry meant that competitive advantage was not purely a matter of meeting the requirements for success in a market economy: 'Competitive advantage Russian style is not simply a matter of profitability and cost control, it's a matter of minding your political fences' (energy consultant, Western). Neither Lukoil nor Surgutneftegaz had a competitive advantage in terms of competing in a market economy; however, their slow-ness to change, retention of the Soviet model (particularly Surgutneftegaz) and good relations with the Kremlin gave them potential superiority in a 'reversion to state control' scenario.

CONCLUSIONS

The theoretical framework in Figure 9.1, grounded in the empirical data, explains the role of organisational learning and dynamic capabilities in organisational transformation. Exploitation learning includes selection and implementation of techniques and processes which are already in exis-tence in Western companies. Implementation entails the dynamic capabili-ties of resource configuration, divestment and integration, that is, capability deployment. As a result, the organisation develops the opera-tional capabilities which are needed for short-term survival in a market economy. Exploration learning, on the other hand, involves search, innovation and risk-taking which is linked with the dynamic capabilities function of search, selection, creation and innovation. This builds the strategic flexibility of the organisation, leading to sustainable competitive

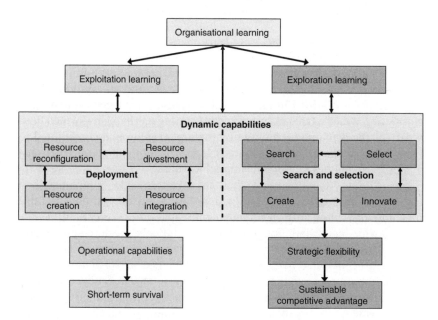

Figure 9.1   Organisational learning and the development of dynamic capabilities

advantage. The discussion that follows further develops the theory and locates it within the literature.

Exploitation Learning and Dynamic Capabilities (Deployment)

The Russian oil companies had few of the capabilities to survive in a market economy (Newman, 2000; Uhlenbruck et al., 2003). They lacked the 'zero-level' capabilities, or the 'how I earn a living now' capabilities (Winter, 2003: 992). These operational capabilities (Helfat and Peteraf, 2003) are the threshold requirement for survival and therefore determine the robustness of the organisation. The acquisition of operational capabilities thus formed the initial focus for organisational learning in the Western-style companies. The emphasis was on exploitation learning since it involved refinement, choice, production efficiency, selection, implementation and execution in relation to business techniques and processes that were already in existence in Western companies. This implied much more than that which Newman (2000) called incremental change in routines within the existing schema, since these changes in routines were radical for the Russian organisations. Nevertheless it was adaptive (or survival) learning (Senge, 1992). The Russian oil companies were merely catching up with their Western counterparts, developing threshold operational capabilities for a market economy.

Dynamic capabilities arise from learning and constitute the firm's systematic methods for modifying operating routines (Zollo and Winter, 2002). The Western-style companies acquired, internalised and disseminated knowledge largely from Western sources and in so doing they modified the operating routines of their organisations to correspond more closely to a Western business model. The learning mechanisms formed both a part of the dynamic capabilities of the organisation and contributed to them – hence the arrow in Figure 9.1 goes in both directions between dynamic capabilities and organisational learning.

The findings demonstrated that the Western-style companies had engaged in resource reconfiguration, divestment and integration (see Table for summary) thus demonstrating dynamic capabilities (Teece et al., 1997). By deploying their capabilities (Helfat et al., 2006) the Western-style organisations had developed the competences which were normally lacking in transition economies, namely marketing, finance and HR capabilities, information sharing and the fostering of innovation. The Soviet-style companies largely failed to develop such capabilities. In Surgutneftegaz there was no evidence of any dynamic capabilities apart from technology development by copying Western techniques. In Lukoil attempts were being made to reconfigure, divest and integrate resources, however there was a high degree of resistance within the organisation to Western ideas. The operational capabilities typically required for survival in a Western organisation were therefore still at very early stage of development.

The effect of exploitation learning and the deployment function of dynamic capabilities on the Western-style organisations was a significant improvement in their operational capabilities. Yukos, in particular, developed many of the operational capabilities required for success in a market economy. Russian competitors readily acknowledged that Yukos were ahead of their peers in this regard.

The Soviet-style companies had made significantly less progress in developing operational capabilities, which was consistent with the reduced level of exploitation learning in these companies. The technical skills of Surgutneftegaz were respected by the Western community, but there was no evidence of the development of Western management capabilities. Lukoil had started to improve some functional areas, particularly finance and business planning, however progress was slow.

The analysis of the process of organisational transformation in the two Western-style companies contributes to the understanding of the interrelationship between exploitation learning and the deployment function of dynamic capabilities. Furthermore I have shown that these are a prerequisite for organisational transformation in this context. Exploitation learning and resource deployment occurs at the first stage of organisational transformation, as a consequence of which basic operational capabilities are developed.

Exploration Learning and Dynamic Capabilities (Search and Selection)

The development of operational capabilities, increasing experience in Western systems and processes and the adoption of Western routines meant that the Western-style companies further developed their absorptive capacity. The organisations, as a result of their prior learning, were ready for the second development stage in organisational learning, namely exploration learning. There was some evidence that the Western-style companies were engaging in exploration learning in terms of learning by mistakes, encouraging innovation and limited delegation of decision-making. Yukos emphasised innovation; however the CEO largely failed to empower managers, meaning both delegation of authority to act and increased motivation to act (Conger and Kanungo, 1988). This constrained exploration learning.

In TNK-BP, the development of operational capabilities was not so far advanced; therefore the focus remained on bringing the organisation up to Western standards, utilising the expertise of the large numbers of expatriates and Russians with Western experience, who generated a critical mass of knowledge and experience within the organisation. BP's concept of establishing boundary conditions, and allowing managers the freedom to innovate within them, was important for facilitating exploration learning and many respondents saw great potential for this in TNK-BP.

The Western-style companies were both at an early stage of exploration learning, but increasing empowerment of the organisation was likely to further encourage innovation and experimentation throughout the organisations. In contrast, the Soviet-style companies had demonstrated little exploitation learning, and showed no evidence of exploration learning.

Search and selection, innovation and resource creation, implicit within exploration learning, represent dynamic capabilities that provide the organisation with strategic flexibility, which is necessary for long-term survival in an uncertain and changing institutional environment (Hitt et al., 1998). The problem for the Western-style companies was that they had failed to empower their organisations, which inhibited strategic flexibility within the organisation. Strategic flexibility remained still largely vested in the top managers. This impaired the capability of the Western-style organisations to achieve sustainable competitive advantage, given the complexity, unpredictability and speed of change in the institutional environment. Being aware of, and adapting to the environment, is critical for newly-privatised firms in transition economies. Firms have to be able to develop strategic responses and adapt to crisis caused by external factors, such as general environmental instability, contraction of demand and other industry-specific influences (Filatotchev et al., 2000). Strategic flexibility is particularly important in transition economies since political and economic changes are frequent, the institutional environment is unstable and markets are poorly developed (Hoskisson et al., 2000; Uhlenbruck et al., 2003). Since the collapse of the Soviet Union in 1991, Russian firms experienced progress and setbacks on the road to a market economy. This placed constant pressure on firms to adapt or proactively develop strategic responses to change, in order to secure sustainable competitive advantage.

The development of operational capabilities for survival in a Western market economy is thus an insufficient prerequisite for sustainable competitive advantage for a company operating in a transition economy. Once the basic operational capabilities have been developed, companies need to engage in exploration learning, typified by new and original thinking, because the challenges of transition economies may require new business models that add value in the specific context (London and Hart, 2004; Prahalad, 2004). In other words, merely importing Western business techniques is not enough to secure sustainable competitive advantage for the Russian oil companies. Firms have to learn through experimentation and internal development of new routines and capabilities adapted to the specific context, rather than the wholesale imposition of imported routines from others (Kogut and Zander, 1996), and thus develop dynamic capabilities and the strategic flexibility to act in a volatile environment (Teece et al., 1997; Hitt et al., 1998).

By identifying the second stage of organisational learning (and the third stage of organisational transformation) and linking it with the search and selection function of dynamic capabilities, I contribute both to organisational learning and dynamic capabilities theory. The identification of the process and timing provides a contribution to the organisational change literature.

10. Conclusions

The preceding chapters have examined the process of organisational transformation in four Russian oil companies and developed theoretical frameworks explaining the role of the top management team in breaking with administrative heritage, the creation of absorptive capacity to enable exploitation and exploration, and the interaction of these with the deployment and search/selection functions of dynamic capabilities. Of the four Russian oil companies, two exhibited a high degree of transformation (the Western-style companies) and two did not (the Soviet-style companies). These case studies thus permitted both literal and theoretical replication. This work has implications for theory and practice and should motivate further research. This chapter first summarises the contributions to theory and areas for further research and second, elicits the critical success factors for business practitioners faced with transforming large, conservative business enterprises.

IMPLICATIONS FOR THEORY

The objectives of this research were twofold: to investigate the process of organisational transformation in the Russian oil industry and to contribute to resource-based theory in the context of the Russian oil industry. In pursuing these objectives I sought to understand how and why the process of organisational transformation differed between Russian oil companies and to what extent the resource-based view helped to explain this. The following sections explain how these objectives were met.

Integrative Framework for Organisational Transformation

Iteration between theory and empirical data from the case studies led to the development of four theoretical frameworks explaining the process of organisational transformation in transition economies, three of them being the constituent parts of an integrative framework for organisational transformation. The first framework (Chapter 3), which integrates the other three, explains the process of organisational transformation as a whole and demonstrates that the top management team adopts different management styles at three different stages: first, a top-down approach to break with the past; second, a contingent approach utilising both a top-down approach and empowerment at the stage of learning and resource reconfiguration in order to secure short-term survival; and third, an empowering approach at the advanced stage of organisational transformation, leading to sustainable competitive advantage. The second framework (Chapter 7) explains the role of the top management team in breaking with administrative heritage in order to bring about organisational transformation. The third (Chapter 8) explains the role of organisational learning in organisational transformation and the fourth (Chapter 9) elaborates the role of dynamic capabilities.

The resource-based view is supplemented with key insights from organisational learning, dynamic capability, organisational change, top management team, leadership and institutional theory to form an integrative framework for organisational transformation. The top management team is isolated as a source of competitive advantage and the specific managerial characteristics associated with organisational transformation are described. The linkages between organisational learning and organisational capability are explained and dynamic capability theory is elaborated in terms of the deployment of resources to develop operational capabilities, and the search and selection function to develop strategic flexibility. The integration of these theories addresses a criticism of management theory that it is too fragmented. Furthermore, a consideration of how the external context (institutional embeddedness) and internal context (administrative heritage) of the firm affect organisational transformation addresses the criticism that the resource-based view neglects context. Thus the framework represents a refinement of resource-based view theory, building on core elements of resource-based view, but also addressing some key limitations.

Processual Analysis of Change

The rapid pace of change in some Russian oil companies permitted processual analysis of organisational change over a ten-year period. The theoretical framework for organisational transformation in transition economies identifies a three-stage process of organisational change and explains the changing role of the TMT over time. At the first stage, an authoritarian management style enables the break with administrative heritage and thus increases the absorptive capacity of the organisation. This facilitates exploitation learning and the deployment function of dynamic capabilities which lead to the development of operational capabilities for survival in a market economy. At a second stage, the TMT adopts a more participatory style, promoting experimentation. This enables exploration learning and the search and selection function of dynamic capabilities. The combination of exploration learning and search and selection helps to develop the strategic flexibility needed for securing sustainable competitive advantage in a changing environment.

By explaining the process of organisational transformation over time, I help to explain the temporal and organisational processes by which change unfolds. The comparison of Western-style and Soviet-style companies furthermore highlights that change can be successfully managed and how this is done. The research also suggests key insights into how large, conservative companies in the West, anchored in their own administrative heritage, may achieve organisational transformation.

Organisational Learning

Three crucial additions to the organisational learning literature are as follows. First, I incorporate the influence of the TMT and leadership style in the analysis of organisational learning processes over time. The framework helps us to understand the process by which TMTs influence organisational transformation in companies in transition economies and indicates a change in role and leadership style for the TMT between the early, and later stages of the organisational transformation.

Second, I contribute to the debate on ambidexterity versus punctuated equilibrium by showing that exploitation and exploration learning do not coexist in the initial stages of organisational transformation, but that exploitation learning is required first, for the development of basic operational capabilities. Exploration learning, if achieved at all, occurs only after prolonged exploitation learning, intensive interfaces with advanced players, and changes in the leadership style. This suggests the punctuated equilibrium model of organisational learning. The first stage of exploitation learning with an authoritarian management style corresponds to the 'induced (variation reducing)' strategy described by Burgelman (2002: 354), whereas the second stage of exploration with a participatory management style corresponds to the 'autonomous (variation increasing)' strategy (ibid.: 354).

Third, the case studies and theoretical framework help to explain what exploration and exploitation actually mean. Exploitation learning refers to the pursuit and acquisition of knowledge, that is new for the companies in a transition economy, but already in existence in the West. Exploration learning is the creation of new knowledge to develop strategic flexibility, leading to sustainable competitive advantage. The link between exploitation learning and the development of operational capabilities and between exploration learning and the development of strategic flexibility adds to understanding of these concepts.

The case studies and theoretical framework contribute to defining exploitation and exploration learning (Gupta et al., 2006). I demonstrated the linkages between exploitation learning and the development of operational capabilities for survival in a market economy, and between exploration learning and the development of strategic flexibility for sustainable competitive advantage. So long as the capabilities being acquired are in existence already, albeit in other organisations, then the learning involves exploitation, not exploration – however radical the organisational transformation. Exploitation learning thus involves the acquisition and assimilation of new knowledge, but it is a different kind of new knowledge to that which is *created* in exploration learning. The latter is the source of competitive advantage, whereas the former secures survival.

Dynamic Capabilities

Grounded in empirical research, I explained how exploitation learning is linked to the deployment function of dynamic capabilities, involving the reconfiguration, divestment, creation and integration of resources to provide the operational capabilities required to survive in the market economy in the short term. On the other hand, exploration learning relates to the search and selection function of dynamic capabilities, involving search, monitoring, reacting and creation to generate the strategic flexibility required for sustainable competitive advantage vis-à-vis their Western peers. In explaining these relationships I make two main contributions. First, I build understanding of the relationships between organisational learning and dynamic capabilities, and second, I explain how these affect organisational transformation in organisations in transition economies.

Many authors have studied exploitation and exploration learning, and dynamic capabilities, but no theory has yet established the link between exploitation learning and the deployment function of dynamic capabilities and between exploration learning and the search/selection function of dynamic capabilities. The theoretical framework of organisational transformation relates these concepts to explain the process of organisational transformation in a transition economy, and thus contributes to the dynamic capabilities and organisational change literature.

Conclusions

I have elaborated a theory of organisational transformation based on empirical research in the Russian oil industry. I have found that Western-derived constructs of organisational learning and dynamic capabilities add to the understanding of the process of organisational transformation in this context. Conversely, I believe that this study in a transition context has helped to enhance these theories and that the insights, moreover, provide new ways to think about the processes of organisational transformation in Western companies, particularly large well-established ones, anchored in their administrative heritage and needing to undergo organisational transformation.

LIMITATIONS OF THE RESEARCH

The research has limitations that may be addressed by future studies. The empirical examination of the concepts of exploration learning and the search and selection function of dynamic capabilities has demonstrated the complexity and interconnectedness of these concepts. For instance, it was difficult to differentiate between search as exploration learning and search as a dynamic capability. Further theorising may help to differentiate more clearly between these two concepts.

Exploration learning and the search and select function of dynamic capabilities were still at an early stage in the Western-style companies and practically non-existent in the Soviet-style companies. Further research in this area in TNK-BP would increase the understanding of the linkage between exploration learning, dynamic capabilities and strategic flexibility.

The context of the oil industry setting limits the generalisation of the inferences to other contexts, as it would constrain any single-context study on organisations. For instance, the national importance of the industry and the high value of the assets meant that there was an increased level of political scrutiny of the businesses. One result was the jailing of Khodorkovsky and the dismemberment of Yukos – an erstwhile highly successful company, representing rapid organisational transformation towards a Western model. The value of the assets, oil, reduced the financial constraints faced by firms during the organisational transformation, a common challenge in other industries in transition economies. Oil is an export commodity in high demand. This meant that the Western-style companies could afford costly expatriates and training programmes to increase the pace of organisational learning. Conversely, the valuable resource base allowed Surgutneftegaz to continue its old strategy of extensive growth even when faced with a changing economic environment. This is not the case for many other organisations in transition economies. Therefore, the theoretical framework would benefit from evaluation in other industry contexts or in other emerging economies. Moreover, a large-scale survey of privatised companies within Russia and the former Soviet Union would be suitable to test the theoretical model and thus to assess the transferability of the findings of this research to other contexts. A fruitful avenue for further research would be to evaluate the framework for organisational turnaround and strategic renewal in Western organisations.

IMPLICATIONS FOR PRACTICE

Understanding the process of organisational transformation and establishing the critical success factors for achieving change is of practical value not only for managers operating in the environment of a transition economy, but also for managers of any large organisations faced with the need to adapt to radical changes in the environment. This research has established that there are three stages of organisational transformation and the following sections focus on the critical success factors for managing change at each stage. This is illustrated in Figure 10.1.

Stage I   Break with the Past

In Stage I it is imperative to break with old practice. The first critical success factor for this is to introduce entrepreneurial outsiders onto the TMT. This

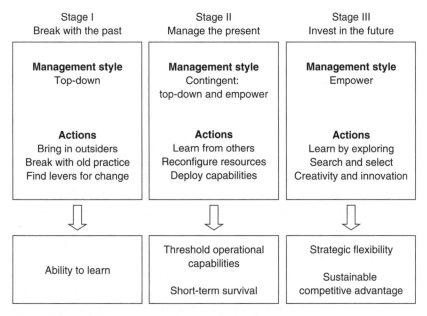

Figure 10.1   Managing organisational transformation

immediately raises a problem for the majority of organisations, which have an inherited management team, or one which has changed little. The conclusion that the characteristics of the TMT are critical for breaking with administrative heritage is akin to the situation criticised by Priem and Butler (2001), whereby it is of little help to practising managers to know that they are the source of the problem and should leave the company. It should however encourage company directors to invite outsiders with targeted expertise onto the management team. Whilst in transition economies they may not be able to afford the expense of expatriates, they could recruit one of the growing band of local managers with experience in a Western company or a 'Western style' company.

The second critical success factor is to identify which mechanisms are effective in breaking with administrative heritage. These have been described in the case study analysis and include, for example, the removal of blockers, rotation of managers, promotion of young managers with a business education, utilisation of project teams, favouring analysis over experience, the achievement of early successes and last, but not least, designing a suitable bonus/incentive system.

The third critical success factor in Stage I is to leverage aspects of the administrative heritage that are beneficial to the change process. In this case the command-and-control management style was leveraged to achieve more rapid implementation of change. This works in a Russian environment which has a heritage of top-down, hierarchical management, however it may not work in environments where a more democratic leadership style is the norm. It may be more appropriate to leverage other factors.

The result of breaking with the past is that the organisation develops the ability and willingness to learn new practices and routines.

Stage II   Manage the Present

Managing the present involves a contingent approach to leadership. In Stage II the first critical success factor therefore relates to the ability of the TMT to vary its leadership style according to requirements of different parts of the organisation. The top-down approach may still be required to break with the past in some parts of the organisation, particularly in subsidiaries. However other parts of the organisation may by this stage already have the ability to learn and therefore may be given authority and encouragement to act.

The second critical success factor is to exploit best practice in other organisations (exploitation learning). This involves knowledge acquisition, knowledge internalisation and knowledge dissemination. In the case of companies in transitions economies, knowledge acquisition included the employment of expatriates, the establishment of alliances, conducting benchmarking studies, training and development. Knowledge internalisation was a function of learning by doing, project work, job rotation, finding the cultural key, learning from mistakes and demonstrating success. Knowledge dissemination was a function of changing cultural attitudes to sharing information, encouraging networking, breaking down organisational silos, setting up communication systems, publishing best practice, organising masterclasses, establishing working groups, using change agents and promoting shared values.

The third critical success factor is reconfiguring, divesting, creating and integrating resources (deploying capabilities). In the Russian oil companies, resource reconfiguration involved asset consolidation, restructuring, the establishment of new business systems, the replacement of 'blockers' in the system and job rotation to break down organisational silos. The divestment of non-core activities was an important element of this reconfiguration. Resource creation involved setting up new systems for HR, corporate governance, finance, etc. and developing new technical capabilities. Resource integration involved aligning the organisation behind common goals and managing conflicts of interest. In the case of the TNK-BP international joint venture it also involved managing the synergies and dealing with the cultural differences and conflicts between expatriates and locals.

By meeting these critical success factors the organisation will secure the threshold operational capabilities required for short-term survival.

Stage III   Invest in the Future

Investing in the future involves empowering the whole organisation. In Stage III the first critical success factor therefore relates to the ability of the TMT to empower the organisation by delegating to employees as well as motivating and enabling them to act.

The second critical success factor is to enable the organisation to engage in exploration. This may be achieved by encouraging innovation, trial and experimentation and by developing a culture which enables learning from mistakes. Exploration enables the organisation to develop new capabilities fitted to its specific context, rather than just imported systems and routines from other contexts.

The third critical success factor is the search and selection capability – organisational processes and routines need to include the search for new ideas and ways of selecting the appropriate ideas for implementation in a given context. In the Russian oil companies, the search and selection functions included the setting up of working groups and networks.

The development of an exploration learning approach, a capability to search and select and an innovative and creative approach enhance an organisation's strategic flexibility and thus its ability to adapt to changes in the environment, thereby securing sustainable competitive advantage.

Conclusions

In conclusion, the framework outlining the process of organisational transformation, together with the rich descriptions of the processes occurring, should assist managers involved in organisational transformation both in transition economies and in other contexts characterised by radical change. It is appropriate for organisations in transition economies to combine both exploitation and exploration learning, although the emphasis is initially more on exploitation learning to develop the threshold operational capabilities required for survival. An understanding of the characteristics of dynamic capabilities will help managers to focus first on the deployment function (resource reconfiguration, divestment, creation and integration) at the early stage and second, on the search and selection function at the more mature stage of organisational transformation. It is important to note that capability deployment is not sufficient in itself for sustainable competitive advantage within contexts of institutional upheaval – managers need to encourage strategic flexibility within their organisations by fostering innovation and devolving decision-making.

Many academic studies fail to generate useful implications for practitioners. I hope that this book will prove the contrary. It is anticipated that managers will be able to recognise similar issues in their own companies by reading the stories of successful and less successful organisational transformation. The cross-case analysis, whilst not prescribing how organisational transformation should be managed, nevertheless explains the process in the two companies that were successful, thus providing guidelines for practising managers. The rich comparative case studies provide insight into the constraints and enablers of organisational change. The three-stage framework for organisational transformation, developed from this research, could equally apply to any large, conservative organisation undergoing change – the case of the Russian oil industry merely makes the topic more interesting and the features clearer.

Postscript

By 2007 the Russian oil landscape had changed radically from the situation described in Chapter 2. By May 2007, the last Yukos asset had been transferred to the state, transforming Rosneft, the state-controlled oil company, from Russia's number 8 oil producer, worth $6 billion, to the country's largest producer with a market capitalisation of $90 billion. The acquisition of Sibneft, one of the five integrated oil majors, by Gazprom, the state gas company, had also propelled Gazprom into the oil business. By January 2007, Gazprom was number 2 behind ExxonMobil in terms of market capitalisation rankings for energy companies and Rosneft had appeared in the rankings at number 13. Lukoil and Surgutneftegaz were at 16 and 17 respectively (PFC Energy, 2007). Both Rosneft and Gazprom are heavily influenced by President Putin. Rosneft is chaired by Igor Sechin, Putin's deputy chief of staff and one of the Kremlin insiders. Gazprom is chaired by Dmitry Medvedev, first deputy prime minister and one of Putin's colleagues from St Petersburg. TNK-BP has also not escaped the growing influence of the state – it was obliged to sell its majority stake in the Kovytka gas field to Gazprom, because it had failed to meet the production quotas stipulated by the licence. However, it had been unable to meet production quotas because of Gazprom's refusal to develop an export pipeline.

In the meantime, although Russian oil production has continued to rise (Figure PS.1), growth rates have declined (Figure PS.2). Output growth for the industry was only 2.8 per cent in 2005 and 2.2 per cent in 2006 compared with an average 8.5 per cent between 2000 and 2004. Yukos had been achieving growth rates of 20 per cent in 2001–03 and had been classified as the most successful oil company in Russia.

In the light of the demise of Yukos and renationalisation of its assets a key question has to be as follows: if organisational transformation in Yukos was so successful, what was the reason for its fall from grace? The corollary to the question was posed by Suhomlinova (2006) in her study of property and power in the Russian energy industry: By what criteria should we judge the post-socialist transformation of an industry and the companies within it? (ibid.: 37). Institutional theory may prove helpful on this matter. The behaviour of firms cannot be separated from their institutional environment – it is embedded in the broader socio-political environment in which competition takes place (Granovetter, 1985; North, 1990; Spicer et al., 2000). A set of

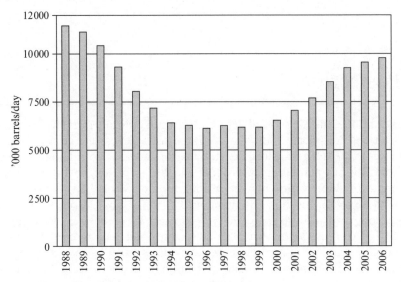

Source: BP Statistical Review of World Energy 2007

Figure PS.1   Russian oil production, 1988–2006

values, norms and organisational templates exists outside particular firms and influences the way in which they are managed (Meyer and Bowman, 1977; Zucker, 1983). Normally, organisations that adapt to institutional pressures are more successful than those that do not (Meyer and Bowman, 1977). However Newman (2000) maintains that this cannot apply when the institutional context itself is changing radically. The institutional context no longer provides organising templates, models for action and sources of legitimacy (Greenwood and Hinings, 1993). Newman (ibid.) therefore argues that radical institutional change inhibits organisational transformation. Similarly, Suhomlinova postulates that the apparent rise in favour of the Soviet-style companies (Lukoil and Surgutneftegaz) as a result of 'the reversion to state control' illustrates one of the paradoxes of evolution described by Lant and Mezias (1992), whereby conditions of high environmental uncertainty favour organisations that are less responsive to environmental change.

   These theoretical propositions conflict to a certain extent with the findings of this research, which suggested that the companies that managed to overcome the genetic coding of the organisation and interact with the emerging institutional frameworks of a market economy (the Western-style companies) were more successful than their peers that still clung to the old institutional frameworks of state ownership (the Soviet-style companies). But to what extent do Suhomlinova and Newman's propositions assist

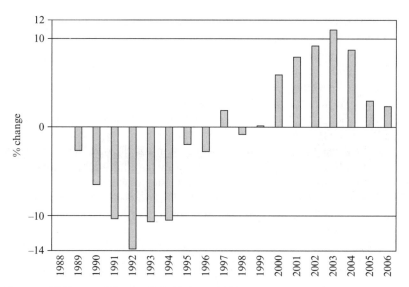

Source: *BP Statistical Review of World Energy 2007*

Figure PS.2   Growth rates for Russian oil production, 1988–2006

understanding of the collapse of Yukos, despite its 'successful' organisational transformation?

An explanation may lie in the Granovetter's (1985) notion of embeddedness – he maintained that economic action is embedded in structures of social relations between business enterprises in modern industrial society. As Suhomlinova (2005) also suggests, the notion of social relations between economic actors in business could be extended to incorporate the state. She refers to the notion of co-evolution in the Russian oil and gas industry, whereby organisational changes in the industry were 'shaped by, but also shaped the way in which the Russian state attempted to influence the processes in an emerging market economy' (Suhomlinova, 2005: 13). This is akin to Sztompka's concept of social becoming (1991) whereby:

> direction, goals and speed of change are contestable among multiple agents . . .; action occurs in the context of encountered structures, which it shapes in turn, resulting in the dual quality of structures (as both shaping and shaped) and the dual quality of actors (as both producers and products); and . . . the interchange of action and structure occurs in time, by means of alternating phases of agential creativeness and structural determination. (Sztompka, 1991: 24)

The multiple actors in the Russian oil industry were the state, the oil companies and the TMTs. The speed of change in Yukos perhaps moved out of step with that in the institutional environment creating conflict in trying to shape the state, rather than allowing itself to be shaped by it. There appears to have been a clash between what Sztompka would call the 'capacity for self-transcendence' and the 'capacity for social learning' (ibid.: 116). The former was represented by the creativeness of Khodorkovsky and his ability to conceive of new business formats, whereas the latter was represented by his unwillingness to learn from experience and to be shaped by the preceding historical process.

Khodorkovsky himself, with his pretensions to the presidency, was out of step with the state. It is interesting to draw parallels with the early days of capitalism in the US and the rise of Rockefeller's Standard Oil as described by Daniel Yergin (1991) in *The Prize*, a classic history of the oil industry. While Rockefeller himself saw the role of Standard Oil as highly beneficial to the US economy:

> the public at large . . . [saw] a powerful, devious, cruel, entrenched, all-pervasive and yet mysterious enterprise. It was accountable to no one except a handful of arrogant directors.. . . The growth of Standard Oil had not occurred in a vacuum. It was a product of the swift industrialisation of the American economy in the last few decades of the nineteenth century. (ibid.: 98)

In 1909, the US Federal Court finally ordered the dissolution of Standard Oil on the basis that the business was against the public interest. By substituting the word privatisation for industrialisation there was a clear parallel with the unpopularity of Khodorkovsky and Yukos with the Russian public and the perceived threat to the state of a man such as Khodorkovsky with vast wealth and with pretensions to the presidency.

The final question relating to Yukos' fall from grace is to what extent was it due to a lack of strategic flexibility in the organisation. I have explained that strategic flexibility was required to secure sustainable competitive advantage for the organisation in a rapidly changing environment. The increasing power and influence of the state from 2003 represented a new challenge which perhaps Khodorkovsky was unable to perceive. Would the outcome have been different if he had had more time to switch to a democratic leadership style and had been able to empower the organisation? Was sole reliance on his judgement the source of his downfall?

The measurement of success in unstable institutional environments presents a conundrum. On the one hand the Western-style companies appear to be the most efficient, well-run companies with a clear source of competitive advantage in market economy terms. On the other hand, the move back to the pre-eminence of the state casts some doubt on the longevity of the Western-style business models and appears to benefit those companies which have changed least from their state-owned heritage.

Perhaps some consolation may be drawn from the demise of Yukos in terms of the large numbers of managers, trained in Western business approaches, who will either stay within their newly nationalised industry or move out into the wider economy to act as ambassadors of new ways of thinking. Let me finish with the the words of one of the 'Heriot-Watters' in Yukos in 2004, when the company was already under siege:

> I, at least, am never embarrassed to say where I work. . . . I always pronounce the word loudly and with pride, even today, knowing what a difficult situation the company is in, knowing that many people are criticising the company. I have never removed the badge from my jacket, never . . . I will always remember this company as the one which made me the person I am. Not anything else, but Yukos. I joined Yukos, I developed, I trained and I grew up in Yukos. I have no one other than Yukos to thank. (senior manager, Yukos, regional, Russian)

Appendix: methodology

RESEARCH PHILOSOPHY

The objective of the research was to examine the process of organisational transformation in the Russian oil companies and to identify how and why it differed between the companies. The theoretical perspective adopted was the resource-based view since this helps to explain why intra-industry company performance differs by highlighting how the deployment of unique and idiosyncratic organisational resources and capabilities generates competitive advantage (Wernerfelt, 1984; Barney, 1991; Peteraf and Barney, 2003).

Since the process of organisational transformation is complex and poorly understood, an interpretive approach was taken, viewing the organisation as a social site, where the people researched and the researcher are active sense-makers (Deetz, 1996). The research method was qualitative: 'an umbrella term covering an array of interpretive techniques which seek to describe, decode, translate, and otherwise come to terms with the meaning, not the frequency, of . . . phenomena in the social world' (Van Maanen, 1979: 520). The interpretive approach helps to gain an understanding of the complex world of lived experience from the point of view of those who live it (Schwandt, 1998). The approach is holistic – context and behaviour are interdependent. It is appropriate where the phenomena to be investigated are not well understood (Ritchie, 2003), such as in the confusing and complex context of the oil industry undergoing change in Russia. The purpose of the research was to develop concepts, models and schemes to make sense of (Schwandt, 1998) what is going on in the transformation of the Russian oil companies by interaction with oil company managers and experts in the field, whilst acknowledging that the different participants in the research have their own view of 'reality' and do not necessarily understand all the processes. Strategic developments are evolutionary processes only roughly understood by the firms involved (Dosi and Marengo, 1994). Thus the methodology provides an in-depth and interpreted understanding within the companies by learning about the circumstances, experiences, perspectives and histories of the respondents (Snape and Spencer, 2003).

A qualitative approach is appropriate for research into organisational processes, since they are complex and contextually situated and they cannot be understood in isolation from the role of the manager and other employees (Barr, 2004). It is the approach most often adopted for studies of organisational change since 'symbolic meaning and unfolding history are necessarily central features of any account of collective identity or social change' (Van Maanen, 1998: 194). It is not feasible to understand the complex nature of organisational transformation by reducing the analysis down to relationships between independent and dependent variables; instead, change should be viewed as 'an interaction between context and action' (Pettigrew et al., 2001: 699). The positivist approach was not appropriate for this research because organisations are not governed by law-like regularities. They are mediated through meaning and human agency, thus I sought to explore and understand the Russian oil companies using the participants' understanding (Snape and Spencer, 2003).

The theoretical perspective for this research is the resource-based view (RBV). RBV has been criticised for involving concepts, such as capabilities, which are difficult to test (Godfrey and Hill, 1995). Large sample, multi-industry, single time-period samples using secondary sources of data are unlikely to identify the key sources of sustained competitive advantage (Rouse and Daellenbach, 1999). However, the norm in published RBV research is to use publicly available data sets to test theory (for instance: Miller and Shamsie, 1996). More can be learnt about the relationship between resources and strategies by 'getting inside' the firm, where resources reside, rather than correlating aggregate measures of resources with aggregate measures of the value of a firm's strategies as is done in quantitative studies (Rouse and Daellenbach, 1999; Barney and Mackey, 2004). This resulted in the decision for this research to 'get inside' Russian oil companies to examine how resources affect organisational transformation.

RESEARCH STRATEGY

A criticism of most RBV studies is that they do not simultaneously account for the effects of strategy, industry, environment, or time, which may interact with the complex of organisational factors (Rouse and Daellenbach, 1999). However, organisational change is typically studied over time and within an historical and organisational context (Pettigrew, 1987). For these reasons an in-depth longitudinal case study approach was adopted (Eisenhardt, 1989, 1991; Stake, 1998; Yin, 2003). Case studies on four Russian oil companies were conducted, covering a ten-year period from full privatisation of the oil industry in 1995 up till 2005. Interviews were conducted from 2001 to 2005 and respondents were asked to talk about organisational change in the 10-year period since privatisation. Choosing a period of rapid change enabled a processual analysis of change (Pettigrew, 1997; Dawson, 2003) over a relatively short period of time.

A case represents a complex entity operating within a number of contexts – in this research the complex entities are the Russian oil companies operating within the context of Russian political, social and economic environment and within the global oil industry. A case study examines a contemporary phenomenon in its real-life context, especially when the boundaries between phenomenon and context are not clearly evident (Yin, 2003). This research has a focus on a specific phenomenon – namely the organisational transformation of Russian oil companies in the period since privatisation. The boundaries between the topic of organisational transformation and the transition economy context are not clearly evident. An advantage of case study research is the opportunity to take a holistic view, to utilise the researcher's capacity for understanding in studying many different aspects, examining them in relation to each other and viewing the process within its total environment (Gummesson, 2000). To summarise, the case study method is appropriate when the objective is (a) to define research topics broadly and not narrowly, (b) to cover contextual or complex multivariate conditions and not just isolated variables, and (c) to rely on multiple and not singular sources of evidence.

The selection of companies for the study was similar to the process suggested by Rouse and Daellenbach (1999) for RBV studies. The performance of different companies in an industry was examined on the basis of secondary data and the companies were clustered into strategic groups – in this case the focus was on the major integrated oil companies. Then performance differences were compared within the group based on secondary data. The final step was to identify the high and low performers in the group. The same approach is used by Pettigrew (1990) in the study of organisational change.

Four case studies were undertaken to enable literal and theoretical replication. Due to the openness of the Western-style companies to Western business concepts it was feasible to gain deep-level access to a range of managers. On the other hand the closed nature of the two Soviet-style companies, in particular Surgutneftegaz, meant that access to these companies was either limited (Lukoil) or non-existent (Surgutneftegaz). Nevertheless substantial additional third-party information was gathered on these companies enabling a comparison to be made. The selection of two sets of extremes of organisational transformation was consistent with the maximum variation approach, which seeks to obtain a range of information and perspectives on a subject, challenging the researcher's preconceived understandings of the phenomenon under study (Kuzel, 1999) and documenting 'unique or diverse variations that have emerged in adapting to different conditions' (Patton, 1990: 182).

Bechhofer and Paterson (2000) argue that comparison and control lie at the heart of good research design. In this research the comparison is between four different oil companies. Control is concerned with having a reference against which to compare competing explanations. Already at the outset of the research, on the basis of pre-existing knowledge, it was assumed that the 'control' case would be the organisation which had adapted least to the market economy, namely Surgutneftegaz.

The purpose of the case studies is to explore 'what is happening; to seek new insights; to ask questions and to assess phenomena in a new light' (Robson, 2002: 59) and to explain why it is happening, thus combining both exploratory (answering the question: what was the process of organisational transformation?) and explanatory approaches (answering the question: how and why did the process differ between oil companies?) (Robson, 2002; Saunders et al., 2003; Yin, 2003). Case researchers seek out both what is common and what is particular about the case, but the end result presents something unique. Uniqueness extends to the nature of the case, its historical background, the physical setting, other contexts (including economic, political, legal and aesthetic), other cases through which this case is recognised and those informants through whom the case can be known (Stake, 1998). Thus case studies can be used where the intention is to explore not typicality but unusualness or extremity with the intention of illuminating processes (Hartley, 1994). This research demonstrates two extremes in the Russian oil industry – the rapid transformation of Yukos and TNK-BP compared to the stagnation of Surgutneftegaz. The exaggerated example, where processes may be more stark, may suggest processes which are occurring in more mundane or common settings (ibid.).

To understand the complexity of change it is important to examine change temporally, as it happens, rather than to take a snapshot of events: 'Change does not occur in a neat linear fashion, but is messy, murky and complicated. It involves twists and loops, turns and returns, omissions and revisions, the foreseen and unforeseen, and is marked by the achievement of planned targets, failures, resistance, celebration, ambivalence, fatigue, conflict and political manoeuvring' (Dawson, 2003: 144). A longitudinal approach was therefore adopted, with rounds of interviews in two periods: 2001 and 2004/5. Respondents were asked to talk about the period since privatisation in 1995. Hartley (1994) maintains that a key strength of case studies lies in their capacity to explore social processes as they unfold in organisations, allowing for a processual, contextual and longitudinal analysis of the various actions and meanings which take place with organisations. For studies into transition economies both longitudinal and cross-sectional approaches are recommended (Hoskisson et al., 2000; Meyer and Peng, 2005). The cross-section for this study comprises the four oil companies.

The objective of the case studies is to explain the relationships (Robson, 2002; Saunders et al., 2003; Yin, 2003) between the constructs leading to organisational transformation in order to increase understanding about the determinants of organisational performance and to explain how managers can create superior performance (Meyer, 1991). Failure to explain how internal capabilities affect organisational performance is a central criticism of RBV (Priem and Butler, 2001). Since organisational performance is multidimensional, the constructs used to represent organisational transformation include dimensions of both operational performance, which is represented by non-financial indicators of organisational operations, and organisational performance, which includes financial and economic outcomes. In this research, staff development and training, health, safety and environment, corporate governance systems and marketing innovations are examples of dimensions of organisational performance which are indicative of organisational transformation. Financial and economic indicators include growth in oil production, cost of oil per barrel and share value/market capitalisation.

The relevance of generalisation of case study research is much discussed (Lewis and Ritchie, 2003). Opposing the drive for generalisability of qualitative research, Boulding emphasises the importance of retaining the particularity of social systems: 'The thing that distinguishes social systems from physical or even biological systems is their incomparable (and embarrassing) richness in special cases. Generalisations in the social sciences are mere pathways which lead through a riotous forest of individual trees, each a species unto itself' (Boulding, 1958: 14). Stake also argues against the need to generalise: 'the purpose of a case report is not to represent the world, but to represent the case' (Stake, 1998: 156). However, Gummesson (2000) emphasises the benefits of in-depth studies based on detailed investigations to identify certain phenomena and lay bare mechanisms which one might suspect could also exist in other companies.

> The description of the process of organisational transformation should thus provide the reader with reason to believe that a similar process could occur in other companies.

Thus, although external validity through generalisation is difficult to achieve for qualitative case studies, due to the unlikelihood of their being statistically representative of some population, nevertheless there is an argument that such studies are strong on 'naturalism' or 'ecological validity' (Seale, 1999) and thus achieve 'transferability' (Lincoln and Guba, 1985) 'Thick' description (Geertz, 1988) of the case provides the reader with a vicarious experience of having 'been there' with the researcher (Seale, 1999). It enables the reader to follow a thought process sequentially under successively unfolding social situations and leads to a deep under-standing of the managerial processes (Numagami, 1998). The detailed cross-case analyses of the four Russian oil companies, together with the detailed description of the context, provide this experience for readers who may wish to generalise from this study.

DATA GATHERING

Semi-structured interviews were conducted over a five-year period from 2001 to 2005 in order to gain an in-depth knowledge and understanding of the organisation and its processes (Rouse and Daellenbach, 1999). Triangulation of source data was achieved by interviewing different man-agement levels (top, senior and middle managers), representing different functions (for example strategy, public relations, human resources, finance, manufacturing and production) at two types of location (head office and regional subsidiaries). The key geographic locations are illustrated in Figure App. 1. External experts with knowledge and experience of the case companies were also interviewed. These included other Russian oil com-panies, Western oil companies, journalists, energy consultancies, manage-ment consultants, headhunters and investment bankers. This group of respondents provided both industry-level contextual data and insight into the operations of the organisations, especially in the case of audit compa-nies or management consultancies. This triangulation of source data avoided over-reliance on perspectives of senior managers who might present events in a favourable light, which has been a characteristic of much organisational learning research (Easterby-Smith, 1997). The sampling approach was criterion-based or purposive (Patton, 1990; Ritchie et al., 2003). Seventy-one interviews were conducted in which 74 respondents were involved, eight of whom had worked in more than one of the compa-nies. In 2003, while the research was still being conducted, two important events happened: TNK merged with BP to form a 50/50 international joint venture; and the CEO of Yukos, Mikhail Khodorkovsky, was jailed for alleged tax crimes. The subsequent partial dismantling of Yukos meant that several employees transferred from Yukos to the new TNK-BP JV – five of these were interviewed. Additionally two respondents had worked both in TNK-BP and Lukoil and one respondent had transferred from TNK to Yukos. Interviews with these respondents provided a unique opportunity for cross-case comparisons.

The interviews were conducted by the author, a fluent English and Russian speaker, who has lived and worked in Russia. They were conducted in English or Russian, according to respondent wishes, and lasted around

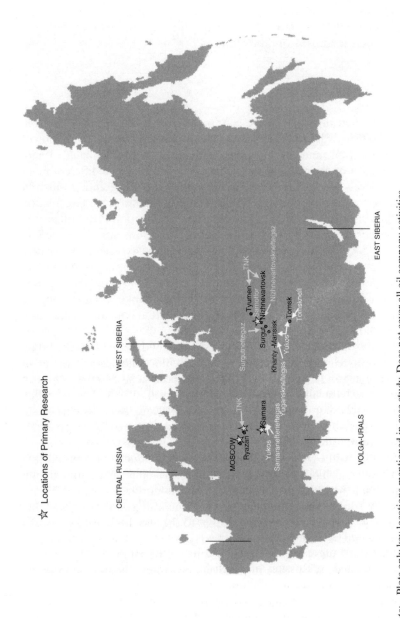

Note: Plots only key locations mentioned in case study. Does not cover all oil company activities

Figure A.1   Key geographic locations

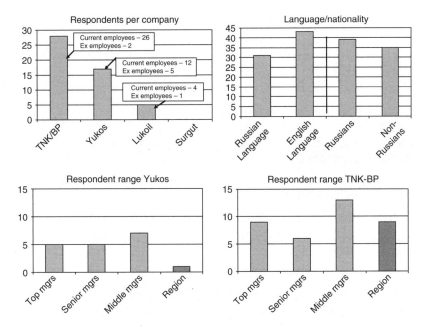

Figure A.2   Respondent details

one hour. They took place mainly in Moscow but also in the regions (for example, Siberia for oil production and European Russia for oil refining).

No access was secured to Surgutneftegaz employees due to the closed nature of this organisation. In retrospect the approach made to Surgutneftegaz was inappropriate and unlikely to secure their participation since the fax[1] sent to the General Director, Bogdanov, requesting a meeting, described the research in terms of organisational transformation. Since there had been no transformation in Surgutneftegaz there was no response. Problems of access were also encountered with Lukoil; only four in-company interviews were secured and one with an ex-employee. Because both of these 'Soviet-style' organisations demonstrated a low degree of transformation, they provided the counterpoint to the two Western-style companies – Yukos and TNK/TNK-BP, which provided the empirical date on which the theory on organisational transformation was based (see Chapter 3).

Information on respondents is given in Figure App. 2. The interviews were conducted in Russian or English, according to the wishes of the respondents, and lasted around one hour. Forty-three were in English and 31 were in Russian; however, the ratio was the other way round on nationality – 39 were Russian nationals or by origin and 35 were English native speakers. The interviews were conducted largely face-to-face in Moscow,

Table App. 1.   Questions, and prompts, used in 2001 interviews

---

1. To what extent can you envisage Russian oil companies competing with the international oil majors in the world arena?

Dynamic organisation; performance

2. What factors about the Russian oil industry inhibit it from becoming a major global player?

Resource-based: historical firm resources; organisational learning: capacity to learn, information processing

3. Do you think that the Russian oil industry can transform/revolutionise itself in the short to medium term?

Resource-based: resource upgrades/divestment/acquisition /integration

4. What do you believe are the major sources of competitive advantage for the Russian oil companies?

Resource-based; performance

5. How could Russian oil companies improve their performance?

Resource-based; organisational learning; dynamic organisation; performance

6. To what extent can Russian oil companies manage the need to balance structure versus flexibility, efficiency versus innovation?

Dynamic organisation: internal consistency, strategic flexibility

7. To what extent does politics play a role in the activities of the Russian oil companies?

Environment

8. Can you envisage a Russian oil company merging with a Western oil major?

Organisational learning: knowledge acquisition. Resource-based: resource acquisition

---

but also in the regions – Nizhnevartovsk, Siberia (for oil production), Samara, Volga Region (for oil production) and Ryazan, Central Region, (for oil refining). See Figure A.1 for key geographic locations. Five interviews were conducted by telephone. The interviews were taped and transcribed in the original language. The Russian interviews were not translated, except for purposes of inclusion as quotations in the book.

The initial interviews in 2001 sought to establish the sources of competitive advantage of the Russian oil companies, while later interviews focused on organisational transformation from a resource-based and organisational learning perspective. (See Tables App. 1 and App. 2 for guideline questions and prompts). The respondents were encouraged to talk freely about organisational change from the time since privatisation (mid-1990s) to the

Table App. 2   Questions used in 2004/05 interviews and their links to constructs

---

1. What do you think are the basic/threshold requirements for survival in the Russian oil industry?

Threshold resources
Operational capability – efficiency, effectiveness, management skills, processes
Do you meet these requirements?
Performance compared to Western companies

2. What is unique about your company? In what ways is it better than competitors?

Unique resources: valuable, rare, non-imitable, non-substitutable
Core competences: managerial and operational processes, present position,
    paths available
Sources of competitive advantage, sustainability of competitive advantage
Balance between flexibility/robustness
Learning
Key weaknesses

3. What are your main performance measures? How do you compare with the competition?

Quantitative shareholder value added (SVA) return on capital employed
    (ROCE), production etc; productivity measures, for example cost/unit, cost per
    employee.
Softer measures: innovative internal processes, corporate governance/corporate
    social responsibility(CSR) learning, growth, leadership, strategic positioning

4. What key changes have there been in the organisation since privatisation?

Resource integration, resource reconfiguration, resource leverage, learning
Successful/unsuccessful examples

5. What are the greatest challenges in the external environment and how does your company cope with them?

Politics, oil price, legal, turbulence, corruption
Russia compared to West

6. What are the greatest challenges within the internal context of the firm and how do you cope with them?

Culture, history, leadership/power, politics, definition of success, genetic coding
Internal consistency/resource integration

7. Who is on the top management team?

Characteristics: heterogeneity, degree of participation/interaction,
    entrepreneurial, empowering, learning orientation, external power/influence

---

present day (up to 2005), thus covering the main period of change. The outline questions were used as prompts as necessary. The interpretive process was ongoing and informed each subsequent interview, thus the understanding gradually emerged within the research process (Miller and Crabtree, 1999).

Interviews were the predominant type of data gathering; however, some documentation was collected and limited amount of observations were recorded to provide triangulation of method (Denzin, 1978; Jick, 1979).

DATA ANALYSIS

The data analysis process broadly followed the recommendations of Miles and Huberman (1994) for data display and Strauss and Corbin (1998) for coding and was facilitated by computer aided qualitative data analysis (CAQDAS) – Atlas-ti. The interviews were imported into Atlas-ti in the original (Russian or English), but the coding was done in English. This had the advantage of retaining the original nuance and enabling a mental recreation of the scene.

Initially an open coding approach was taken to allow themes to emerge from the data. Patterns were formed when groups of properties aligned themselves along various dimensions (Strauss and Corbin, 1998), for example management style ranged from top-down and centralised to open and empowering. As patterns began to emerge, the codes were clustered into groups (for example, management style, dynamic capabilities, company structure), which formed categories. This was an early approach to axial coding in which data, that were fractured during the open coding, were reassembled into categories (Strauss and Corbin, 1998). Once a category was identified (for example management style), it became easier to remember it, to think about it, and to develop it in terms of its properties and dimensions and further differentiate it and explain it by breaking it down into its subcategories (for example Western-style, Soviet-style); that is, by explaining the when, where, why, how and so on of a category that was likely to exist (ibid.). Following Eisenhardt's (1989) suggestions for developing theory, evidence was tabulated for each category and evidence was consolidated for the 'why' behind the relationships.

Associative analysis was conducted to find links or connections between two or more phenomena (Ritchie et al., 2003). Extensive use was made of Atlas-ti facilities to theorise about codes and their relationships, to conceptualise the data and to develop a more integrated understanding of events, processes and interactions in the case. This was facilitated by the network functionality within Atlas-ti which was used to display relationships and patterns in the data. The paradigm approach (Strauss and Corbin, 1998) was used to sort out and organise the emerging connections. The paradigm consisted of three elements: the conditions, the actions/interactions and the consequences (ibid.). The conditions were the internal and external context – the why, where, how come, and when, that is the structure or set of circumstances in which phenomena are embedded (for example Soviet heritage, transition economy, privatisation). The actions/interactions were the strategic or routine responses made by individuals or groups to issues, problems, happenings or events which arose under those conditions (for example the actions of TNK-BP and Yukos to acquire Western management skills). The consequences were the outcomes of such actions/interactions (for example improved performance and organisational transformation) or the failure to respond to situations (for example in the case of Surgutneftegaz – no organisational transformation). Time-ordered or conceptually ordered data display tables illustrate the application of the paradigm approach. However, the complexity of the process meant it was not possible to talk of one variable having a direct effect on another: 'We are not talking a language of cause and effect . . . [t]his is too simplistic' (Strauss and Corbin, 1998: 130). Thus many different actions/interactions (for example training and development, introduction of new business processes, incentivisation) were moderated by the internal context (for example Soviet administrative heritage, Russian *spetsifika* – specifics) and the external environment (for example lack of institutions, move towards a market economy) to produce a range of consequences (for example lower production cost, increased transparency).

Initial relationships between conditions, actions and consequences were developed into relational statements because they linked two or more concepts, explaining the what, why, where and how of a phenomenon (Strauss and Corbin, 1998). These relational statements were abstractions; that is statements at the conceptual level which required further validation and elaboration through continued comparison of data (ibid.) within and between the cases. For example, an initial relational statement that expatriates had a major influence on organisational transformation (established by analysing several Yukos interviews) could then be compared with TNK-BP interviews. This process was facilitated by the query tool in Atlas-ti which generated outputs of co-occurring codes such as expatriates and transformation. Discovering contradictions or 'outliers' led to further questioning of the data (Ritchie et al., 2003). For example, there were contradictory views on whether Khodorkovsky, CEO of Yukos, was empowering managers within the organisation or restricting decision-making to key members of the 'clan'. An explanation for the contradiction seemed to be related to the conditions, that is the timing. In the early days the 'clan' predominated, but over time, as more Western business practices were introduced, there began to be increased empowerment of the organisation.

As the topic of the research was the process of organisational transformation over time it was necessary to code for process by looking at actions over time to note how things change. Actions/interactions can both change in response to shifts in the context and can bring about changes in the context. Different stages of development were identified over the ten-year period after privatisation as explained in Chapter 2, for example time of troubles, reversion to state control. 'Reversion to state control' could be described as a change in context as a partial result of the actions/ interactions of Yukos CEO Khodorkovsky with the State. The growing wealth of Yukos and Khodorkovsky's PR campaigns in the West (positioning himself for a political career) were factors affecting the reversion to state control and the confiscation of the Yukos assets.

Theory was 'constructed' from the integration of major categories into relational statements to form a larger theoretical scheme (Miles and Huberman, 1994; Strauss and Corbin, 1998) – the conceptual frameworks of organisational transformation which are described in Chapters 3, 7, 8 and 9. These frameworks were then reviewed for internal consistency and logic. At this stage, standing back from the data, an important insight was gained:

> Sometimes, it is simply that the analyst is almost there but, without realising it, has taken the wrong stance toward the data; that is, it is easy to look at the data from the perspective of the analyst and not the respondents while thinking that he or she is doing the opposite. (Strauss and Corbin, 1998: 157)

It became obvious why Surgutneftegaz had not consented to any interviews, quite apart from its closed nature and lack of familiarity with Western business research – it had simply not been appropriate to describe the research in terms of organisational transformation to a company which had not transformed. In retrospect it would have been better to couch the topic of the research in terms of sources of competitive advantage of Russian oil companies.

As mentioned in the section on data gathering above, the interpretive process and theory development was ongoing, with a constant iteration between the literature review and the data analysis and between deduction and induction following conventions established by Strauss and Corbin:

> To us, an interpretation is a form of deduction. We are deducing what is going on based on data, but also based on the reading of that data along with the assumptions about the nature of life, the literature that we carry in the heads, and the discussions that we have with colleagues. . . . In fact, there is an interplay between induction and deduction (as in all science). (Strauss and Corbin, 1998: 136–7)

Thus theory was allowed to 'emerge' during the research process – this flexibility of theory being an important feature of interpretive research (Kuzel, 1999). This interplay between academic pre-conceptualisation and detailed empirical descriptions of emerging themes is typical for processual research into organisational change (Dawson, 2003) and has also been used in other studies, for example Barr et al.'s study of organisational renewal (1992), Regner's investigations of inductive versus deductive strategy making (2003) and Orlikowski's research into knowing in practice (2002).

Emergent concepts and theory were compared with the extant literature in a process Eisenhardt called 'enfolding literature' (1989: 544). Thus a pattern-matching logic was applied whereby the empirically based pattern was compared with the literature (Yin, 2003).

Construct validity, which derives from establishing the correct operational measures for the concepts being studied (Yin, 2003), was enhanced by referencing the multiple sources of evidence (vertical and horizontal cross-sections, the regions and head offices, external experts) and by the chain of evidence of the interviews and data analysis (within Atlas-ti) from initial research propositions through to final conclusions. Internal validity, which establishes causal relationships which are not spurious (Yin, 2003), derived from the process of pattern matching, utilising the emerging patterns to build explanations and tabulating evidence for the constructs and relationships. The external validity, or the domain to which a study's findings can be generalised (Yin, 2003), relates to the replication logic within the case study groups and from analytical generalisation where the particular set of results are generalised to a broader theory, that is theory of organisational transformation in transition economies. A top TNK-BP manager checked the TNK-BP case study, providing an element of respondent validation. Taken together, these methods of ensuring validity then result in credibility and transferability (Lincoln and Guba, 1985) and plausibility (Glaser and Strauss, 1967). The reliability of the study rests on the documentation of the research processes, for example the case study protocol and the database and audit trail in Atlas-ti (Seale, 1999; Lewis and Ritchie, 2003). This provides trustworthiness (Guba and Lincoln, 1989), consistency (Hammersley, 1992) and dependability (Fontana and Frey, 2000).

METHODOLOGICAL CONTEXTUALISATION

Methodological contextualisation is particularly important in transition economies. Michailova (2004) proposes two routes for this: field contextualisation and researcher contextualisation. This section examines, first, the specificity of the field of research, highlighting some of the issues associated with conducting management research in the transition economies of Eastern Europe and, second, the specificity of the researcher, as 'not merely an outsider to the field, but as a complex individual engaged in playing a variety of roles while being in the field' (Michailova, 2004: 368).

Field Contextualisation

A difficulty of research on strategy in emerging market economies is that theories established for developed market economies may not be appropriate for emerging economies (Hoskisson et al., 2000). It may be difficult to replicate research from developed markets in emerging markets and research designs may be mis-specified if essential conceptual differences between developed and emerging economies are not taken into account (ibid.). These issues are investigated in answering the question: how does RBV help to explain the process of organisational transformation in the Russian oil industry, what are its limitations, and to what extent does its application in this context lead to a refinement of the theory?

Strategy research requires the collection of subjective information from enterprise directors – this may be hindered by the tendency of managers in transition economies to monopolise information (Hoskisson et al., 2000). Furthermore, problems of data collection and reliability of responses may be exacerbated in emerging economies by a lack of understanding of terms and concepts familiar to managers in developed economies (ibid.). In this research, this risk was minimised due to the researcher's fluency in Russian and ability to explain any terms which were not immediately understood. Furthermore the semi-structured interviewing approach provided the researcher with the ability to check and probe responses.

Given the significant changes in transition economies it is important to distinguish between changes that are exogenous and those that are attributable to the effects of organisational variables (Hoskisson et al., 2000). In this study, for example, it has been shown that the Yukos collapse was linked with exogenous issues (government intervention) and organisational shortcomings (in particular, CEO Khodorkovsky's crossing of the boundary between business and politics).

The types of resources creating and sustaining competitive advantage vary across contexts both cross-sectionally (for example, in this study between the Soviet-style and Western-style companies) and longitudinally (for example in this study between the different development phases of the companies over time) (Meyer and Peng, 2005). Given the pace of change in transition economies there is a danger that purely cross-sectional studies may produce misleading results about the impact of particular strategies

(Hoskisson et al., 2000). Longitudinal studies can help to mitigate these effects. For this study the research was conducted over a period of five years and respondents were asked to talk about the ten years since privatisation of the oil industry. For longitudinal studies in emerging economies the normal difficulties arising from respondent drop-out are compounded by high rates of firm attrition through failure and acquisition (Hoskisson et al., 2000). The Yukos case study provided an example of this since the company was collapsing and being renationalised at the end of the research period. This had specific advantages for the cross-case analysis since former Yukos employees were interviewed in TNK-BP and were thus able to provide a first-hand view on the similarities or differences between the two companies.

During the transition era, given that most local firms do not possess many of the normal resources of Western businesses, at least initially, adaptation of existing resources and development of new context-specific resources through organisational learning are crucial. To better understand these processes, researchers applying the RBV often have to engage in exploratory, case-based research first to ascertain which resources may be crucial in the given context (Meyer and Peng, 2005). This is the approach adopted in this study.

Michailova (2004) highlighted the different approach needed to gain access to respondents in transition economies compared to research in the West. There is no history of cooperation with researchers (Michailova and Liuhto, 2000) and the vast majority of managers in East European organisations are highly suspicious of Western research (Michailova, 2004). This was evidenced in this study by the difficulties gaining access to the two companies which had changed least towards a Western model (Lukoil and Surgutneftegaz). Another characteristic of research in Eastern Europe is the importance of personal networking, using the researcher's informal networks to gain access. This was the approach taken in this research since the researcher had lived and worked in Russia and had existing contacts in oil companies which could be utilised to gain access to other respondents in a snowballing technique (Patton, 1990).

CONTEXTUALISING THE RESEARCHER

According to Michailova (2004) the researcher's age, nationality and language skills play a key role in fieldwork. Since I had 23 years' experience in the Western oil company, Shell, my age was rather advantageous – most often the conversations with respondents could be conducted as equals.

I am a British national but have a history of more than 30 years living and working in Russia, with the first period spent in Moscow as a language student in 1972. My job has been connected with Russia on and off through my working life. I travelled widely throughout Russia both on business and for pleasure. From 1992–96, a period of rapid change in Russia, I lived and worked in Moscow as the Chemicals Manager for Shell. At this time many of the contacts were established that were then utilised to gain access for field work. Having studied, worked and lived in Russia for a long time I have a good feel for the Russian culture.

Languages spoken affect research, in particular where and how research is conducted (Usunier, 1998). Language helps to shape individual views and ideas shared with those who speak the same language:

> People's understandings are not uniform, and concepts and terms are not used in a vacuum. They involve different associations in different cultural environments. In that sense, concepts themselves might be viewed as cultural artefacts and language as a means of communication in a particular culture rather than a universal means of communications. Therefore, mastering the language of the field is of critical importance. (Michailova, 2004: 379)

I am a fluent Russian speaker and the interviews with Russian speakers were mostly conducted in Russian. Occasionally Russian-speaking respondents preferred to be interviewed in English; for example, where English was the working language for that individual. In two cases this was a source of regret, since the respondents were not able to express themselves as fluently and expressively in English as they could have done in their native language. Having conducted the interviews and experienced the context, I was then also best placed to translate those parts of the transcribed interviews which are included as quotations in the thesis. In my early career, after graduating as a linguist, I had worked as an interpreter and translator.

PRESENTATION OF FINDINGS

Representative quotations are given in the text, with references to the respondent provided in brackets, as well as an indication as to whether the text was translated or not (translation). A series of within-case and cross-case displays (Miles and Huberman, 1994) assist understanding. The within-case findings for the two main case studies of organisational change are presented as time-ordered and conceptually ordered data displays. The cross-case analyses include conceptually ordered cross-case displays across all four case companies, focusing on the key elements of the framework for organisational transformation. This is helpful for both literal and theoretical replication purposes.

The rich case studies contributes to the validity of the research: 'The validity, meaningfulness, and insights generated from qualitative inquiry have more to do with the information-richness of the cases selected and the observational/analytical capabilities of the researcher than with sample size' (Patton, 1990: 185). Validity also derives from the presentation of the cases accurately in accordance with the emerging themes, since 'an account is valid or true if it represents accurately those features of the phenomena that it is intended to describe, explain or theorise' (Hammersley, 1992: 69). Similarly King (1994) maintains that in qualitative research, a study is valid if it truly examines the topic which it claims to have examined – in this case the process of organisational transformation in Russian oil companies.

NOTE

1. Fax is the only way to communicate.

References

Antill, N. and R. Arnott (2003), *Oil Company Crisis*, Oxford: Oxford Institute for Energy Studies.

Argyris, C. and D.A. Schön (1978), *Organisational Learning. A Theory of Action Perspective*, Reading, MA: Addison-Wesley.

Avolio, B.J., B.M. Bass and D.I. Jung (1999), 'Re-examining the components of transformational and transactional leadership using the multifactor leadership questionnaire', *Journal of Occupational and Organizational Psychology*, **72**, 441–62.

Barker, V.L., P.W. Patterson and G.C. Mueller (2001), 'Organizational causes and strategic consequences of the extent of top management team replacement during turnaround attempts', *Journal of Management Studies*, **38** (2), 235–69.

Barney, J.B. (1986), 'Strategic factor markets: expectations, luck and business strategy', *Management Science*, **42**, 1231–41.

Barney, J.B. (1991), 'Firm resources and sustained competitive advantage', *Journal of Management*, **17** (1), 99–120.

Barney, J.B. and T.B. Mackey (2004), 'Testing resource-based theory', in D.J. Ketchen and D.D. Bergh (eds), *Research Methodology in Strategy and Management*, Oxford: Elsevier, pp. 1–13.

Barr, P.S. (2004), 'Current and potential importance of qualitative methods in strategy research', in D.J. Ketchen and D.D. Bergh (eds), *Research Methodology in Strategy and Management*, Oxford: Elsevier, pp. 165–88.

Barr, P.S., J.L. Stimpert and A.S. Huff (1992), 'Cognitive change, strategic action, and organizational renewal', *Strategic Management Journal*, **13** (special issue), 15–36.

Bartlett, C.A. and S. Ghoshal (1989), *Managing across Borders: The Transnational Solution*, Boston: Harvard Business School Press.

Bass, B.M. (1985), *Leadership and Performance Beyond Expectations*, New York: Free Press.

Bass, B.M. (1998), *Transformational Leadership: Industry, Military, and Educational Impact*, Mahwah, NJ: Lawrence Erlbaum Associates.

Bechhofer, F. and L. Paterson (2000), *Principles of Research Design in the Social Sciences*, London: Routledge.

Benner, M.J. and M.L. Tushman (2003), 'Exploitation, exploration, and process management: the productivity dilemma revisited', *Academy of Management Review*, **28** (2), 238–56.

Bettis, R.A. and M.A. Hitt (1995), 'The new competitive landscape', *Strategic Management Journal*, **16** (summer special), 7–16.

Boue, J.C. (2004), *Will Russia Play Ball with OPEC?*, accessed 22 May at www.oxfordenergy.org/comment.php?0401.

Boulding, K.E. (1958), 'Evidences for an administrative science: a review of the *Administrative Science Quarterly*, vols 1 and 2', *Administrative Science Quarterly*, **3**, 1–22.

Bowman, C. and V. Ambrosini (2003), 'How the resource-based and the dynamic capability views of the firm inform corporate-level strategy', *British Journal of Management*, **14** (4), 289–304.

BP (2005), *Table of World Oil Production 2005*, accessed 23 January 2006 at www.bp.com/liveassets/bp_internet/globalbp/globalbp_uk_english/ publications/energy_reviews_2005/STAGING/local_assets/downloads/ pdf/table_of_world_oil_production_2005.pdf.

BP (2007), *The Statistical Review of World Energy 2007*, accessed 13 January 2008 at www.bp.com/productlanding.do?categoryId=6848& contentId=7033471.

BP Statistical Review of World Energy (2003), accessed 23rd May 2004 at www.bp.com/subsection.do?categoryId=95&contentId=2006480.

Brada, J. (1995), 'A critique of the evolutionary approach to the economic transition from communism to capitalism', in K. Poznanski (ed.), *The Evolutionary Transition to Capitalism*, Boulder, CO: Westview, pp. 183–210.

Brown, C. (2001), *Russian Oil Companies Gear up for Expansion into the West*, *European Downstream Oil Report*, London: Wood Mackenzie.

Burgelman, R.A. (2002), 'Strategy as vector and the inertia of coevolutionary lock-in', *Administrative Science Quarterly*, **47** (2), 325–57.

Burns, T. and G.M. Stalker (1961), *The Management of Innovation*, London: Tavistock.

Child, J. and A. Czegledy (1996), 'Managerial learning in the transformation of Eastern Europe: some key issues', *Organization Studies*, **17** (2), 167–79.

Clark, E. and A. Soulsby (1995), 'Transforming former state enterprises in the Czech Republic', *Organization Studies*, **16** (2), 215–42.

Clark, E. and A. Soulsby (2005), 'Organizational change in a transforming enterprise: demography and process in the study of top management', Presentation to the 21st EGOS Colloquium, Berlin.

Clark, E. and A. Soulsby (2007), 'Understanding top management and organizational change through demographic and processual analysis', *Journal of Management Studies*, **44** (6), 932–54.

Cohen, W.M. and D.A. Levinthal (1990), 'Absorptive capacity: a new perspective on learning and innovation', *Administrative Science Quarterly*, **35** (1), 128–52.

Conger, J.A. and R.N. Kanungo (1988), 'The empowerment process: integrating theory and practice', *Academy of Management Review*, **13** (3), 471–82.

Dawson, P. (2003), *Reshaping Change: A Processual Perspective*, London: Routledge.

De Chazeau, M.G. and A.E. Kahn (1959), *Integration and Competition in the Petroleum Industry*, Port Washington, NY and London: Kennikat Press.

DeCastro, J. and K. Uhlenbruck (1997), 'Characteristics of privatization: evidence from developed, less developed, and former Communist countries', *Journal of International Business Studies*, **28** (1), 123–43.

Deetz, S. (1996), 'Describing differences in approaches to organization science: rethinking Burrell and Morgan and their legacy', *Organization Science: A Journal of the Institute of Management Sciences*, **7** (2), 191.

Denzin, N.K. (1978), *The Research Act*, New York: McGraw Hill.

Dess, G.G., R.D. Ireland and M.A. Hitt (1990), 'Industry effects and strategic management research', *Journal of Management*, **16** (1), 7–27.

Dixon, S.E.A. (2004), 'The globalisation potential of the Russian oil industry: an empirical study', *Journal for East European Management Studies*, **9** (1), 40–60.

Dixon, S.E.A., K.E. Meyer and M. Day (2007), 'Exploitation and exploration learning and the development of organizational capabilities: a cross-case analysis of the Russian oil industry', *Human Relations*, **60** (10), 1493–523.

Dosi, G. and L. Marengo (1994), 'Some elements of an evolutionary theory of organisational competences', in R.W. England (ed.), *Evolutionary Concepts in Contemporary Economics*, Ann Arbor, MI: University of Michigan Press, pp. 157–78.

Dosi, G., R.R. Nelson and S.G. Winter (2000), *The Nature and Dynamics of Organizational Capabilities*, New York: Oxford University Press.

Dupree, J. (2004), 'Technology delivery models', *TNK-BP Insight*, 6–8.

Earle, J. and S. Estrin (1996), 'Employee ownership in transition', in R. Frydman, C. Gray and A. Rapaczynski (eds), *Corporate Governance in Central Europe and Russia*, Budapest and London: Central European University Press, pp. 1–61.

Earle, J., R. Frydman and A. Rapaczynski (eds) (1993), *Privatization in the Transition to a Market Economy*, New York: St. Martin's Press.

Easterby-Smith, M. (1997), 'Disciplines of organizational learning: contributions and critiques', *Human Relations*, **50** (9), 1085–113.

Ebel, R. (2003), 'Untapped potential. The future of Russia's oil industry', *Harvard International Review*, 26–31.

Economides, M. and R. Oligney (2000), *The Color of Oil*, Katy, TX: Round Oak Publishing.

Economist (2000), 'Oil and the new economy', accessed 14 April 2002 at www.economist.com/finance/displaystory.cfm?story_id=E1_PPTJQD.

The Economist (2000), *Oil and the New Economy*, 20 March.

EIA (2005) *Russia Country Analysis Brief* accessed 24 September at www.eia.doe.gov/emeu/cabs/russia.html.

Eisenhardt, K.M. (1989), 'Building theories from case study research', *Academy of Management Review*, **14** (4), 532–50.

Eisenhardt, K.M. (1991), 'Better stories and better constructs: the case for rigor and comparative logic', *Academy of Management Review*, **16**, 620–7.

Eisenhardt, K.M. and J.A. Martin (2000), 'Dynamic capabilities: what are they?', *Strategic Management Journal*, **21** (10), 1105–21.

Elenkov, D.S. (1998), 'Can American management concepts work in Russia?', *California Management Review*, **40** (4), 133–56.

Elenkov, D.S. (2002), 'Effects of leadership on organizational performance in Russian companies', *Journal of Business Research*, **55** (6), 467–80.

Elfring, T. and H.W. Volberda (2001), 'Schools of thought in strategic management: fragmentation, integration or synthesis', in H.W. Volberda and T. Elfring (eds), *Rethinking Strategy*, London: Sage Publications, pp. 1–25.

Ellis, S. and N. Shpielberg (2003), 'Organizational learning mechanisms and managers' perceived uncertainty', *Human Relations*, **56** (10), 1233–54.

Emery, F.E. and E.E. Trist (1965), 'The causal texture of organizational environments', *Human Relations*, **18**, 21–32.

Estrin, S. (2002), 'Competition and corporate governance in transition', *Journal of Economic Perspectives*, **16**, 101–24.

Estrin, S., J. Brada, A. Gelb and I. Singh (1996), *Restructuring and Privatization in Central and Eastern Europe: Case Studies of Firms in Transition*, Armonk, NY: M.E. Sharpe.

Fey, C.E. and D.R. Denison (2003), 'Organizational culture and effectiveness: can American theory be applied in Russia?', *Organization Science*, **14** (6), 686–706.

Filatotchev, I., T. Buck and V. Zhukov (2000), 'Downsizing in privatized firms in Russia, Ukraine, and Belarus', *Academy of Management Journal*, **43** (3), 286–304.

Filatotchev, I., R.E. Hoskisson, T. Buck and M. Wright (1996), 'Corporate restructuring in Russian privatizations', *California Management Review*, **38** (2), 87–105.

Filatotchev, I., M. Wright and M. Bleaney (1999), 'Privatization, insider control and managerial entrenchment in Russia', *Economics of Transition*, **7**, 481–504.

Filatotchev, I., M. Wright, K. Uhlenbruck, L. Tihanyi and R.E. Hoskisson (2003), 'Governance, organizational capabilities, and restructuring in transition economies', *Journal of World Business*, **38**, 331–47.

Fiol, C.M. and M.A. Lyles (1985), 'Organizational learning', *Academy of Management Review*, **10** (4), 803–13.

Fontana, A. and J. Frey (2000), 'Interviewing: the art of science', in S. Deetz and Y.S. Lincoln (eds), *Handbook of Qualitative Research*, Thousand Oaks, CA: Sage, pp. 361–76.

Gaddy, D.E. (2000), 'Fresh opportunities arise in Russia as country's oil majors respond to lessons learned from the 1990s', *Oil and Gas Journal*, **98** (9), 23–6.

Geertz, C. (1988), *Works and Lives: The Anthropologist as Author*, Stanford, CA: Stanford University Press.

Giddens, A. (1979), *Central Problems in Social Theory*, London: Macmillan.

Ginsberg, A. and J.A.C. Baum (1994), 'Evolutionary processes and patterns of core business change,' J.A.C. Baum and J.V. Singh (eds), *Evolutionary Dynamics of Organizations*, New York and Oxford: Oxford University Press, pp. 127–51.

Gladyshev, A. (2001), *Investor Meetings September 2001*, Moscow: Yukos.

Glaser, B.G. and A.L. Strauss (1967), *The Discovery of Grounded Theory. Strategies for Qualitative Research*, London: Weidenfeld and Nicolson.

Godfrey, P.C. and C.W.L. Hill (1995), 'The problem of unobservables in strategic management research', *Strategic Management Journal*, **16** (7), 519–33.

Grace, J.D. (2005), *Russian Oil Supply: Performance and Prospects*, Oxford: Oxford Institute for Energy Studies, Oxford University Press.

Granovetter, M. (1985), 'Economic action and social structure: the problem of embeddedness', *American Journal of Sociology*, **91**, 481–501.

Grant, R.M. (2003), 'Strategic planning in a turbulent environment: evidence from the oil majors', *Strategic Management Journal*, **24** (6), 491–517.

Greenwood, R. and C.R. Hinings (1993), 'Understanding strategic change: the contribution of archetypes', *Academy of Management Journal*, **36**, 1052–81.

Greenwood, R. and C.R. Hinings (1996), 'Understanding radical organizational change. Bringing together the old and the new institutionalism', *Academy of Management Review*, **21b**, 1022–54.

Greenwood, R. and C.R. Hinings (2006), 'Radical organizational change', in S.R. Clegg, C. Hardy, T.B. Lawrence and W.R. Nord (eds), *The Sage Handbook of Organization Studies*, London: Sage Publications, pp. 814–42.

Grewal, R. and P. Tansuhaj (2001), 'Building organizational capabilities for managing economic crisis: the role of market orientation and strategic flexibility', *Journal of Marketing*, **65** (2), 67–80.

Guba, E.G. and Y.S. Lincoln (1989), *Fourth Generation Evaluation*, Newbury Park, CA: Sage.

Gummesson, E. (2000), *Qualitative Methods in Management Research*, Thousand Oaks, CA, London and New Delhi: Sage.

Gupta, A.K., K.G. Smith and C.E. Shalley (2006), 'The interplay between exploration and exploitation', *Academy of Management Journal*, **49** (4), 693–706.

Gurkov, I. and S. Maital (2001), 'How will Russia's future CEOs manage? A survey of attitudes toward loyalty, leadership and teamwork', *Journal for East European Management Studies*, **1**, 28–42.

Gustafson, T. (1999), *Capitalism Russian-Style*, Cambridge: Cambridge University Press.

Hambrick, D. and P. Mason (1984), 'Upper echelons: the organization as a reflection of its top managers', *Academy of Management Review*, **9**, 193–206.

Hambrick, D.C. (2004), 'The disintegration of strategic management: it's time to consolidate our gains', *Strategic Organization*, **2** (1), 91–8.

Hammersley, M. (1992), *What's Wrong with Ethnography: Methodological Explorations*, London: Routledge.

Hartley, J.F. (1994), 'Case studies in organisational research', in C. Cassell and G. Symon (eds), *Qualitative Methods in Organisational Research. A Practical Guide*, London, Thousand Oaks, CA and New Delhi: Sage, pp. 208–29.

He, Z.-L. and P.-K. Wong (2004), 'Exploration vs. exploitation: an empirical test of the ambidexterity hypothesis', *Organization Science*, **15** (4), 481–94.

Helfat, C.E., S. Finkelstein, W. Mitchell, M.A. Peteraf, H. Singh, D.J. Teece and S.G. Winter (2006), *Dynamic Capabilities: Understanding Strategic Change in Organizations*, Oxford: Blackwell.

Helfat, C.E. and M.A. Peteraf (2003), 'The dynamic resource-based view: capability lifecycles', *Strategic Management Journal*, **24** (10), 997–1010.

Heller, F.A. and G. Yukl (1969), 'Participation, managerial decision-making, and situational variables', *Organizational Behavior and Human Performance*, **4**, 227–41.

Hendry, C. (1996), 'Understanding and creating whole organizational change through learning theory', *Human Relations*, **49** (5), 621–41.

Hitt, M.A., M.T. Dacin, E. Levitas, J.–L. Arregle and A. Borza (2000), 'Partner selection in emerging and developed market contexts: resource-based and organizational learning perspectives', *Academy of Management Journal*, **43**, (3) 449–67.

Hitt, M.A., B.W. Keats and S.M. DeMarie (1998), 'Navigating in the new competitive landscape: building strategic flexibility and competitive advantage in the 21st century', *Academy of Management Executive*, **12** (4), 22–42.

Hodgkinson, G.P. and P.R. Sparrow (2002), *The Competent Organisation*, Buckingham: Open University Press.

Hoffman, D. (2002), *The Oligarchs: Wealth and Power in the New Russia*, New York: Public Affairs.

Hoskisson, R.E., L. Eden, C.M. Lau and M. Wright (2000), 'Strategy in emerging economies', *Academy of Management Journal*, **43** (3), 249–67.

IEA (2004), *IEA Oil Market Report May 2004*, Washington, DC: International Energy Agency.

Jick, T.D. (1979), 'Mixing qualitative and quantitative methods: triangulation in action', *Administrative Science Quarterly*, **24**, 602–11.

Johns, G. (2001), 'In praise of context', *Journal of Organizational Behavior*, **22** (1), 31–42.

Johnson, G. (2000), 'Microprocesses of institutional change in the context of privatization', *Academy of Management Review*, **25** (3), 572–80.

Johnson, J. (1997), 'Russia's emerging financial industrial groups', *Post-Soviet Affairs*, **13**, 333–65.

Keck, S.L. (1997), 'Top management team structure: differential effects by environmental context', *Organization Science*, **8** (2), 143–56.

Kets de Vries, M.F.R. (2001), 'The anarchist within: clinical reflections on Russian character and leadership style', *Human Relations*, **52** (5), 585–627.

Khartukov, E.M. (2001), *Russia: Oil Companies, Privatizations, Alliances and Overseas Ventures*, Moscow: International Center for Petroleum Business Studies.

Khartukov, E.M. and E. Starostina (2003), 'Post-Soviet oil exports: are the Russians really coming?', *OPEC Bulletin*, 11–22.

King, N. (1994), 'The qualitative research interview', in C. Cassell and G. Symon (eds), *Qualitative Methods in Organizational Research. A Practical Guide*, London, Thousand Oaks, CA and New Delhi: Sage, pp. 14–36.

Kogut, B. and U. Zander (1996), 'What firms do? Coordination, identity, and learning', *Organization Science*, **7** (5), 502–18.

Kogut, B. and U. Zander (2000), 'Did Socialism fail to innovate? A natural experiment of the two Zeiss companies', *American Sociological Review*, **65** (2), 169–90.

Kornai, J. (1992), *The Socialist System: The Political Economy of Communism*, Oxford: Clarendon.

Kraatz, M.S. and E.J. Zajac (2001), 'How organizational resources affect strategic change and performance in turbulent environments: theory and evidence', *Organization Science*, **12** (5), 632–57.

Kuzel, A.J. (1999), 'Sampling in qualitative inquiry', in B.F. Crabtree and W.L. Miller (eds), *Doing Qualitative Research*, Thousand Oaks, CA, London and New Delhi: Sage, pp. 33–46.

Landes, A., E. Savchik and R. Smith (2004), *Russia Oil and Gas Yearbook Counting Barrels*, London and Moscow: Renaissance Capital.

Lane, D. (1999), *The Political Economy of Russian Oil*, Lanham, MD: Rowman & Littlefield.

Lane, D. and I. Seifulmulukov (1999), 'Structure and ownership', in D. Lane (ed.), *The Political Economy of Russian Oil*, Lanham, MD: Bowman & Littlefield, pp. 15–45.

Lane, P., J.E. Salk and M.A. Lyles (2001), 'Absorptive capacity, learning, and performance in international joint ventures', *Strategic Management Journal*, **22** (12), 1139–61.

Lant, D. and S.J. Mezias (1992), 'An organizational learning model of convergence and reorientation', *Organization Science*, **3**, 47–71.

Lavigne, M. (1999), *The Economics of Transition, from Socialist Economy to Market Economy*, Basingstoke and London: Macmillan.

Lawrence, B.S. (1997), 'The black box of organizational demography', *Organization Science*, **8** (1), 1–21.

Levinthal, D.A. and J.G. March (1993), 'The myopia of learning', *Strategic Management Journal*, **14** (Winter), 95–112.

Levitt, B. and J.G. March (1988), 'Organisational learning', *Annual Review of Sociology*, **14**, 319–40.

Lewin, K., R. Lippitt and R. White (1939), 'Patterns of aggressive behavior in experimentally created "social climates"', *Journal of Social Psychology*, **10**, 271–99.

Lewis, J. and J. Ritchie (2003), 'Generalizing from qualitative research', in J. Ritchie and J. Lewis (eds), *Qualitative Research Practice*, London, Thousand Oaks, CA and New Delhi: Sage, pp. 263–86.

Lincoln, Y.S. and E.G. Guba (1985), *Naturalistic Enquiry*, Beverly Hills, CA: Sage.

Liuhto, K. (2003), 'Rossiiskaya Neft': Proizvodstvo I Eksport', *Voprosi Ekonomiki*, **9**, 136–46.

London, T. and S.L. Hart (2004), 'Reinventing strategies for emerging markets: beyond the transnational model', *Journal of International Business Studies*, **35**, 350–70.

Luo, Y. and M.W. Peng (1999), 'Learning to compete in a transition economy: experience, environment, and performance', *Journal of International Business Studies*, **20** (2), 269–95.

Lyles, M.A. and I. Baird (1994), 'Performance of international joint ventures in two Eastern European countries: a case of Hungary and Poland', *Management International Review*, **34**, 313–29.

Lyles, M.A. and J.E. Salk (1996), 'Knowledge acquisition from foreign parents in international joint ventures: an empirical examination in the Hungarian context', *Journal of International Business Studies*, **27**, 877–903.

Mabro, R. (2001), '11 September 2001', *Oxford Energy Forum*, (47), 12.

Mahoney, J.T. (1995), 'The management of resources and the resource of management', *Journal of Business Research*, **33** (2), 91–101.

Makadok, R. (2001), 'Toward a synthesis of the resource-based and dynamic-capability views of rent creation', *Strategic Management Journal*, **22** (5), 387–401.

March, J.G. (1991), 'Exploration and exploitation in organizational learning', *Organization Science*, **2**, 71–87.

March, J.G. (2005), 'Parochialism in the evolution of a research community: the case of organization studies', *Management Organization Review*, **1**, 5–22.

Martin, R. (1999), *Transforming Management in Central and Eastern Europe*, Oxford: Oxford University Press.

McCarthy, D.J. and S.M. Puffer (1995), '"Diamonds and rust" on Russia's road to privatisation', *Colombia Journal of World Business*, 56–9.

McCarthy, D.J. and S.M. Puffer, O.S. Vikhanski and A.I. Naumov (2005), 'Russian managers in the new Europe: need for a new management style', *Organizational Dynamics*, **34** (3), 231–46.

McLean, J.G. and R.W. Haigh (1954), *The Growth of Integrated Oil Companies*, Boston, MA: Harvard University Press.

Meyer, A. (1982), 'Adapting to environmental jolts', *Administrative Science Quarterly*, **27**, 515–37.

Meyer, A.D. (1991), 'What is strategy's distinctive competence', *Journal of Management*, **17** (4), 821–33.

Meyer, A.D., G.R. Brooks and J.B. Goes (1990), 'Environmental jolts and industry revolutions: organizational responses to discontinuous change', *Strategic Management Journal*, **11** (5), 93–110.

Meyer, A.D., J.B. Goes and G.R. Brooks (1993), 'Organizations reacting to hyperturbulence', in G.P. Huber and W.H. Glick (eds), *Organizational Change and Redesign*, New York: Oxford University Press, pp. 56–111.

Meyer, J.W. and B. Bowman (1977), 'Institutionalized organizations: formal structure as myth and ceremony', *American Journal of Sociology*, **83**, 340–63.

Meyer, K.E. (2007), 'Contextualizing organizational learning: Lyles and Salk in the context of their research', *Journal of International Business Studies*, **38**, 27–37.

Meyer, K.E. and I.B. Møller (1998), 'Managing deep restructuring: Danish experiences in Eastern Germany', *European Management Journal*, **16** (4), 411–21.

Meyer, K.E. and M.W. Peng (2005), 'Probing theoretically into Central and Eastern Europe: transactions, resources and institutions', *Journal of International Business Studies*, **36** (6), 600–21.

Michailova, S. (2004), 'Contextualising fieldwork: reflections on conducting research in Eastern Europe', in R. Marschan-Piekkari and C. Welch (eds), *Handbook of Qualitative Research Methods for International Business*, Cheltenham, UK and Northampton, MA, USA: Edward Elgar, pp. 365–83.

Michailova, S. and K. Husted (2003), 'Knowledge-sharing hostility in Russian firms', *California Management Review*, **45** (3), 59–77.

Michailova, S. and K. Liuhto (2000), 'Organisation and management research in transition economies: towards improved research methodologies', *Journal of East West Business*, **6** (3), 7–46.

Miles, M.B. and A.M. Huberman (1994), *Qualitative Data Analysis: An Expanded Sourcebook*, London: Sage.

Miller, D. (1983), 'Correlates of entrepreneurship in three types of firms', *Management Science*, **29**, 770–91.

Miller, D. and J. Shamsie (1996), 'The resource-based view of the firm in two environments: the Hollywood film studios from 1936 to 1965', *Academy of Management Journal*, **39** (3), 519–43.

Miller, W.L. and B.F. Crabtree (1999), 'Depth interviewing', in B.F. Crabtree and W.L. Miller (eds), *Doing Qualitative Research*, Thousand Oaks, CA, London and New Delhi: Sage, pp. 89–108.

Minbaeva, D., T. Pedersen, I. Bjorkman, C.F. Fey and H. Park (2003), 'MNC knowledge transfer, subsidiary absorptive capacity, and HRM', *Journal of International Business Studies*, **34** (6), 586–99.

Murray, I. (2004), *Russian Energy Developments and IEA Cooperation since the Russian Economic Survey 2002*, accessed 13 January 2008 at www.iea.org/textbase/speech/2003/sincsurv.pdf.

Naumov, A.I. and S.M. Puffer (2000), 'Measuring Russian culture using Hofstede's dimensions', *Applied Psychology*, **49** (4), 709–18.

Nelson, R.R. and S.G. Winter (1982), *An Evolutionary Theory of Economic Change*, Cambridge, MA: Harvard University Press.

Newman, K.L. (2000), 'Organizational transformation during institutional upheaval', *Academy of Management Review*, **25** (3), 602–19.

Nickolov, R. and P. Kushnir (2001), 'Russian oil sector', *ABN-AMRO Oil and Gas Sector Research*, London: ABN–AMRO.

North, D.C. (1990), *Institutions, Institutional Change and Economic Performance*, Cambridge, MA: Harvard University Press.

Numagami, T. (1998), 'The infeasibility of invariant laws in management studies: a reflective dialogue in defense of case studies', *Organization Science*, **9** (1), 2–15.

OPEC (2004), OPEC website, accessed 5 June at www.opec.org/.

Orlikowski, W.J. (2002), 'Knowing in practice: enacting a collective capability in distributive organizing', *Organization Science*, **13** (3), 249–73.

Patton, M.Q. (1990), *Qualitative Evaluation and Research Methods*, Newbury Park, CA: Sage.

Peng, M.W. (1994), 'Organizational changes in planned economies in transition: an eclectic model', *Advances in International Comparative Management*, **9**, 223–51.

Peng, M.W. (2000), *Business Strategies in Transition Economies*, Thousand Oaks, CA: Sage.

Peng, M.W. and P.S. Heath (1996), 'The growth of the firm in planned economies in transition: institutions, organizations, and strategic choice', *Academy of Management Review*, **21** (2), 492–528.

Penrose, E.T. (1959), *The Theory of the Growth of the Firm*, New York: Wiley.

Penrose, E.T. (1968), *The Large International Firm in Developing Countries. The International Petroleum Industry*, London: George Allen & Unwin.

Peteraf, M.A. and J.B. Barney (2003), 'Unraveling the resource-based tangle', *Managerial and Decision Economics*, **24** (4), 309–23.

Petromarket Research (2003), *Russia's Oil Balances: Third Quarter 2003*, Moscow: PetroMarket Research.

Pettigrew, A.M. (1987), 'Context and action in the transformation of the firm', *Journal of Management Studies*, **24** (6), 649–70.

Pettigrew, A.M. (1990), 'Longitudinal field research on change: theory and practice', *Organization Science*, **1** (3), 267–92.

Pettigrew, A.M. (1997), 'What is a processual analysis?', *Scandinavian Journal of Management*, **13** (4), 337–48.

Pettigrew, A.M. and R. Whipp (1991), *Managing Change for Competitive Success*, Oxford: Blackwell.

Pettigrew, A.M., R.W. Woodman and K.S. Cameron (2001), 'Studying organizational change and development: challenges for future research', *Academy of Management Journal*, **44** (4), 697–713.

PFC Energy (2004), *PFC Energy 50*, accessed 18 April 2005 at www.pfcenergy.com/pfc50/PDF/PFC501Q04.pdf.

PFC Energy (2007), *PFC Energy 50*, accessed 13 January 2008 at www.pfcenergy.com/pfc50.aspx.

Pisano, G.P. (2000), 'In search of dynamic capabilities: the origins of R&D competence in biopharmaceuticals', in G. Dosi, R.R. Nelson and S.G. Winter (eds), *The Nature and Dynamics of Organizational Capabilities*, Oxford: Oxford University Press, pp. 129–54.

Pleines, H. (1999), 'Corruption and crime in the Russian oil industry', in D. Lane (ed.), *The Political Economy of Russian Oil*, Lanham, MD: Bowman & Littlefield, pp. 97–110.

Prahalad, C.K. (2004), *The Fortune at the Bottom of the Pyramid: Eradicating Poverty through Profits*, Philadelphia, PA: Wharton School Publishing.

Prahalad, C.K. and R.A. Bettis (1986), 'The dominant logic; a new linkage between diversity and performance', *Strategic Management Journal*, **7** (6), 485–501.

Priem, R.L. and J.E. Butler (2001), 'Is the resource-based "view" a useful perspective for strategic management research?', *Academy of Management Review*, **26** (1), 22–40.

Rainbow, R. (2001), 'Vertical integration', *Oxford Energy Forum*, (47), 13–15.

Regner, P. (2003), 'Strategy creation in the periphery: inductive versus deductive strategy making', *Journal of Management Studies*, **40** (1), 57–82.

Ritchie, J. (2003), 'The applications of qualitative methods to social research', in J. Ritchie and J. Lewis (eds), *Qualitative Research Practice*, London, Thousand Oaks, CA, and New Delhi: Sage pp. 24–46.

Ritchie, J., L. Spencer and W. O'Connor (2003), 'Carrying out qualitative analysis', in J. Ritchie and J. Lewis (eds), *Qualitative Research Practice*, London, Thousand Oaks, CA and New Delhi: Sage, pp. 219–62.

Robson, C. (2002), *Real World Research*, Oxford: Blackwell.

Rouse, M.J. and U.S. Daellenbach (1999), 'Rethinking research methods for the resource-based perspective: isolating sources of sustainable competitive advantage', *Strategic Management Journal*, **20** (5), 487–94.

Sachs, J. (1993), *Poland's Jump to the Market Economy*, Cambridge, MA: MIT Press.

Salaman, G. (2001), 'A response to Snell: the learning organization: fact or fiction?', *Human Relations*, **54** (3), 343–59.

Saunders, M., P. Lewis and A. Thornhill (2003), *Research Methods for Business Students*, Harlow: Pearson Education.

Schoemaker, P.J.H. (2001), 'The elusive search for integration', in H.W. Volberda and T. Elfring (eds), *Rethinking Strategy*, London, Thousand Oaks, CA, and New Delhi: Sage, pp. 92–6.

Schwandt, T.A. (1998), 'Constructivist, interpretivist approaches to human inquiry', in N.K. Denzin and Y.S. Lincoln (eds), *The Landscape of Qualitative Research. Theories and Issues*, Thousand Oaks, CA: Sage, pp. 221–59.

Scott, W.R. (1995), *Institutions and Organizations*, Thousand Oaks, CA: Sage.

Seale, C. (1999), *The Quality of Qualitative Research*, London, Thousand Oaks, CA and New Delhi: Sage.

Sedaitis, J. (1998), 'The alliances of spin–offs versus start-ups. Social ties in the genesis of post-Soviet alliances', *Organisation Science*, **9**, 368–87.

Senge, P.M. (1990), *The Fifth Discipline: The Art and Practice of the Learning Organization*, New York: Doubleday.

Senge, P.M. (1992), 'The leader's new work: building learning organizations', *Sloan Management Review*, 7–23.

Shrivastava, P. (1983), 'A typology of organizational learning systems', *Journal of Management Studies*, **20** (1), 7–28.

Simon, H.A. (1955), 'A behavioral model of rational choice', *Quarterly Journal of Economics*, **69**, 99–118.

Snape, D. and L. Spencer (2003), 'The foundations of qualitative research', in J. Ritchie and J. Lewis (eds), *Qualitative Research Practice*, London, Thousand Oaks, CA, and New Delhi: Sage, pp. 1–23.

Spicer, A., G. McDermott and B. Kogut (2000), 'Entrepreneurship and privatization in Central Europe', *Academy of Management Review*, **25** (3), 630–49.

Stake, R.E. (1998), 'Case studies', in N.K. Denzin and Y.S. Lincoln (eds), *Strategies of Qualitative Enquiry*, Thousand Oaks, CA: Sage, pp. 134–64.

Stake, R.E (2003), 'Case studies', in N.K. Denzin, Y.S. Lincoln (eds), *Strategies of Qualitative Enquiry*, Thousand Oaks, CA: Sage, pp. 134–64.

Steensma, H.K. and M.A. Lyles (2000), 'Explaining IJV survival in a transitional economy through social exchange and knowledge-based perspectives', *Strategic Management Journal*, **21**, 831–51.

Strauss, A. and J. Corbin (1998), *Basics of Qualitative Research*, London: Sage.

Suhomlinova, O.O. (2006), *Property and Power in Post-Socialist Transformation, Human Relations*: University of Leicester.

Suhomlinova, O.O. (2007), 'Property rules: state fragmentation, industry heterogeneity and property rights in the Russian oil industry, 1992–2006', *Human Relations*, **60**, 1443–66.

Surgutneftegaz (2005), 'Management structure', accessed 12 September at www.surgutneftegas.ru/rus/structure_management.xpml.

Swaan, W. (1997), 'Knowledge, transaction costs and the creation of markets in post-Socialist economies', in P.G. Hare and J. Davis (eds), *Transition to the Market Economy*, London and New York: Routledge, pp. 53–76.

Sztompka, P. (1991), *Society in Action: The Theory of Social Becoming*, Chicago, IL University of Chicago Press.

Teece, D.J., G. Pisano and A. Shuen (1997), 'Dynamic capabilities and strategic management', *Strategic Management Journal*, **18** (7), 509–33.

TNK-BP (2004a), *First Corporate Technical Conference of TNK-BP Young Specialists: Summaries of Projects*, Moscow: TNK-BP.

TNK-BP (2004b), *Training and Development Programme for Regional Employees for 2005*, Moscow: TNK-BP.

Tripsas, M. and G. Gavetti, (2000), 'Capabilities, cognition, and inertia: evidence from digital imaging', *Strategic Management Journal*, **21** (10/11), 1147–61.

Tsui, A.S., C.B. Schoonhoven, M.W. Meyer, C.-M. Lau, and G.T. Milkovich (2004), 'Organization and management in the midst of societal transformation: the People's Republic of China', *Organization Science*, **15** (2), 133–44.

Tsui, A.S. (2004), 'Contributing to global management knowledge: a case for high quality indigenous research', *Asia Pacific Journal of Management*, **21** (4), 491–513.

Turner, L. (1978), *Oil Companies in the International System*, London: George Allen & Unwin.

Tushman, M.L. and L. Rosenkopf (1996), 'Executive succession, strategic reorientation and performance growth: a longitudinal study in the U.S. cement industry', *Management Science*, **42** (7), 939–53.

Uhlenbruck, K., K.E. Meyer and M.A. Hitt (2003), 'Organizational transformation in transition economies: resource-based and organizational learning perspectives', *Journal of Management Studies*, **40** (2), 257–82.

Usunier, J.-C. (1998), *International and Cross-Cultural Management Research*, London: Sage.

Van Maanen, J. (1979), 'Reclaiming qualitative methods for organizational research: a preface', *Administrative Science Quarterly*, **24** (4), 520–6.

Van Maanen, J. (ed.) (1998), *Qualitative Studies of Organizations*, Thousand Oaks, CA, London and New Delhi: Sage.

Vera, D. and M. Crossan (2004), 'Strategic leadership and organizational learning', *Academy of Management Review*, **29** (2), 222–40.

Virany, B., M.L. Tushman and E. Romanelli (1992), 'Executive succession and organization outcomes in turbulent environments: an organization learning approach', *Organization Science*, **3** (1), 72–91.

Vlachoutsicos, C.A. and P.R. Lawrence (1996), 'How managerial learning can assist economic transformation in Russia', *Organization Studies*, **17** (2), 311–25.

Wernerfelt, B. (1984), 'A resource-based view of the firm', *Strategic Management Journal*, **5**, 171–80.

Whitley, R. and L. Czaban (1998), 'Institutional transformation and enterprise change in an emergent capitalist economy: the case of Hungary', *Organization Studies*, **19** (2), 259–80.

Wiersema, M.F. and K.A. Bantel (1992), 'Top team demography and corporate strategic change', *Academy of Management Journal*, **35**, 95–121.

Winter, S.G. (2003), 'Understanding dynamic capabilities', *Strategic Management Journal*, **24** (10), 991–95.

Wright, M., T. Buck and I. Filatotchev (1998), 'Bank and investment fund monitoring of privatised firms in Russia', *Economics of Transition*, **6**, 361–87.

Wright, M., I. Filatotchev, R.E. Hoskisson and M.W. Peng (2005), 'Strategy research in emerging economies: challenging the conventional wisdom', *Journal of Management Studies*, **42** (1), 1–33.

Yergin, D. (1991), *The Prize*, London: Simon & Schuster.

Yin, R.K. (2003), *Case Study Research. Design and Methods*, London: Sage.

Zahra, S.A., H.J. Sapienza and P. Davidsson (2006), 'Entrepreneurship and dynamic capabilities: a review, model and research agenda', *Journal of Management Studies*, **43** (4), 917–55.

Ziener, G. (2001), 'The Russian oil sector: finally ready for investors?', *Russian Economic Trends*, **10** (3), 38–44.

Zollo, M. and S.G. Winter (2002), 'Deliberate learning and the evolution of dynamic capabilities', *Organization Science*, **13** (3), 339–51.

Zucker, I.G. (1983), 'Organizations as institutions', in S.B. Bacharach (ed.), *Research in the Sociology of Organizations*, Greenwich, CT: JAI Press, pp. 1–42.

Index